# ANALYSIS OF
# CHINESE CHARACTERS

BY

G. D. WILDER & J. H. INGRAM

DOVER PUBLICATIONS, INC.,

NEW YORK

Published in Canada by General Publishing Company, Ltd., 30 Lesmill Road, Don Mills, Toronto, Ontario.

Published in the United Kingdom by Constable and Company, Ltd.

This Dover edition, first published in 1974, is an unabridged republication of the second edition of the work, published by the College of Chinese Studies in China (no indication of city) in 1934. (The first edition was published by the North China Union Language School, Peking, in 1922.)

*International Standard Book Number: 0-486-23045-7*
*Library of Congress Catalog Card Number: 74-75626*

Manufactured in the United States of America
Dover Publications, Inc.
180 Varick Street
New York, N.Y. 10014

# INTRODUCTION

## TO

## ANALYSIS OF CHINESE CHARACTERS.

---

The author of the great Chinese English dictionary Mr. Giles, has not hesitated to express most trenchantly his contempt of etymology as it has been applied to Chinese Characters. He says that "Much of the etymology of the Shuo Wen is childish in the extreme", and that the phonetic principle of combination is the only one of which we can pretend to know anything. Notwithstanding the ridicule heaped upon it, scholars, like Chalmers, Chalfant, Wieger and others have continued to pursue the fascinating study of the origin of these symbols and have given us most interesting results. These results are so convincing that in the teaching of character writing we have unhesitatingly adopted the principle that the etymology of the earliest Chinese writers on the subject. childish though it may often be and fanciful, is yet superior to the numerous mnemonics that have been invented by foreign students to assist in the difficult task of memorizing the forms of a few thousand characters. The student of these pages may often consider the etymology suggested fanciful and the logic of the combinations far fetched but the following consideration should be borne in mind. They are the products of Chinese fancy and imagination and to some extent show the workings of the Chinese mind. Therefore they interest us who are students of Chinese thought. Moreover they often may only seem to be fanciful because we are ignorant of the ancient customs out of which they arose, or of the forms of the utensils of which they are pictures, or of the variations of pronunciation in the different dialects. If any one of us were entrusted with the task of inventing written symbols for both concrete objects and abstract ideas it is doubtful if we would produce anything much less fanciful and we could produce nothing of such rich historic interest, as certainly invests the 3000 most primitive characters.

Writing Chinese characters is a task of memory. Modern pedagogy insists on the value of logical or even fanciful links between ideas for fixing them in mind. Those who try to learn Chinese characters almost invariably grope for some association of ideas, some logic in the formation by which to hold them in memory. We have no doubt that the groupings which have been arrived at already by a study of the ancient inscriptions of the early seal writings and etymologies are more interesting, more logical, and wider in range than any memory system that has been or can be invented by ihe superficial study of the characters as written with the modern Chinese pen. These etymological studies enlist the interest of the historic imagination to aid the dry-as dust task of committing to memory these curious symbols of the thought of three or four milleniums.

Missionaries in China have been spared the task which their brethren in many places have had, of reducing the language of the people to writing. The genealogy of Chinese characters takes us back nearly 4000 years. For an interesting historical sketch the student is referred to Wieger's introduction, of which we here give a summary. Tradition confirmed by well grounded induction ascribes the idea of writing to the mythical Emperor Fu² Hsi 伏羲 and the systemization of written characters to Ts'ang¹ Chieh⁴ 倉頡 in the 27th century B.C. Emperor Huang² Ti⁴ 黃帝, B.C. 2697-2598, had recorders trained in official schools under a 太史 t'ai⁴ shih³ or Grand Master. Bronzes of the 18th century B.C. with characters on them are extant. The stone drums exhibited in the gateway of the Confucian Temple in Peking, referred by some to the 12th century, by others to the 9th century B.C. show inscriptions in the style used by an imperial recorder 籀 Chou⁴ in a catalog of characters called the 籀文 Chou⁴ wen² or large seal, 大篆 ta⁴ chuan⁴. Later they became known as tadpole characters, (B.C. 200) 蝌蚪字 k'o¹ tou³ tzu⁴, because so many of the penstrokes suggest the form of a tadpole. Confucius, B.C. 500, complained, of scribes who were dishonest and instead of leaving blanks when they forgot characters, made new ones. These he called 奇字 ch'i² tzu⁴ or odd characters. Ch'in² Shih³ Huang² 秦始皇, 213 B.C. had his prime minister Li³ Ssu¹ 李斯 make a new catalog called the 三倉 san¹ ts'ang.¹ It contained 3300 characters which are known as the small seal 小篆 hsiao³ chuan⁴. Li³ Ssu¹ invented no new symbols but combined the primitive picture characters with phonetics. Thus the creation of new characters ceased before 200 B.C. and probably long before that, as the phonetic principle, which renders unnecessary the invention of new symbolic elements, was in use in 800 B.C. Li³ Ssu¹ was deceived by the "odd characters" and as he had not enough ancient documents to ascertain the meaning of many who consults the lines. 网 *wang*³ is a picture of a fishing net. By extension of the primitive meaning it means any network, cobweb or reticulate design; also to catch with a net, to catch in general, to envelope or wrap, to gather. These meanings are gotten by turnings 轉 of interpretation. Primitives are usually pictures of concrete objects. Abstract terms are usually extensions of meaning or turns of thought from the original concrete characters. 父乀 *fu*⁴ is a hand holding a stick of authority therefore, father, by a metaphorical extension.

6. 假借 *chia*³ *chieh*⁴ or false borrowing, refers to the use of a character in a sense which is not its own originally, either by (1) error, substituting it for another existing character or (2) by convention to designate an object which has a name in the spoken language but which has no written name e.g. to take the character for some obsolete utensil arbitrarily to stand for some new idea for which a symbol is wanted. See No. 4. 也丣 *yeh*³. As an example of the former we have in the first chapter of the Analects 說 now pronounced in other places *shuo*¹ meaning to speak, but in this place always pronounced *yüeh*⁴, meaning to rejoice. *Yüeh* to rejoice is written 悅, but a scribe once wrote 說 for 悅 by mistake, and it was not corrected out of respect for the classical text. 哥 *ko*¹, to sing, was taken by convention to mean elder brothers.

Another interesting method of forming characters was by inverting an old character to make a new one of opposite meaning. For example 下 *hsia*⁴ below is the inversion of 上 *shang*⁴ above: 亠 *t'u*⁴, an inversion of 子 *tzu*³, son, means an unnatural child; 屮 *t'a* to go on, is only, 止 *chih*² to stop, turned bottom up; 步 *pu*⁴ walking is a combination of the two preceding containing both stopping and going owing to the advancing and stopping alternately of the feet in walking. 人 *jen*² inverted is 匕 *hua*⁴, to change.

Some characters are formed by doubling and trebling other characters either to emphasize the meaning, as 幺 *yao*¹ the finest thread, 玆 *yu*¹ an almost invisible filament or to express simple reduplication or multiplication as 口 *k'ou*³ mouth and 吅 *hsüan* clamor of many voices; 木 *mu*⁴ tree and 林 *lin*² forest, 森 *sen* many trees, green, many.

This book explains a thousand characters. After the student has studied these he will have learned about 1400 useful characters. We recommend that he proceed then to read Wieger's Etymological lessons in order, and to learn to write all the list of "340 Characters selected for the phonetic and 口 *k'ou*³ mouth to signify the meaning of ask, but a mouth in a doorway certainly suggests asking. So too in 聞 *wen*³ to hear, an ear at a crack in the door, the phonetic 門 is suggestive.

We give the following examples of the four classes mentioned above,—

1.  Imitative symbols or pictures such as 又 彐 *yu*⁴, right hand; 𠂇 left hand; 門 *men*², door, of the Chinese two leaved style with projecting pins at top and bottom for hinges.

2.  Indicative symbols, that suggest meaning often with the idea of motion as, 丨 *kun*³ representing suspension from above or action of force or authority from above downwards; 旦 *tan*⁴, the sun 日 just above the horizon—, suggesting the meaning of morning.

3.  Logical combination, in which the meaning of the character results from the meaning of all the elements. 占 *chan*¹ is a mouth 口 *k'ou*³, meaning to ask, under a 卜 *pu*³, a diviner or the lines on a tortoise shell, so the whole character means to consult the diviner or simply to divine, i.e. to ask the tortoise shell lines.

4.  Phonetic compounds, in which one part has to do with the meaning and the other with the sound only. 沾 *chan*⁴ to moisten, naturally has the water radical 水 *shui*³ to suggest moisture and has the 占 *chan*¹ for the phonetic, to indicate the sound. In many cases the phonetic has little likeness in sound to that of the character of which it forms a part. Such discrepancies will be understood if one remembers that the Chinese custom requires that only the latter part of the sound of the phonetic shall be like that of the character whose sound it indicates. Thus 尚 *shang*⁴ is, considered a perfect phonetic for 鞺 *t'ang*⁴, and 童 *t'ung*² for 鐘 *chung*¹, 般 *pan* for 盤 *p'an*² etc. Moreover many of the phonetic combinations were invented in parts of the country where the dialect varies greatly from that familiar to the student.

These four classes are based on the form or composition of the characters. The Shuo Wen distinguishes two more classes of characters based upon use.

5.  轉注 *chuan*³ *chu*⁴, is an acceptation of a character in a meaning more extended, or derived, generalized, metaphorical, analogous, adapted, figurative, or even inverted and opposite to the original meaning. For instance in 卜 *pu*³ the original meaning seems to be a horizontal and a perpendicular line from the lines appearing in a heated tortoise shell, that is, what the diviner consults; then by extension it meant the diviner or one

Melion Menzies has pointed out, and these abbreviations have become precedents for permanent forms.

About 120 A.D. there was printed a posthumous work of Hsü[3] Shen (B.C. 86). It was the first publication of genuine archaeological and etymological studies. This father of Chinese archaeology had travelled ex'ensively and studied Li[3] Ssu's catalog. His great work is the 說文解字 Shuo[1] Wen[2] Chieh[3] Tzu. It contains 10516 standard characters arranged under 534 to 544 primitive symbols which are the origin of our 214 radicals. All Chinese dictionaries claim to be based upon the Shuo Wen, though they often show ignorance of it and few scholars to-day are acquainted with it. Our Character Analysis is based upon Wieger's Etymological Lessons which is drawn largely from the Shuo Wen. Our references usually mean that our explanation is taken from Wieger. But it is not always so, for the original Shuo Wen as well as the works of Chalfant, Chalmers and others have been used. Original or at least modern suggestions have been made and usually placed after the reference to Wieger. In Wieger's Lessons will often be found the quotation from the Shuo Wen in Chinese justifying the explanation.

We shall use a few technical expressions which are best explained by the ancient classification of characters into six categories. All characters are divided into the 文 wen[2] or simple figures and the tzu[4] or compound. On the basis of form or composition these two classes are each divided into two other classes. 1. The wen[2] or SIMPLE characters may be either (1) pictures 像 hsiang[4] or imitative symbols, 像形 hsiang[4] hsing[2], of which there are 364 in the Shuo Wen or they may be (2) indicative symbols 指事 chih[3] shih[4], pointing to things, affairs. The Shuo Wen has 125 of these. 2. The COMPOUND characters 字 are divided into (1) logical combinations, 會意 hui[4] i[4], in which each component part of the character has a meaning relevant to the meaning of the character as a whole. There are 1167 of these in the Shuo Wen: (2) phonetic combinations 形聲 hsing[3] sheng[1] (form and sound), also called 諧聲 hsieh[2] sheng[1], in which one part has a significant meaning and the rest points out the pronunciation only. Of these the Shuo Wen explains 7697. We should note however that in many of these phonetic combinations the phonetic part was chosen because its meaning had some suggestion of the meaning of the character so that they incline towards the logical combination class and may be called suggestive phonetics. e.g. 問 wen[4] to ask has 門 men[2] door symbols he fixed wrongly the meaning of many characters. We can now correct some of his mistakes. In the period of literary enthusiasm following Li[3] Ssu[1] many new characters were invented by the easy process of phonetic combination. As there were many literary centers with different dialects prevailing and no standard or center of control, countless useless and duplicate characters were formed. Li[3] Ssu's catalog was reedited seven times until it contained 7380 at the time of Christ and two hundred years later over ten thousand. The modern standard dictionary of Kang Hsi finished A.D. 1717 has 40,000 characters. Of these 34,000 are monstrosities and useless doubles ; 2000 more are surnames and doubles of little use, leaving 4000 that are in common use. Of these 3000 are all that need be studied for etymological purposes, although there are also some rare or obsolete characters that are of etymological and historical interest. Fortunately the 3000 ancient primitives are still the most useful characters and anyone who gets a mastery of them and their combinations will have a magnificent vocabulary for all departments of literature. Let no one be appalled by the popular misstatement that there are 80.000 characters or even by the fact that there are 40.000 in the dictionary The vocabularies of Goodrich and Soothill have but 10.000 and the larger Chinese English dictionaries but 14.000. One who masters 2000 will find himself fairly well equipped for public speech. Dr. Goodrich after his many decades of experience is surprised that he can catalog but 4000 colloquial characters.

Besides the multiplication of characters there have been many transformations for ease in writing or condensations for the sake of speed. Many of these changes occurred as writing materials changed. At first the metal stylus, writing on wood made uniform strokes equally easy in all directions. Curves and circles were common. Then the wooden pencil used on silk caused poor writing and some peculiar changes. Finally fine pointed hair brushes used on paper gave great Power of shading and speed in execution but still further distorts the shapes of the classic small seal characters. The brush has produced the modern 楷字 k'ai[3] tzu[4], in which curves are reduced to straight lines and angles, and the grass characters, 草字 ts'ao[3] tzu[4]. or running hand which still further obliterates the classic forms.

Other transformations are due to abbreviation for securing more space for inscriptions on small pieces of bone, shell or metal, as Mr. J.

from those Lessons which do not occur in the First list." Then a study of Wieger's Phonetic series, learning to write the "second thousand selected characters" will place all the student has learned in phonetic groups enabling him to remember them much more easily. The study of the phonetic groups in Soothill's pocket dictionary or in Wieger throughout the course will rapidly increase the numbers of characters the student can write.

# SUGGESTIONS TO THE BEGINNER
# FOR WRITING CHARACTERS.

----

If the student begins with the first character and studies them in order he very soon comes to very complicated symbols. It will ease his task if he takes one or two lessons on simpler forms such as the numerals and simple characters occurring early in the book as designated below, in the suggested first lesson.

It will be found a pleasing diversion to practice under the guidance of a teacher with a Chinese pen and the red copy forms that schoolboys use. In this way one will at the same time learn the order of the strokes which the Chinese follow. It is highly important to learn this order if one wishes to write at all, as a regular habit formed by the hand in making the strokes of each character is a great assistance to the memory. The Language School also has a table giving the order of strokes for the first 150 of the characters in this book. From this the student can easily acquire the principles of order in writing. Mr. Baller's suggestions in the Introduction to his Mandarin Primer will also give the same. P. xxv,

In writing with either pen or pencil, the following rules should be observed in order to secure as much of proportion and style as possible. 1. Each character should occupy as nearly as possible a square space of equal size with those above and below, no matter how many strokes it may contain. 2. The elemental strokes are as follows — ｜ ､ ノ ＼ ７ Ｌ Ｌ ５ ｜ . 3. Where space is enclosed the perpendiculars slope inwards, making the space broader at the top than at the bottom. 4. Perpendiculars in the middle of the character should be absolutely upright, but the horizontals tend to slope upwards toward the reader's right hand.

We suggest the following for the

## FIRST LESSON.

$i^1$ One, represents the primordial unity. The first in the series of numerals, it represents the source of all beings. It is the first radical.

In composition to make up another character it has the following symbolic meanings.

1. —$i^1$ at the top of any character usually means heaven, a roof or any cover as in 天 $t'ien$, heaven, 雨 $yü^3$ rain.

2. At the bottom it means the surface of the earth, a base, or foundation. 本 $pen^3$ trunk of a tree or base; 旦 $tan^4$, morning, the sun just above the horizon. 立 立 $li^4$ to stand, is a man 大 on the ground,—.

3. A barrier or hindrance as in 丂 $ch'iao$, a difficult breathing, 勹 representing the breath. 門 $shuan^1$ a bolt to a door. 4. Something contained, as 勺 $shao^2$ a spoon with something in it.

二

$erh^4$ Two. The number of the earth, because it makes a pair with heaven. It signifies the masculine and feminine principles 陽 $yang^2$ and 陰 $yin^1$. It is the 7th radical. In composition it has three uses. 1. The meaning of two as in 仁 $jen^2$, two men, love each other. 2. Two extremes as in 五 $wu^3$ five 羊 $ko^2$ a sheen skin 丫 stretched on a frame 二. An old form of 上 $shang^1$ above, or of 下 $hsia^4$ below. e.g. 示 $shih^4$, a revelation from above. 元 $yüan^2$, head, that which is the top 二 on man 儿.

三

$san^1$ Three, the order of humanity coming after heaven and earth. The Chinese commonly explain 王 $wang^2$ king, as the one who unites heaven, earth and man.

十

$shih^2$, Ten. The number that includes all the rest of the simple numbers, a symbol of separation, extent in two dimensions, and the cardinal points of the compass. It is the 24th radical. e.g. 米 $mi^3$, is a 十 separating the kernels of grain 㐅. It means threshed out grain or any such substance.

For the rest of the numerals study the following numbers in the book, 29 to 33, inclusive, 58, 59. For more easy characters first study No. 57, 1, 5, 6, 14, 15, 35, 27, 19, 12, 2, 3, 4, after mastering these one may as well begin with No. 7 and go on in the order given in the book.

# ANALYSIS OF CHINESE CHARACTERS, FROM BALLER'S MANDARIN PRIMER.

BASED MAINLY ON DR. L. WIEGER'S ETYMOLOGICAL
LESSONS AND THE SHUO WEN.

(W. with a number and letter refers to these lessons. A comma after the Romanization in the first
column means that it is a colloquial character. The form given at the right is
the seal writing of 100 A.D.)

### BALLER, LESSON I.

**1 字,宧**

*tzu*[4], To have children 子 *tzu*[3] under one's roof ⼧ *mien*[2]. Logical composition, to shelter, to nurse, to bear. By extension it refers to the characters produced or born by combining the simple 文 *wen*[2], into compound characters, 字, either by logical composition 會意 or phonetic combination, 諧聲 (See introduction, Page 6, in Wieger; also W. 94 A.)

**子,�złᵖ**

*tzu*[3], The radical of the character, a picture of a newborn child swathed so that its legs are not visible. In an ancient form  it has the hair. By extension it means disciple, then sage or teacher because the emperors honored the sages by calling them *tzu*[3] or sons. It is the 39th radical, relating to children. (W. 94 A.)

**⼧,∩**

*mien*[2] Picture of a roof, a shelter, a house. It is the 40th radical of characters relating to dwellings. (W. 36 A.) Called 寶蓋 *pao*[3] *kai*[4].

**2** 我, 𢧵, 戎    wo[3], I, me. Two spears, 戈 ko[1], pointing towards each other, two rights opposing each other, and by extension my right, me. (W. 71 Q.) 戈 is the radical. Williams says it is a hand 手 grasping a spear, defending my rights, therefore I.

戈, 犬    ko[1], Picture of a spear with a hook or crescent on top, a crosspiece below and a sword knot at the handle; the 62nd radical, of characters relating to spears and weapons generally. (W. 71 F.)

**3** 你    ni[3], You. 人 jen[2], man (picture) 9th radical, is the radical of ni[3].

尔, 尒, 尒, 尔    erh[3] you, is a contraction of 爾 the classic character for you. It is final expletive equivalent to a full stop, or " There now!" (At the end of a phrase the voice is drawn in 入 ju[4], and the reserve of breath 亅 is separated, 八 pa[1], sent forth. The character is borrowed for you.) (W. 18 O, and 35 L.)

**4** 他    t'a[1], He, the other, she, it. 人 jen[2], man is the radical, combined with yeh[3], also; therefore the other man, he. (Man 人 also 也.)

也, 丩    yeh[3], This character is a picture of an ancient utensil, either a funnel or a drinking vessel; borrowed for the conjunction, also. (W. 107 B.)

**5** 們    men[2], Sign of plural in pronouns and other words indicating persons. The radical is 人, called 立人兒 or standing man when written 亻 at the left of a character.

門,門 門 *men²*, gate, radical 169, is a picture of a two-leaved gate turning on pivots (*hu⁴* 戶 being a one-leaved door). (W. 129 C.) This may have been taken to form the sign of the plural because it is a door with two leaves.

**6** 的     *ti⁴*, Target, mark; clear, true. Adjectival particle, sign of possessive.

白, 白 *pai²*, white, is the radical, No. 106. The sun just appearing and making white daylight, cf. 白天 *pai² t'ien¹*. (W. 88 A.) Chalmers says it is the white cocoon.

勺, 勹 *shao²*, A ladle, a spoon. 勹 is a primitive picture of a kind of spoon, and the — is something in it. (W. 54 H.)

The phonetic *shao²* may have been selected owing to its having a straight line pointing to the center, thus indicating the spot where the arrow should strike.

**7** 筆     *pi³*, Pen, (made of bamboo and a hair brush).

竹, 竹 *chu²*, bamboo is the radical, No. 118. The seal writing represents the drooping whorl of leaves, 屮 the inverse of 屮 *ch'e⁴*, a sprouting plant. When written above another character in composition it is 艹, called 竹字頭 *chu² tzu⁴ t'ou²*. (W. 77 B.)

聿, 聿 *yü⁴* A stylus, = a 彐 hand holding a | pen writing — lines on a ⌐ tablet.

**8** 紙, 紙     *chih³*, Paper. From 糸 *ssu¹*, silk, the radical, and 氏 *shih⁴*, a flat floating plant, the phonetic.

糸, 糸 *ssu¹*, Silk, a strong thread. The upper part represents two cocoons, 幺 *yao¹*; the lower part, 小 is a primitive representing the twisting of several threads into a big one,

—the threads from two or more cocoons twisted. It is the 120th radical of characters relating to textile matters. (W. 92 A.)

氏, 氐, 乇 shih[4], A surname. A family, clan, sect. Used in married women's surnames. Originally a floating plant, that ramifies and branches and finally fixes itself by a root to the bottom and develops greatly. Therefore by extension, development, multiplication; a wandering horde of primitive times, a clan, family. It is the 83rd radical, here used as a pure phonetic. (W. 114 A.)

Silk was used for writing on before paper was invented; hence the radical 糸. The plant spreads out flat on the water; hence the fitness of this element 氏 to form the character for paper.

9 書, 喬

日, 屮    shu[1], To write, a writing, a book.

回    yüeh[1] to speak, is the radical, No. 73. The mouth 口 k'ou[3] exhaling a breath — or a word; therefore by extension, emanation, exhalation. A more ancient form exhibits the breath as forming a cloud over the mouth (W. 73 A.)

聿 yü[4] A stylus (see No. 7).

While yüeh is given as the radical by Kang Hsi, yet the seal form shows that historically it is but a contraction for 者 che[3], phrase speech, document. (See No. 270. W. 159 B.) A book 書 is the emanation or speech 曰 of a pen 聿.

**10** 這 辶, 辵, 辵
止, 屮

che⁴, This, here, now.   This 這 word 言 goes 辵.
cho⁴ is the radical, No. 162, to run and to stop;
from 彳 ch'ih⁴, to step with the left foot,
and 止 chih³, to stop, which is a representation of a foot standing, heel at the left,
toes at the right, and ankle above. (W.
112 A and E.)   In combination 辵 written 辶, is called 走 之 兒.

言, 宮 yen², Words.   The 口 k'ou³, mouth with words
舌 issuing from it.   149th radical (W.
73 C.)

**11** 那

na³¹, Where? in third tone; there, in fourth
tone.

阝, 邑, 邑 i⁴, A city.   The radical, No. 163, in combination written 阝 and always. at the right.
The 口 seat of 巴 chieh² authority.   The 口
represents the walled town, and the 巴 is
a seal or stamp of authority.   (W. 74 C.)

冄, 枀 The 冄 is a modification of 枀 by the
scribes.   The whole character 那 was the
name of a city west of Szuchuan, whose
inhabitants wore furs 枀.   It also means
weak, and was borrowed for the meaning
there, that.   (W. 116 B.)

**12** 是 昰
日
正

shih⁴, Right, exact, to be, yes.
iih⁴, the sun, is the radical, No. 72,—a picture.
cheng⁴, from — i¹, one, limit and 止 chih³ to
stop.   Stopping only at the proper limit set
beforehand, upright, correct.   (W. 112 I.)
The sun 日 exactly 正 on the meridian,
right, straight＝是.

**13** 錢

ch'ien², Money.

金,金 *chin*[1], metal, is the radical, No. 167. 今 *chin*[1], "now, present," is phonetic. (See No. 18.) 土 *t'u*[3], earth, bearing in its bosom two nuggets 八 of gold or metal. In earth 土 there are present 今 two nuggets 丷 of gold 金.

土 *t'u*[3], earth, is the 32nd radical. The earth 土 that produces all things. The top line represents the surface, the lower line the rock or subsoil, and | the upright, the things that it produces. (W. 81 A and 14 K. T.)

戔 *chien*[1] To exterminate, to destroy. The common work of two or many spears 戈. (W. 71 R.) Most of the characters of which this forms a part have the sense of small, mean or to ruin, as 賤 *chien*[4] cheap, 踐 *chien*[4] trample, 淺 *ch'ien*[3] shallow.

**14** 外,外

*wai*[4], Outside, foreign.

夕 *hsi*[1] Evening. The radical, No. 36; represents the half moon which appears in the evening. One line is left out of 月 *yüeh*, the moon.

卜 *pu*[3], A soothsayer, to divine. The 25th radical. (W. 56 A and F.) The divination is by looking at the veins appearing in a heated tortoise shell, and the 卜 *pu*[3] represents a perpendicular and horizontal vein. 外 outside, is a diviner, 卜 in the evening 夕 i. e., a person must consult the diviner outside of working hours, before a new day.

**15** 生 生

*sheng*[1], Grow, beget, produce. Radical No. 100.

A plant that grows more and more. A whorl was added to 业 之. (W. 79 B, F.) Others make it a combination of 土 t'u³ (earth) and 屮 ch'e⁴ (grass). That is, the earth 土 produces 生 grass 屮.

**16** 要, 覺 yao⁴, (Loins, waist), to want, to wish. Originally written as a picture of a woman, with face ⊗, two hands 臼, and figure with enlarged bust 虎. It was taken for waist, that part being more marked in wonran's figure than in man's; but in this sense it is now written with the 月 肉 jou⁴ radical added 腰. The primitive meaning is now lost, and the character is borrowed for the meaning to want. (W. 50 M.)

西 hsi¹, West radical No. 146 was taken arbitrarily by Kang Hsi as the radical for classification of the character in his dictionary. (See No. 26.)

女, 舟, 虎 nü³, woman, is a picture character. The 38th radical. Originally ♠ a woman standing in respectful attitude, altered to 虎 for ease in writing! "What China wants— the Western woman" is a convenient mnemonic for 要.

**17** 做 tso⁴, To make, to act as.

亻, 人 jen², is the radical, No. 9.

故 ku⁴, Cause, purpose, old. Combined with 人 man, we have man as cause, that is, doing, making.

古 ku³, Ancient, that is, what has passed through ten 十 shih², mouths or generations, 口

*k'ou*[3], picture of a mouth, 30th radical. (W. 24 F.).

**攴, 攵, 与** *p'u*[1] To tap, rap. 66th radical. From a 又 *yu*[4] (hand, 29th radical) holding a ⼘ *pu*[3] diviner's rod.

**18 念, 念**

**心, 心** *nien*[4], To read, to chant. To think, to study.

*hsin*[1], Heart, a picture in the seal writing. 61st radical. It shows the pericardium opened, the lobes and the aorta below. (W. 107 A.) In combination at the left it is written ⺖.

**今** *chin*[1], now, is made up of a triangle 亼, *chi* meaning union, and 𠃌 *chi*[2], an abbreviation of 及 meaning contact, up to, (W. 19 D.) (a hand 又 holding a man 人). The combination is thus tautological. (W. 14 K.) The idea of the character may be that all past time unites in the present. Therefore 念 to read or think, is to make present 今 to the mind 心.

**19 不, 帀**

*pu*[1], Not, a negative. Primitively a bird 帀 flying up to the sky—" not able to get there " for a mnemonic. The radical, — *i*[1] is often used as a limit, or the sky, at the top of a character. (W. 1 B and 133 A.)

**20 些**

*hsieh*[1], A little, some. Sign of comparative, several.

**此** *tz'ŭ*[3], This, here. Originally it meant to turn 匕 on one's heel 止. " This " is a borrowed meaning. 匕 *pi*[3] is an inverted man 人, to turn. (W. 26 A 112 A.)

二 *erh*[4], Two. The number of the earth because it is paired with heaven. Also the number of the two principles 陰 *yin*[1] and 陽 *yang*[2], (W. 2 A.) The radical of 些, the 7th.

The combination of 此 *t'zu*[3], this, and 二 *erh*[4], two, means pointing to this and that, sign of plurality.

**21 誰**

    *shui*[2], Who? who; any one. 言 *yen*[2] is the radical, the 149th.

隹, 隼, 𨾴 *chui*[1] Short-tailed birds (a picture), the 172nd radical. (W. 168 A.) A phonetic combination.

**22 懂**

    *tung*[3], To understand. The radical is 心, here written 忄 and called 豎 *shu* 心 *hsin*[1], vertical heart, the 61st radical.

董 *tung*[3] To lead or influence, to rule or lead people on to right ways.

With 心 heart meaning to influence the mind, or to understand.

艸, 艹 *t'sao*[3], grass, a picture, the 140th radical, is its radical. It is written 艸 when standing alone, and 艹 in composition.

重 *chung*[4], Heavy, important. Composed by superimposing *t'ing*[2] 壬 upon 東 *tung*[1], the two oblique strokes of the latter being reduced to a horizontal stroke.

壬, 𡈼 *t'ing*[2] is a man 人 standing at his place on the earth 土, the earth denoting the business of life, position. The positions on the east of the throne were the more important and honorable, hence the combination with 東 *tung*[1], east, to mean important or heavy. (W. 81 D.)

東 *tung*[1], The sun 日 shining through the trees, 木 *mu*[4] i.e., on the horizon where it appears in the morning, so, east. (W. 120 K.)

木, 朩 *mu*[4], Tree, a picture of trunk, roots and branches the 75th radical. (W. 119 A.)

**23** 甚, 是 *shen*[24], Very, superlative, what? Before 麼 read *shen*[2].

甘, 日 *kan*[1], sweet, the 99th radical is the radical, from 口 *k'ou*[3], mouth, and something held in it,—i.e., agreeable to the taste, sweet, satisfaction. (W. 73 B.)

匹, 匹 *p'i*[3], To pair, a pair. It is a half of the whole which is represented by 四 *ssu*[4]. A little more than half of the character is retained so as to be recognizable. (W. 42 A.)
Therefore 甚 means affection for the mate. As this is the strongest affection, the character comes to mean superlative, very.

**24** 麼 *ma*[1], *mo*[1], An interrogative particle, a sort; also used ironically. These are borrowed meanings. The primitive meaning is small, delicate, from 麻 *ma*[2] hemp fibre, and 幺 *yao*[1], the finest thread. (W. 90 A.)

麻, 麻 *ma*[2], Hemp, hemp fibre, pockmarked; the 200th radical; it is *the* radical of this character. It is made up of the following:

朩 *p'an*[4] To strip hemp; from 八 *pa*[1], to divide (12th radical) the fibres from the 屮 *ch'e*[4], stalk. (Distinguish from 木 *mu*[4].) When doubled it forms 林 *p'ai*[4], textile fibres. When the stalks are soaked and stripped off and brought under cover or stored in a shed 广 *yen*³, it is called 麻 *ma*², prepared hemp or tow, kept under shelter. (W. 79 H.) In combination this character has the idea of entanglement, troublesome.

幺, 吕 *yao*¹ The finest thread as obtained from winding the filaments of only two cocoons which are represented in the character. By extension, any fine thread, tow, slender, tender, 52nd radical. (W. 90 A.)

**25** 東, 東    *tung*¹, East. Sun 日 shining through the trees, 木 *mu*⁴. See No. 22. 木 *mu*⁴ is the radical, the 75th.

**26** 西, 圆 卤    *hsi*¹, West. The primitive writings picture a bird settling on its nest. The birds go to roost at sunset; hence the use of the character for west; the 146th R. (W. 41 D.)

**27** 先, 㞢    *hsien*¹, First. The radical is 儿 *jen*², a man. It sometimes means feet, support. The 10th radical. (W. 29 A.)

生, 之, 㞢 *chih*¹ A small plant ψ issuing from the ground 一; to grow; development, continuity, progress. It is borrowed as the sign of the possessive. (W. 79 B.) Accordingly the combination 先 *hsien*¹ means to advance 㞢 on one's feet 儿, to be first.

**28** 個 箇 个, 巾    *ko*⁴, The culm of the bamboo, a joint of bamboo with a knot and a whorl of leaves, in the primitive writing. An article, a classifier. (W. 77 A.) In the common form 人 *jen*² is the radical, combined with the phonetic 固 *ku*⁴, shut up, to make firm, fortified;

12

composed of 口 *wei²*, an enclosure, (the 31st radical) and 古 *ku³*, ancient (see No. 17) as phonetic. Only when written with the 竹 *chu²*, as radical has it the meaning of bamboo.

---

BALLER, LESSON II.

**29** 四, ꝗ

*ssŭ⁴*, Four. An even number easily divided into halves by the 八 *pa¹*, to divide ; all around. The radical is 口 *wei²*, No. 31, used in words relating to enclosures. (W. 42 A.) The old form represents the division into halves. For 八 see under No. 32.

**30** 五, 乂

*wu³*, Five. At first written × being four lines and a center, or five ; then placed between 二 heaven and earth, as the dual powers 陰 *yin¹* and 陽 *yang²*, begetting the five elements, 五行 *wu³ hsing²*. (W. 39 A.). The radical is 二, the 7th.

**31** 六, ꝗ 介

*liu⁴*, Six. The even number that comes after four marked with a dot. Note that all the even digits are written so as to show their divisibility, 二 *erh⁴*, two, and 八 *pa¹*, eight. (W. 42 A.) The radical is 八, 12th.

**32** 七, 丂

*ch'i¹*, Seven lines, in old writing. All the digits are found written in this style in old inscriptions, i.e., with the number of lines indicated by the digit. (W. 33 A.). Radical is 一 *i¹*.

八, 八 — pa[1], Eight; to divide. The meaning is indicated by the form. Also written with eight lines in the angular form. The 12th radical. (W. 18 A.)

**33** 九, 九 — chiu[3], Nine. A numerical sign without other meaning. An original writing contains nine lines. Radical is 乙 i[4] a hook, the 5th.

**34** 幾, 幾 — chi[3], Few, nearly. The radical is 幺 yao[1], No. 52 (See No. 24.)

It is a guard 戍 shu[4], of soldiers on the frontier who are watching the slightest movements and are attentive to the least things 絲 yu[1]. Therefore to examine, subtle, hidden, small, few.

絲, 絲 yu[1], has the meaning of 幺 yao[1] reinforced, i.e., very small, slender, almost invisible. (W. 90 D.) (See No. 24.)

戍, 戍 shu[4], To guard the frontiers; from 人 man carrying a 戈 ko[1], spear. See No. 2. (W. 25 D.)

**85** 兩, 兩 — liang[3], Two. An ounce, a pair. From a picture of a standing scale 巾 the upper stroke having been added in modern times to indicate the beam (or equilibrium). The idea of a pair may have been suggested by the balanced scale pans. (W. 35 H.)

入, 人 ju[4], is the radical, No. 11, meaning to enter, or to put on either pan of the scales. It represents roots entering the ground 人 the opposite of 出 ch'u 'to go out, which represents a plant growing up. (W. 15 A.)

**36** 本, 米

**běn**

pen³, The trunk of a tree. The line across the 木 mu⁴, tree, represents the surface of the ground, drawing attention to the part of the tree below ground, the roots. So root, source, natural, native; capital. Books. (W. 120 A.) 木 mu⁴, wood, is the radical, No. 75.

**37** 認

jen⁴, To know well; to recognize; to acknowledge. 言字傍 yen² tzu⁴ p'ang² is the radical, No. 149. Words and 忍 jen³, patient (phonetic combination).

忍, 忍 jen³, Patient, to bear, suffer, endure, patience, harsh. 心 hsin¹ is the radical. 刃 jen⁴, a cutting weapon, formed of 刀 tao¹, with a stain on the edge, or something being cut by it. Tao¹ 刀 is the 18th radical, 𠃌 a picture of the Chinese razor or cleaver. A heart under a knife-edge means to suffer, (W. 52 B.) In composition at the right 刀 is written 刂. A heart that has endured 忍 the monotony of continual practise knows well its lesson 認.

**38** 買, 買

mai³, To buy. Mencius says, "net 网 the market gains 市利"; better explained by "to wrap up a thing with its price in cowries 貝 in a net 网." (W. 161 D.)

貝, 貝 pei⁴, A cowrie shell. These were used for money in early times. The seal character shows the feelers of the live shell. It is the radical, No. 154, of things relating to values and trade. (W. 161 A.)

网 wang³, Net, radical No. 122 (called 四字部 ssu⁴ tzu⁴ pu⁴ by the writers, because modified to look like a 四 *szu*[4] when used at the top of characters); in some it is written 宀 or 网. To entangle. (W, 39 C.)

**39 識**

言, 音 *shih*[34], *chih*[4] To keep in mind, know, recognize. *yen*[2], word is the radical, No. 149.

戠, 誅 *chih*[1] A sword, to gather; potters' clay; office, official duty (now written 職). Ancient chiefs or officials. These held a 戈 *ko*[1], when they gathered the people 戠 and announced their will 意 *i*[4] (shortened to 音 *yin*[1]). (W. 71 H.)

音, 音 *yin*[1], sound, is the 180th radical, formed of 言 *yen*[2], utterance, and — a sound. The — is placed in the 口 mouth to represent a word or sound issuing and in the seal character this line is the only difference between 言 *yen*[2] and 音 *yin*[1]. (W. 73 E.) "When the people could repeat the words 言 of the officials 戠 they were said to know." 識.

**40 茶**

*ch'a*[2], Tea. 艸 *t'sao*[3] *tzu t'ou*[2] is the radical. (See No. 22.) The plant 艸 like a tree, 木 for man 人. This may do for a mnemonic. This is a modern phonetic combination. It uses 舍 *she*[4], house and 八 *pa*[1], to distinguish, the 口 being replaced by

余 *yü*[2] 八 *Pa*[1] as in 余 *Yü*,[2] I, me in Wen li, 舍 *She*[4], contracted, is a phonetic for *ch'a*[2] 茶 and no logic need be sought. Tea seems not to have been widely used in ancient China. Mencius uses 檟 *chia*[3], for some kind of tea tree in Shantung in the phrase, 舍 其 梧 檟 養 其 樲 棘

"Discarding his wood oil and tea trees, to cultivate brambles and thorns."

舍, 舍 she[4] A shed, booth, house. It is the joining 스 chi[2] of 口 walls and of the thatch roof ψ to form a house. (W. 14 C.)

**41** 寫, 寫 hsieh[3], To write. Primitively to set in order the things in a house, 宀 mien[2]. 宀 is the radical, 40th. By extension, to set in order one's ideas, to write. The lower part is a phonetic only.

舄, 舄 yeh[4] A magpie. It is a modification of 鳥 niao[3], with a special head given it. 鳥 niao[3], is a long-tailed bird, a picture, the 196th radical. (W. 138 A. & C.) The magpie is a bird of neat, trim appearance, which may suggest the idea of order in the combination.

**42** 碗 wan[3], Basin, cup, bowl.

石, 石 shih[2], Stone. It is a piece of rock 口 fallen from a cliff 厂 han[4] (27th radical). It forms the 112th radical. (W. 59 D.)

宛, 宛 wan[3] Good behavior 夗 yüan[3], in the house 宀, to comply with the demands of others, therefore the derived meaning, to bend, to cover; yield. Yüan[3] 夗 to turn in bed, a curling up, dignity or modesty 巳 chieh[2], during the night, 夕 hsi[1] (See No. 14) "It is not decent," says Confucius, "to lie like a corpse." "Stand like a pine (立 li[4] 如 ju[2] 松 sung[1];) Sit like a bell (坐 tso[4] 如 ju[2] 鐘 chung[1];) Lie like a bow (臥 wo[4] 如 ju[2] 弓 kung[1];) Walk like the wind (走 tsou[3] 如 ju[2] 風 feng[1].") These are models of behaviour. From modesty in lying down, *yüan*[3], comes by extension to mean good behaviour in general. (W. 64 D.)

巴, 弓 *chieh*[2], A seal. Some say the form where one has slept. It is one half of the character 弓=卯 *ch'ing*[3] or seal. One half of the seal is kept at the yamen and the other given to the individual concerned in the case. (W. 55 A, B.) The phonetic 宛 has the idea of order, and bowls 碗 are a means to secure order in eating.

**43** 有, 匀

*yǒu*

*yu*[3], To have. Primitively it meant the phases of the moon 月 as if a hand covered it. Some say the eclipse of the moon, with the same interpretation. To have, is a borrowed meaning. (W. 46 H.) To have the hand on the moon might well be called possession.

月, ⽉ *yüeh*[4], the moon, is the radical, No. 74. A pic-

*yüe* ture of the crescent moon completely visible (compare 夕 *hsi*[1], No. 14). (W. 64 G.)

ナ, 又, 彐 *yî*[4], The right hand. The fingers reduced to three for ease in writing. It is the 29th radical. (W. 43 B.) It means also, again. The right hand returning repeatedly to the mouth in eating suggests "again."

**44** 意, 悥

*xīn*

*î*[4], Intention, thought.

心 *hsin*[1], heart, is the radical, No. 61. The heart or mind 心 of the speaker is known by the sounds 音 that he utters. By extension it means also the thought that the mind of the hearer gets from the words 音 of the speaker. (W. 73 E.)

音 *yin*[1], A sound.   (See No. 39.)

**45** 思, 㠯   *ssu*[1], To think; the wish of the heart.  心 is
the radical, No. 61.

田, 囟, 囟 *hsin*[1] The skull, the cover of the brain (altered
to look like 田 *t'ien*[2], field).  " When one
thinks, 思 the vital fluid of the heart 心
acts on the brain 囟 *hsin*[1]."  Shuo Wen.

**46** 出, 㞷, 㞷 *ch'u*[1], To go forth, to go out.  To issue, to beget,
to eject.  Primitively it represents stalks
growing out of the ground, the opposite
of 入 *ju*[4], No. 35.  The 屮 small plant has
grown another pair of leaves.  (W. 78 E.)
In combination often reduced to 土.  The
radical is 凵 *k'an*[3], a receptacle, the
17th.

**47** 氣   *ch'i*[4], Vapor, the 气 *ch'i*[4] or fumes rising from
fermenting 米 *mi*[3] rice; ether, breath,
air.  It is substituted in common use for
the radical 气 and is in much use in philosophy for the primal aura or vital fluid.

气, 气 *ch'i*[4], vapor, is the radical, No. 84, meaning
curling vapors rising from the ground and
forming clouds.  Ancient forms show the
sun 日 and 火 fire which cause the vapors.
Contracted into 乞 *ch'i*[3] it means to beg.
(W. 98 A.)

米 *mi*[3], Rice after it is hulled; other small grains
and things small like rice.  It represents
four grains 㸚 separated 十.  The 十 often
means separation toward the four quarters North, South, East and West.  (W.
122 A.)  It is the 119th radical.

**48** 朋

*p'eng²*, A friend, companion, peer. Now composed of two moons; but it has nothing to do with 月 *yüeh⁴*, the radical of classification in Kang Hsi, but comes from an ancient primitive 羸 *feng⁴*, representing the tail of the phoenix, and by extension meaning the bird itself, now written 鳳. The character 朋 was then changed in pronunciation to *p'eng²*, and taken to mean friend, because the phoenix draws all other birds after it; or two birds together, therefore friend, (Chalfant) 鵬 *p'eng²*, was a fabulous bird, the roc, from which the 朋 may have derived its pronunciation of *p'eng²*. (W. 64 I.)

**49** 友 彐
yŏu

*yu³*, Friend, associate. From two hands 又 acting in the same direction. 又 *yu⁴*, is the radical, No. 29. (W. 43 P.)

**50** 件

*chien⁴*, Classifier of many things, item, to divide, distinguish. 人 is the radical.

牛, 半 *niu²*, Cow, ox. The 93rd radical, a picture of head, horns, legs and tail. Anything from man to beast.

**51** 衣 衮
衤

*i¹*, Clothes, especially upper garments. 145th radical of many characters relating to clothing. In composition it has the following forms: 1. when at the left of the character 衤; 2. cut into halves, the 亠 being at the top and the 𧘇 being at the bottom of the character. (It must not then be confused with ㇀ the eighth radical, the ㇆ at the bottom being the test) ; 3. both parts may be changed by fusion with other parts of the character when split, e.g., 表袁卒. It also is placed either at the top or the bottom of a character unchanged. It *pictures the sleeves and the skirts hanging below*. (W. 16 A.)

**52 裳**

shang[1], Clothes for the lower part of the body. 衣 is the radical (see No. 51.)

尚, 尚 shang[4], is a phonetic here. 尚 is contracted to 丷 when in composition, meaning a roof or a house. It represents the ridgepole and sides of the house as in 宀 *mien*[2], but has a window 口 added and a 八 *pa*[1], divide, indicating that the ridgepople divides the wind and water, or 風水 *feng*[1] *shui*[3]. This ridge raised at both ends is placed last of all, and so the character means to add to, still, elevated, noble, superior. It is a suggestive phonetic as the *clothing is a house or cover for the body*. (W. 36 E.)

**53 把**

*pa*[3 4 1], To take hold of, grasp, classifier of things held in the hand. Read *pa*[4], a handle, *pa*[3], a handful. "To clap 巴 the hand 手 on something."

手, 手 *shou*[3], The hand, handy, skill, workman. It is 手 the radical, No. 64. When written at the side called 提手 *t'i*[2] *shou*[3]. 又 彐 is the picture of a side view of the hand, 手 is the full palm. In the ancient writing the 仌 represents the lines in the palm. (W. 48 A.)

巴, 弓 · *pa*[1], A kind of boa, short and thick. It is represented raised on its tail. It is found in the south; its flesh is eaten and its skin is used to cover guitars, 琶 *pa*[1]. (W. 55 L.) It also means a slap, clap.

54 **椅**

*i*[2], A chair. The radical is 木 *mu*[4], the 75th. (See No. 25.)

奇 *ch'i*[2], Unusual, strange, rare. That which causes men 大 to exclaim in admiration 可.

大 *da*[4], Great, 37th radical, in combination
dà means man, representing head, arms and legs.

可, 可 *k'o*[3], To send forth a breathing of approbation 弖 from the mouth 口, to express satisfaction, to be willing, permit, admire. Logical combination (W. 58 I). The Chinese, being used to sitting on their heels, or flat on the *k'ang*, the chair seems so much more comfortable as to be a surprising or strange thing.

55 **張**

*chang*[1], To draw a bow, stretch, extend. Classifier of things of extended surface.

弓, 弓, B *kung*[1], a bow, is the radical, No. 57. A picture. Ancient forms also represent it bent or vibrating. (W. 87 A.)

長, 开 *chang*[3,4], To grow, excel, senior.

長, 髟 *ch'ang*[2], Long. The primitive form represents locks of hair so long that they must be tied by a band — and a hairpin Y. With 匕, an inverted or changed man, added, it means manhood, grown up so the hair is long. By extension it means long in time or space, to grow. The modern form is

an arbitrary contraction.  168th radical.
(W. 113 A.)

**56** 棹

cho¹, Table.  木 mu⁴ is the radical.  (See No.
25.)

卓, 桌 cho¹, Surpassing, high, elevated.  It represents
*a mast surmounted by a globe and a
flame*, an ornament of which the Chinese
are fond.  It is imitated in the yamen flag
staffs.  (W. 143 F.)  A table being high
as compared with chairs and stools, this
phonetic meaning high  is selected appropriately.

--------

BALLER, LESSON III.

**57** 中, 串
串

*zhōng*

zhong¹, The middle, among, in.  *Chung⁴*, to hit
the mark, attain, pass an examination.
The character represents a  square  target
pierced in the center by  an  arrow.  The
form of the target is lost  in  this  modern
writing, but is retained in 用 *yong*.⁴  (W.
109 A.)  (See No. 225.)

kun³, A down stroke, a  perpendicular,  is the
radical, No. 2.  It has  a  symbolic  signification in many characters, e.g.: the trunk
in 木 *mu⁴*, tree ; an arrow in 中 *zhong¹;* a
spindle running  through  two  objects  in
串 *ch'uan⁴*, i.e., to string  together ; a bow
string in 引 *yin³*, to draw a bow, to lead ;
a man standing in 申 *shen¹*,  to gird  one's
self.  (W. 6 A.)

**58** 百, 百

bai³, One hundred, many, all.  The unity  of
hundreds is represented by — *i¹*, one, and

白 *pai*², white. It is purely a phonetic combination. 白 is the radical, 106th. (See No. 6.) (W. 88 A. and B.)

**59** 千, 千

*ch'ien*¹, Thousand, very many. Ten 十 hundred (but the 百 *pai*³ is not here).

十 *shih*², Ten, symbol of extension in two dimensions, is the radical, No. 24. The 丿 at the top of the character is the abbreviation for 人 *jen*², which is phonetic in this character. (W. 24 D. and A.)

**60** 萬, 蠆

*wan*⁴, Ten thousand; an indefinite number, wholly, emphatic particle. Written 卍 it is the Indian swastika, symbol of Buddha's heart, also meaning 10,000. The radical in Kang Hsi's dictionary is 艹 *t'sao*³, but the character has nothing to do with that radical, originally it being the picture of a scorpion, 㔾 艹 being the feelers, ⊗ 囟 being the head, and 禸 内 the legs and the tail. It was then pronounced *ch'ai*⁴, but as there were other words for scorpion it was borrowed for the meaning 10,000. (W. 23 H.)

**61** 零

*ling*², Small rain, or last drops of a shower, a fraction, residue.

雨, 雨 *yü*³, rain, is the radical, the 173rd. It represents drops of water ⼊ (the same primitive as in 米 *mi*³, No. 47), falling | from a cloud 冂 hanging in the sky — *i*¹. (W. 1 B and 125 B.)

令, 金 *ling*⁴, A law, an order, to command, your honored. It is formed of 亼 *chi*², the notion of union, assemblage, being the joining of three lines (see No. 18), and 卩 *chieh²*, a seal (see No. 42.) Therefore 令 an order, is the uniting 亼 of the written document and the 卩 seal,—i.e., the stamping of the order. (Note that when 口 *k'ou³*, is added, we have 命 *ming⁴*, an order or command by word of mouth, and the decree of heaven). (W. 14 A. 1.)

**62** 回, 回 回

*hui²*, To return to or from ; a time. Mohammedan. A turn or revolution. It represents an eddy (like the curling clouds of smoke, or whirlpools in water) or an object that rolls, turns on an axis ; hence the abstract idea of revolving, return.

口 *wei²* is the radical, twice written. (See No. 28.) (W. 76 G.) Also written 囘.

**63** 請

請

言 *yen²*, is the radical, the 149th. (See No. 10.)

*ch'ing³*, To invite, to request, to engage.

青, 靑 *ch'ing¹*, The green of sprouting plants, also blue, black, gray, white of an egg. The 174th radical. It is made up of 生 *sheng¹*, plants, and 丹 *tan¹*, their color (red), as if the makers of the character were color blind. 丹 *tan¹* is cinnabar, a red mercury ore, represented by the 丶 for the ore in a crucible 月 where it was sublimed by the alchemists in search of the philosophers' stone for turning base metals to gold. (W. 115 D.) 月 may be the Chinese stove with the round hole red with fire.

**64** 來，来

*lai*[2], To come; in the future. The radical is 人 *jen*[2]. It is formed of 木, a primitive representing a plant and 从 or ears of grain hanging from it; a sort of bearded barley, used as food in the Chou Dynasty. The Shuo Wen says it means come, because the grain eaten by men *comes* from heaven. It is more probably a borrowed meaning without logical explanation. (W. 13 B.)

**65** 問

*wen*[4], To ask, inquire. The radical is 口 *k'ou*[3], mouth, No. 30. The 口 placed in a 門 *men*[2], door, is a suitable character for the meaning, to ask. (See Nos. 5 and 9.)

**66** 坐，坐

*tso*[4], To sit down, to rest, to place, to reign. The radical is 土 *t'u*[3], the 32nd. Two men 从 sitting on the earth 土 *t'u*[3], face to face to talk. (W. 27 D.)

**67** 去，杏

*ch'ü*[4], To go. 厶 *ssu*[1], is the radical, the 28th. It is made, however, from a picture of an empty vessel ∪ *ch'ü*[1] and its cover 土; hence the meaning of to empty, to remove, leave, go, all being ideas connected with the removing of the cover of a vessel and its contents. The top resembles 土 *t'u*[3] in the modern writing, and 大 *ta*[4] in the old. The bottom is like 厶 *ssu*[1], but here stands for ∪ *ch'ü*[1], a basin. (W. 38 F.) See 89.

**68** 了，𗊯

*liao*[3], A child in swaddling clothes. (Compare 子, No. 1.) This character being of no use was borrowed for the common suffix to denote past time in a verb, or the end of a sentence, conclusion, intelligent. clear. (W. 94 H.)  ╎ *kun*[3] is the radical, No. 2, perpendicular.

**69** 對

*tui*[4], Opposite; parallel sentences on scrolls hung opposite each other; to correspond to, to suit, match, agreeing with; sign of dative.

寸, ⼹ *t'sun*[4], inch, is the radical, the 41st, to measure. The dot represents the pulse on the wrist about an inch from the hand. In composition used often for ⼹ hand. (W. 45 B.)

丵 *tsao*[2] Luxuriant vegetation, being a representation of its branching into many twigs from a single stem; emanation, multitude, faggot. (W. 102 I.)

士 *shih*[4], A scholar, gentleman; the 33rd radical; from 一 *i*[1] and 十 *shih*[2], because all things are comprised between the numerative one and ten, therefore an affair (same as 事), a thing, and by extension a sage, scholar (W. 24 C.). Before 100 B.C. 口 *k'ou*[3] was in the place of 士 *shih*[4]. *Tui*[4] therefore means to apply a measure 寸 *t'sun*[4] to the luxuriant emanation 丵 of men's mouths 口 *k'ou*[3], i.e., men's testimonies. Emperor Wen Ti, in 100 B. C. changed the writing to 士 *shih*[4] to remind his officers that men's testimonies 口 must not be believed, but only the words of the 士 sages, which alone deserve to be examined 寸. (W. 102 I.)

**70** 國, 國

guó

*kuo*[2], A state, country. From 口 *wei*[2], a boundary (the radical, No. 31) and

或 { *yü*[4] a primitive appanage, post, a center; the *huo*[4], land 一 that one baron defended with the weapons 戈 of his retainers, around his 囗 castle, or town, whose limits are not indicated because there were none. Pronounced *huo*[4] it means by extension an indeterminate person, whose name is not given, being known only as from a certain estate; by extension, again, uncertain, perhaps, "a certain one." With the 囗 *wei*[2] or boundary added, it becomes an estate well defined, a country 國. (W. 71 J.)

**71 聲**

*sheng*[1], Sound, music, voice, accent, tone; to declare

耳, 𦣝 *erh*[3], ear, is the radical, the 128th, used in a natural group of characters relating to hearing. It is a picture of the external ear. (W. 146 A.)

殸, 殸 *ch'ing*[4] On the right is 殳 *shu*[1], the 79th radical meaning the right hand (W. 22 D.), making a jerky motion, to strike, a staff, to kill. On the left is a primitive picturing sonorous jade or quartz stones suspended from a frame to make a musical instrument; these stones were in the form of a carpenter's square, and were struck like a triangle. The character is now written with a 石 *shih*[2] 磬. 声 is used as an abbreviation of 聲. The combination of ear 耳 and musical stones 声 struck by the hand 殳 naturally makes 聲 sound. (W. 173 A.)

声

**72 說**

shuo[1], To talk, speak, converse, sayings, doctrines.

言 yen[2], is the radical, No. 149. (See No. 10.)

兌,兌 yüeh[4], To speak, to rejoice, i.e., good words 兄 that dispel 八 grief and rejoice 兒 the hearer. This is made up of 兄 (huang[4], ancient pronunciation, a mouth 口 on top of a man 儿, or to speak authoritatively ; pronounced hsiung[1] it is the oldest brother who must exhort his brothers) and 八 to dissipate the breath or divide it into words, to speak. By an arbitrary modern borrowing the character is read tui[4], and means exchange. (W. 29 D.)

**73 話**

hua[4], Words, discourse, a language. Words 言 of the 舌 she[2], tongue.

言 yen[2], is the radical, No. 149. (See No. 10.)

舌,舌 she[2], Tongue, is a picture of the tongue protruding from the mouth. (Compare 圅 han[2], the tongue drawn back into the mouth 圅.) It is the 135th radical. (W. 102 C.)

**74 吃**

ch'ih[1], To stutter, to swallow, to eat ; to suffer.

口 k'ou[3], mouth is the radical, No. 30.

乞 ch'i[3] To beg. It is a contraction of 气 ch'i[4], vapor, breath,—the 84th radical. (See No. 47.) In this form it is borrowed for 匃 kai[4] to mean beg. (W. 98 A.)

To stammer 吃 is to fill the mouth 口 with breath 乞, and make no progress in speech. In eating one mouths the food as in stammering one mouths the breath, hence to eat.

**75** 飯

*fan*⁴, A meal, cooked **rice** (the chief dish of a meal).

食
食 *shih*², to eat, is the radical, No. 184, relating to food in general. It is formed of △ *chi*², to collect (see No. 18), and 皀皀 *hsiang*¹, boiled grain, the sweet smell of the 飯 *fan*⁴. It is a picture of the bowl ㅎ and its contents—, and a ヒ *pi*³, spoon, to ladle it out. ヒ *pi*³, spoon, is the 21st radical. (W. 26, C.L.M.) Gather △ the family to eat 食 the rice 艮.

反
反 *fan*³, To return, turn back, turn over; opposite; to rebel. From 又 *yu*⁴, hand, and 厂 a representation of the motion of the hand in turning over. (厂 *han*⁴, is a cliff, a retreat, shelter. Radical No. 27.) (W. 43 E.) In eating the hand returns again and again 反 to the mouth with 食 food.

**76** 兒, 臾

*erh*², A male child, a person with the fontanelles not yet closed, a child.

儿 *jen*², man, the 10th radical, is the radical of this character.
The upper part is written like 臼 *chiu*⁴, the 134th radical, but it is really 囟 *hsin*¹, skull, open above, as the skull of an infant. (W. 29 B.)

**77** 曉

*hsiao*³, Dawn, bright, to understand; i.e., a high and bright 堯 sun 日.

日 *jih*⁴, sun, is the radical combined with
堯 *yao*², eminent, lofty. From 垚 *yao*², earth, heaped up (three 土 earths) and 兀 *wu*⁴, a high base, level on top. 堯 *Yao*² is the name of a famous ancient emperor, 2300 B.C.

(W. 81 C.) When the sun 日 is high 堯 one can see and understand 曉.

**78 得**

tê², To get, receive.

彳, 彳 ch'ih⁴ to take a step forward with the left foot, to walk (60th radical) is the radical (W. 63 A). It was added to this character late, and is superfluous.

尋, 冔 tê² to obtain, to get, is the original writing of the character, 得 and in the seal writing shows its etymology, viz., to get the hand 寸 on that which one has in view 見. The 見 *chien*⁴, see, is reduced to 旦. (W. 45 E.) See No. 85.

寸 *t'sun*⁴, Inch. See No. 69.

**79 没**

mo⁴ or *mei*², To sink in the water, to dive, to perish ; none of, not, least, without.

水, 氵 shui³, Water, is the radical (No. 85.) The central stroke represents a rivulet, and the others the ripples on the surface of the water. (W. 12 A, B ; 125 A.)

殳, 뫃 mu² To dive, while turning 回 hui², on oneself in order to get 又 something under the water, the head being below. The 回 hui², is changed by scribes to 刀. (W. 76 I.)

**80 句**

chü⁴, A sentence.

口 k'ou³, mouth, is the radical with

勹, 勹 pao¹ to wrap up, (the 20th radical), from a picture of a man bending over to envelop an object in his apron ; therefore to enfold, a bundle, to contain, a whole. The mouth 口 used to form a whole 勹 phrase or sentence. (W. 54 A, for pao¹.)

**81** 在杜     *tsai*⁴, To be in or at; i.e., to exert one's powers 才 *t'sai*², on the earth 土; or presence in a place 土 *t'u*³, is manifested by one's activity 才. (W. 96 D.)

土 *t'u*³, is the radical

扌,才,丰   *t'sai*², has been modified to 才. It is a tree grown to a size for timber, materials, now written 材 *t'sai*²; then force of expansion, natural activity, mental capacity, talents, the substance of a thing. (W. 96 A.)

**82** 裏,裏    *li*³, The lining of clothes; inner, inside; to the left (in rules of the road).

衣 *i*¹, clothes, is the radical, No. 145; (see No. 51.).

里 *li*³, a village, is the phonetic, but being placed inside the radical for clothes it suggests the meaning of lining or inside. (W. 16 G.) It is the 166th radical, of a few incongruous characters. It is made up of

田 *t'ien*², field, the (102nd radical), being a representation of a furrowed field, and of

土 *t'u*³, earth. Its common meaning of *li*³, or one-third of an English mile, comes from the ancient custom of the smallest village being composed of the fields of eight families being arranged around a ninth public field with a well represented by the pictorial character 井 *ching*³ (the dot being the well.) One side of the square was one *li*³ in length. When the custom went out of use the character 井 *ching*³ lost the dot and retained the simple meaning of well. 田 *t'ien*² being easy to write, is used to represent many objects. (W. 149, A and D.)

83  *wei²*, To be, to make; *wei⁴*, for, because, in order to.

爪 *chua¹*, *chao³*, claws, the prone hand, is the radical (No. 87.)

The seal character represents a mother monkey, sitting with one hand at its head and the other at the bottom of the character mixed up with its tail and feet. In the middle is the character for man 人 because of the monkey's likeness to a man, and the primitive character for breasts to show that it is a mother. The Shuo Wen says that of all animals (literally "birds") the female monkey is most prone to claw 其爲禽好爪 and therefore the character 爪 *chao³*, stands as its symbol. There is an ancient writing consisting solely of two claws ⊖. The character has lost its primitive meaning, and now is borrowed for to be, because, etc. (W. 49 H.)

————

BALLER, LESSON IV.

84 牀, 牀

床 爿, 爿 *ch'uang²*, A bed, couch, sled.

*ch'iang²*, is the radical, No. 90, a heavy slab, a thick, strong plank. It is the left half of the 木 *mu⁴* as written in the seal form (W. 127 A.)

木, 朮 *mu⁴*, Wood. A bed 牀 is made of strong pieces 爿 of wood 木.

85 見, 見 *chien⁴*, To see. This is the 147th radical, of characters relating to sight, perception.

Wieger explains it as an eye 目 *mu⁴*, on a man 人 (W. 158 C.) But Chalfant finds a writing more ancient than the seal writing 允, which is a picture of the eye emitting light. The Chinese believe that light comes out of a normal eye, enabling it to see.

**86** 第

*ti⁴*, An order, series ; before a number it forms the ordinal.

竹 *chu²*, bamboo, the 118th radical, is the radical. (See No. 7.) It is chosen perhaps because of the graduation of joints in a bamboo stalk.

弟, 帝 *ti⁴*, Represents a thread or cord wound around a spindle having a catch on top and a catch or winch below. It is a primitive bobbin or reel, and means by extension a succession of brothers, and now only the younger brothers. This primitive is appropriate for series, as is also the bamboo, 竹 used as its radical. (W. 87 E.)

**87** 章, 章

*chang¹*, A strain in music or a chapter in a book, or an essay ; rules.

立 *li⁴*, to establish, stand, (the 117th radical) is arbitrarily taken for the radical ; but the etymology is from 音 *yin¹* (See No. 39), sound, and 十 *shih²*, ten, a perfect number. Therefore ten 十 sounds or strains 音 constitute a musical composition ; and the meaning is extended to a chapter, or an essay. (W. 73 E.)

**88** 到, 勶

*tao⁴*, To arrive at, to reach.

刀 *tao*[1], knife, is the radical (No. 18.) (See No. 37.) But here it has phonetic force as well.

至, 坣 *chih*[4], To go, to arrive at (classical). The 133rd radical. It represents a bird 乑 flying down to the earth, —, therefore to arrive, reach. (W. 133 B.) It is both pictorial and indicative in its composition.

**89** 紅

*hung*[2], Red, lucky, pleasant.

糸, 枲 *ssu*[1] or *mi*[4] is the radical (No. 120.) (See No. 8.) Textile matters, especially silk, interested the Chinese from ancient times hence the importance given to these elements in their writing. 厶 ㅇ *ssu*[1], the 28th radical, is a single cocoon in which the worm wraps himself up, caring for nothing but self; therefore the meaning, selfish, private, separation. (W. 92 A.)

工, 工 *kung*[1], is purely phonetic. Work, workman, time of work. It pictures the ancient carpenter's square, and so by extension means work, skill, or any ornament requiring skill. (W. 82 A.)

Red 紅 not being a natural color of silk 糸 it requires the work 工 of the dyer to produce red silk.

**90** 好, 𡥫

*hao*[3], Good, right, very; *hao*[4], to be fond of. From 女 *nü*[3], woman, and 子 *tzu*[3], child. Wife 女 and child 子 are what one is most fond of 好. (Or the fondness of a woman for her child.) See No. 1.

女, � nü[3], is the Radical, No. 38. It originally was a woman standing in ceremonial attitude with arms hanging and crossed over the body. So symmetrical a character was hard to write, and the seal is a modification of the more ancient form. (W. 67 A.)

**91** 上, 丄

上

shang⁴, Above, superior, to mount, upon.

一 i¹, representing a horizontal base line, is the radical. The perpendicular line above it represents something above the level. (An indicative character.) It was originally written 二, the short upper line representing something above the longer base line. At the top of some characters it is written ㇊, as in 立帝旁 where it is distinguished from 亠 t'ou², the fictitious eighth radical. (W. 5 A.)

**92** 下, 丁

下

hsia⁴, Below, to descend, inferior.

一 i¹, is the radical, with the perpendicular below it to represent something below as in the preceding character. It was anciently written 二 the longer line representing the base. (W. 5 B.)

**93** 完, 宛

wan², Finished, complete, to settle (as an affair).

宀 mien² house, roof, is the radical, No. 40. (See No. 1.)

元 yüan², That which is upon 二 (equivalent to 上, See No. 91.) a man 儿, i.e., the head, origin, principle. While phonetic in force in this character, we may say, " Putting on the roof 宀 over the head 元 finishes 完 the building." (W. 29 H.)

**94 送**

sung⁴, To escort, to see a guest out ; to give a gift ; to accuse at court.

辵 cho⁴ going, is the radical, No. 162.

关 省 cheng⁴ A fire that can be handled, as to bend planks for a boat or to caulk a boat; charcoal.

A torch 火 carried 𦥑 to escort a guest out 送. 关 is a suggestive phonetic and of no value to the beginner. (W. 47 J.)

**95 關**

kuan¹, A cross bar of a gate, to shut or bar the gate, a custom-house barrier, suburb.

門 men², door, is the radical, No. 169. (See No. 5.)

絲 𦆨 kuan¹ To pass threads through a web with a shuttle. The 絲 ssu¹ (contracted into 𢇁) represents the warp. The down strokes in the lower part represent the shuttle carrying the thread through to form a woof. (See Nos. 8 and 24.) By extension it means to join, to fix transversely. (W. 92 G.) The cross bar of the gate passes through the slots and iron loops like a shuttle passing through the warp.

**96 事, 事**

shih⁴, To serve, affairs, office, matter, anything.
亅 kou¹ is the radical, the 6th. It is from

史, 喦 shih³, shows a hand 彐 holding as tylus. A recorder, to record. In 事 the top is 屮=之 chih¹, the pronoun it. An event 事, record 史 it 之 faithfully.

**97 穿, 𡧫**

ch'uan¹, To bore 穴 with the teeth 牙, to perforate ; to put on clothes, wear ; to thread, to string.

穴 hsüeh²⁴, A cave, a hole, any dwelling, i.e., a

room or space 宀 made by the removal 八 *pa*¹ of the earth; to dig through, bore. The 116th radical. (W. 37 A, D.)

牙,  *ya*², The teeth, the grinders or molar teeth, hooks. It is a picture of the grinding face of a molar. The 92nd radical. (cf. W. 147 A.) Chalfant IV, Williams.

98 就,  *chiu*⁴, To go or come to, to follow; to make the best of; then, soon, immediately.

尢,  *wang*¹ radical No. 43, is the radical under which it is found in the dictionaries. A man 大 who puts his weight on his right leg; to spring; lame, crooked, also written 尣. (W. 61 C.) This classification was an etymological error, however, for it comes from

尤,  *yu*², which in the seal writing pictures a dog with its ears pricked up. By extension, attracted to, surprise, strange. (W. 134 C.)

京,  *ching*¹, The capital; originally high, elevated; being a contraction of 高 *kao*¹, high, the bottom changed by substituting 亅 for 口, adding the idea of elevation, and by reducing 冂 to 八; it has nothing to do with 小 *hsiao*³. The capital is the place to which the people go; hence towards.

就 Admiration or attraction to 尤 something high 高 therefore to go towards, to follow, consequently. (W. 75 C.)

 Chalfant finds an ancient form of 京 picturing the gate tower of a walled city with the opening in perspective.

99 **聽,聽**    *t'ing*[1], To hear, to listen, to understand, to allow.

**耳**   *erh*[3], the ear (see No. 71.), is the R., No. 128.

**壬, 𡈼**   *t'ing*[2] Good, full; from a man standing on the earth in his official position (to be distinguished from 壬 *jen*[2]), is the phonetic. (W. 81 D.)

**悳,悳**   *te*[2], Virtue. Therefore we have 聽 *t'ing*[1] as the virtue 悳 practised by the ear 耳; i.e., hearing, to obey. 悳, *te*[2], used for the Christian term character, virtue, is usually written 德, with the 彳 adding the idea of going out to others, action. Its composition is of 直 *chih*[2], upright, and 心 *hsin*[1], heart; an upright heart.

**直, 直**   *chih*[2], is composed of ㄴ representing a horizontal and a perpendicular, 十 ten and 目 eye. Before the days of square and plumb-line, ten eyes were called on to test the straightness of the frame of a house. The ㄴ is often changed to a single straight line. It is often written incorrectly 直 as if of two strokes. (W. 10, K.)

100 **知, 知**   *chih*[1], To know, perceive; *chih*[4], wisdom.

**矢, 𢞤**   *shih*[3] an arrow, dart, is the radical, No. 111.
**𡗉**     It is a picture, the point above, notch and feathers below. Therefore an action that
**𢎥**     has come to an end, irrevocable, as an ancient form shows the arrow fixed in a man's body. (W. 131 A.)

United with 口 *k'ou*[3], mouth, we have the knowledge possessed by one who can give his word, opinion, with the precision and speed of an arrow. Knowledge 知 is an arrow 矢 mouth 口.

**101** 道

*tao*[4], To go at the head, to lead; a road, a path, principle, doctrine; the progress of a speech, to speak.

辶 = 辵 *cho*[4] is the R., the 162nd, to go. (See No. 10.)

首 *shou*[3], the head, is the primitive 𦣻 *shou*[3], head, 𩠐 with the hair added, being a pictorial character. (巛 is not 巛 *ch'uan*[1], streams,) 185th radical.

To lead, road, 道 is to go 辵 at the head, 首. (W. 160 A.) It is the way not only for the feet to walk in 辵 but also for the thoughts 首 to move in.

**102** 看, 𥄀

*k'an*[4], To look, to see, to regard carefully. It is composed of;—

目, ⊕ *mu*[4], an eye (which is the radical, No. 109), a 𠃊 picture (compressed and often set upright to save room), (W. 158 A.) and

手 *shou*[3], the hand, covering the eye or shading it. "For," says the Shuo Wen, "one shades the eyes in order to see better, cutting off the rays of the sun, and gathering the light" from the eye. (W. 48 C.)

**103** 拿

*na*[2], Hands 手 united 合 *ho*[2]; to take, to sieze; a sign of the accusative when placed before the noun.

手 *shou*[3], hand, is the radical, No. 64. (See No. 53.)

合 *ho*[2], joining, uniting, union, harmony. Formed of △ *chi²*, a triangle, union, being three lines united (see No. 18), and 口 *k'ou³*, mouth. Three or many △ mouths 口 together shows good understanding, harmony. (W. 14 A, B.)

To take with the hand 拿 requires the hand 手 to come in contact with 合 the object.

**104** 邊

*pien¹*, To walk on the edge of a precipice, to fall in and disappear; a bank between fields, margin, edge, boundary, i.e., the place where the thing disappears.

辶 = 辵 *cho⁴* to go, is the radical, the 162nd. (See No. 10.)

 *yen¹* Disappearance, absence. In modern writing the 冂 (double cover) has been changed to 方 arbitrarily. It is made up of:—

自, 白 *tzu⁴*, a picture of the nose; a starting point, origin, beginning, evolution; the nose being, according to Chinese embryology, the starting point in the development of the body; self, I, my behavior, to act; the nose being the projecting part and in a way the characteristic of the person; the 132nd radical; (W. 159 A.) and

穴 *hsüeh²*, a cave, storehouse, and

方 = 冂 a double cover meaning invisibility. Therefore 舁 *yen¹* is an object that was at one time 自 *tzu⁴* in a storeroom 穴 and later on disappeared 冂. Therefore 邊 is to walk 辵 on the disappearing line 舁; the edge. (W. 34 K.)

**105** 頭

*t'ou²*, The head, the end of a beam or street,

etc., the beginning ; a classifier of affairs, cattle, etc.

頁, 𩑞 yeh⁴, Head, page, man.　A picture of a head or face 百 upon a man 人.　It is the radical, the 181st.　(W. 160 C.)

豆, 豆 tou⁴, A sacrificial dish, a dish in which meat was served; beans, (being used for 荳 tou⁴).　The 151st radical.　It is possibly a suggestive phonetic in this character.　The skull encloses the brain as a dish its contents, and the Thibetans use the skull bone for a dish, on a tripod standard.　(W. 165 A.)

106 箱　hsiang¹, A box, a chest.　(Larger than 匣子 hsia² tzu.)

竹 chu², bamboo, is the radical, the 118th, indicating the material.　(See No. 7.)

相, 𥄶 hsiang¹, to examine, to inspect.　It may be from 目 mu⁴, to watch from behind a 木 mu⁴, tree ; or to keep the eye 目 open in the 木 woods so as to avoid danger from foes or beasts.　The more common abstract meaning of mutual, reciprocity, etc., is said to come from a kind of pun, both elements, 木 and·目 being pronounced alike, mu⁴.　It is purely phonetic here.　(W. 158 B.)

---

BALLER, LESSON V.

107 晚　wan³, Late, evening, sunset, twilight, late in life, tardy.

日 jih⁴, sun, is the radical, No. 72, as the character has to do with the declining sun.

免, 𠘟 mien³, a man 儿 whose sides are swollen out

口 with his effort, and whose legs are spread out to prop himself firmly to fight or ward off some evil ; therefore it means to avoid, without. In 晚 it is purely phonetic. (W. 106 A.) According to Mr. Chalmers 免 is a man trying to hide himself by drawing in to his clothing ; hence to avoid. The sun 日 withdrawing 免, it is late 晚.

**108 前, 峎**

*ch'ien²*, To advance, forward, toward, before, formerly.

刀 *tao¹*, is the radical, 18th, arbitrarily fixed without reference to the etymology. The upper part 止 is a contraction of 止, *chih³*, to stop, and the 刖 is a contraction of

舟, 舟 *chou¹* a boat, the 137th radical. It is a picture in the seal writing of a boat with high curved prow, a deck supported by one of the partitions in the hull, an oar in front and a rudder behind. It is straightened and placed upright to save room. (W. 66 A.) A boat 舟 advancing 前 into the harbor where it will stop 止. (W. 66 D.)

**109 快**

*k'uai⁴*, A flow of spirits, cheerful ; promptness, rapid, sharp, quick.

忄 = 心 *shu⁴ hsin¹*, is the radical, the 61st, meaning heart. See No. 18.

夬, 夬 *chüeh²* To divide, to partake, a hand 彐 holding a half of a 中 *chung¹* or object of any kind, that may be equally divided. (W. 43 O.) The splitting is instantanious when sufficient force is applied ;

therefore quick. As quickness depends on the mind, thus the radical 心 is added.

**110** 年, 秊

*nien²*, A year; at first, the crop or harvest, and then the year, for that is the time taken to produce the thousand grains.

干, 丫

丫

*kan¹*, A shield, is the radical, the 51st; a trunk or stem; to look after or concern; originally a picture of a pestle, so to grind. The seal writing is a combination of *jen²* man, and *ch'ien¹*, a thousand. This combination is difficult to explain. (W. 24 D.) In the present edition the writing on the Oracle Bones is followed, 秊 a man bearing home a sheaf of grain. (J.M. Menzies.) Its meaning was identical with the modern meaning of 歲 *sui⁴*, No. 197 and 869.

**111** 早, 早

日

*tsao³*, Early, morning, soon, formerly.

*jih⁴*, sun, is the radical, the 72nd, as the idea early, has to do with the rising sun. The 十 *shih²* is an old writing of 甲 *chia³*, first, a helmet. 早 *tsao³* is the time of day when the sun 日 has risen as high as a man's helmet. It also means first 甲 sun 日. (W. 143 E.)

**112** 挑

手
兆
川

*t'iao¹*, To carry a load from the two ends of a pole, to stir up, to choose, to reduce.

*shou³*, or *t'i² shou³* is the radical. See No. 53.

*chao⁴*, omen, is a picture of the lines on the back of a tortoise shell brought out by heating for divination; in the middle is ⼘ *pu³* in its ancient form; an omen, a million or vast number. (W. 56 D.) This phonetic is the same as in 逃 *t'ao²* to run. It is two 八 *pa¹* characters, one outside the other indicating wide separation. It is probable that this phonetic was selected as in carrying a burden in this way, half at either end of a pole, it must be divided or separated.

113 天, 兲    *t'ien*[1], Heaven, the sky, a day, the weather, celestial; the Emperor, great, high, any superior over an inferior; moral superiority.

大 *ta*[4], great, is the radical, but the meaning of the character is not the one — great 大, as it is often translated, but the one sky — which is over man 大; thus it is an indicative character, not a logical combination. (W. 60 C and 1 C.)

114 節    *chieh*[2], The nodes or joints of the bamboo, any joint, knot, verse; a feast day; temperance.

竹 *chu*[2], is the radical, No. 118, bamboo. (See No. 7.)

即, 皂 *chi*[2] To eat, that which is done as soon as the fragrance of the cooked rice 皀 (see No. 75) is smelt. By extension a conjunction meaning consequence in general, being the equivalent in *wen li* of the 就 *chiu*[4] of common use. (W. 26 M.)

卩, 㔾 *chieh*[2], is a suggestive phonetic in 卽. It is written either 卩 or 㔾. (See No. 42.) It is the 26th radical, meaning joint, the proper quantity. (W. 55 B.)

115 初, 衦    *ch'u*[1], To cut out 刀 *tao*[1] clothes 衣 *i*[1]; i.e., to begin making garments, which is the first step in civilization; to begin, the first, at first.

刀 *tao*[1], knife, is the radical, the 18th. For 衣 *i*[1], see No. 51. 初 The first thing in making clothes 衣 is to cut out 刀. (W. 16 B.)

**116** 給

*kei*[3], To give to, to let, allow, for, instead of, to, Read *chi*[3], to receive, to afford, to give out.

糸 *ssu*[1] silk floss, is the radical, No. 120.

合 *ho*[2], To join, union, harmony. (See No. 103.) To give is to join 合 silk threads 糸. Silk is a popular present.

**117** 叫, 暭

*chiao*[4], To call, to tell, to command, to cause; the cries of the birds and animals; named, termed.

口 *k'ou*[3], mouth, is the radical, No. 30.

斗, 毛 *tou*[3], Measure, ten 十 *sheng*[1] or pints 升. It is a picture of the peck measure, said to be a scoop with a handle: 68th R. (W. 98 B.) 叫 is to call out 口 the measure 斗.

**118** 半, 半

*pan*[4], To divide in two; a half, a large piece of.

十 *shih*[2], ten, is the classification in the standard dictionary, the 24th radical. It comes etymologically from 八, to divide, and 牛 an ox. (See No. 50.) To divide 八 an ox 牛 into two halves as butchers split the beef down the backbone. (W. 18 D.)

**119** 過, 調

*kuo*[4], To pass by, cross over, to pass time, to exceed, sin of ignorance, sign of past time.

辵 *cho*[4] to go, is the radical, the 162nd. The rest is a suggestive phonetic. See No. 10.

咼, 呙 *kua*[3], A wry mouth, hare lip or cleft palate. It is from 口 *k'ou*[3], mouth; and

咼, 咼 *kua*³, Skull and bones, to strip off the flesh, to bone, to disarticulate, broken, and so a defect. The 辵 to go, means action and 咼 *kua*³, defective; defective **action is sin** 過. (W. 118 A.)

**120** 緊

*chin*³, To bind fast, to press tight, urgent, important. From

糸 *ssu*¹, *mi*⁴, a silk thread, the 120th radical and

臤 臤 *chien*¹, firm, solid. To have hold 又 of one's servants 臣, *ch'en*²; 臣 a servant bending before his master, the 131st radical. (W. 82 E.)

**121** 以, 㠯

*i*³, A form of 㠯 or 已 already.

人 *jên*.² man, is the radical.

When preceded by 可 *k'o*³, could, it is equivalent to can be, may be. It is a very ancient primitive representing the exhalation of breath, the virtue of any object, its use, and so use until exhaustion, to end, to be no more, passed, already. It is written in four ways in modern times, 已 㠯 厶 以. When written 以 it means use, by, with, by means. (W. 85 B, F.) is the radical.

**122** 晨

日 *ch'en*², Sun shining forth, morning.

日 *jih*⁴, sun, is the radical, No. 72.

辰, 辰 *ch'en*², A day, time, the 161st radical; 7 to 9 A.M., the heavenly bodies. These are borrowed meanings; the original means to be pregnant, a woman who bends forward 厂 *jen*² to conceal 丏 *mien*⁴ her pregnancy, " her shame," says the Shuo Wen. (W. 30 B.) For another explanation see No. 864. Purely phonetic here.

丏, 丐 *mien*⁴ A woman sitting, — is the girdle, at the left is the seat, at the right is an apron that hides the front of the body, the pregnancy, says the Shuo Wen. Therefore the meaning to hide, conceal. (W. 112 L.)

**123** 昨

日 *jih*⁴, sun, is the radical, the 72nd.

凵亡, 匚 *wang*², A primitive meaning to hide, from 入 *ju*⁴, to enter, and 乚 a hiding place.

乍, 匚 *cha*⁴, is 匚 plus — which represents an obstacle, that is, to seek to hide and to be hindered; therefore the modern meanings of suddenly, hastily, unexpectedly. (W. 10 F.)

昨 yesterday has passed suddenly out of existence. The sun 日 hastily 乍 hid.

**124** 現

*hsien*⁴, The glitter 見 of gems, 玉; to appear, to manifest; at once, now.

玉, 王 *yü*⁴, a gem, (the radical, No. 96), jade, pearly, half translucent stones. The character represents three pieces of jade strung together, the dot being added to distinguish it from 王 *wang*², king. (W. 83 A.)

見 *chien*⁴, to see; the appearance of. (See No. 85.)

**125** 時, 旹

*shih*², Time.

日 *jih*⁴, sun, is the radical, No. 72.

寺 *ssǔ*⁴, temple, is the conventional phonetic for the modern writing. 土＝之 *chih*¹ is a small plant 屮 issuing from the ground —; to grow, development, continuity. Standing alone it is borrowed now for the sign of the genitive or possessive case in the classic language. 寸 *t'sun*⁴, inch, rule, law. Hence the 寺 *ssǔ*⁴ or temple is the

48

place where the law 寸 is applied constantly 业. (W. 79 B.)

者 The ancient writing of 時 shih², was 耂, meaning the time of sprouting of plants under the influence of the sun, or perhaps the continuity 土 = 之 of the solar 日 periods. (W. 79 B.)

126 候 hou⁴, To wait, to expect, to inquire, a time or period.

人 jen², is the radical, the 9th. The character was originally written 侯 meaning a nobleman, and read hou².

侯, 矦, 㘴 hou², The upright stroke was inserted, some say, to differentiate the meaning of wait, time, etc. Others say it is the archer's attendant. The original character is composed of 矢 arrow (see No. 100), sticking in the target above 厂 with a man beside it 𠂆. The man is reduced to 亻 and the target to ユ. Shooting at a target was the means of selecting officials, for the good shot must have an upright heart, so the character means a nobleman. With the 亻 reduced to | and another 亻 added it means to wait 候 as a target marker does. (W. 59 H.)

127 明, 明 ming², bright, the dawn; evident, open; intelligent; illustrious in virtue.

日 jih⁴, sun, is the radical, No. 72.

月 yüeh⁴, moon (see No. 43.) The sun and the moon are the two brightest things. The early seal character has the character 囧 for window instead of 日 sun. Here the idea of brightness **was from** the moon shining in at the window.  (W. 42 C.)

**128** 從,訓    *t'sung²*, To follow, obey.  A man walking after another, **and often written** 从 to represent that idea.

彳 *ch'ih⁴* is the radical, No. 60.  從 is two men 从 walking 彳 and **stopping** 止 together, i.e., to follow, obey.  (W. 27 A.)  In the seal character the 彳 and 止 are united into a 辵 *cho⁴*, going.  See No. 10.

---

### VOCABULARY I OF BALLER'S LESSONS.

**129** 記    *chi⁴*, To remember, **being composed of** 言 word, and 己 self, succession ; to record ; a sign ; to tell 言 the succession 己 of facts.

言 *yen²*, words, is the R., the 149th.  (See No. 10.)

己,己,己 *chi³*, self, in the seal writing represents threads on a loom, two of the warp, horizontal, and one of the woof, perpendicular ; hence the meaning of succession ; the 49th R. It is borrowed to mean self.  (W. 84 A.)

**130** 慢    *man⁴*, Remiss, rude ; to treat haughtily ; slow, easy, sluggish.

忄,心 *hsin¹*, called the *shu⁴ hsin¹*, is the radical, No. 61, as the qualities are those of the heart or mind.  cf. 快 *k'uai⁴*, quick, No. 109.

曼,曼 *man²* the phonetic, means to draw, extend or pull out with the hand, long.  冃 *mao⁴* is a hat or cap (picture 冂 with a — to represent the head).  冒,冒 *mao⁴*, to rush on heedlessly or with the eyes covered. The 目 is written horizontally to make room for the 又 hand, which pulls. (W. 34 J.)

**131** 長,兵 飛

*ch'ang²*, Long. The 168th radical, used in matters relating to hair, as it is a contraction of 髟 *piao¹*, bushy hair, the 190th radical. The seal writing shows that it is hair so long that it must be tied with a band —, and pinned with a brooch Y. It also means growth to manhood when the hair is long, and is read *chang³*, for the meaning growth. It also had the inverted man placed below 匕 to indicate change or growth. The modern form is an arbitrary contraction. (W. 113 A.)

**132** 店 广,广 占

*tien⁴*, A shop, an inn.

*yen³* A single slope shed roof, being half of 宀 *mien²*, or roof; a declivity or slope; the radical of this character, the 53rd; an outhouse or hut. (W. 59 I.) (See No. 24.)

*chan¹*, To ask 口 about some enterprise by heating a tortoise shell 卜; divination. It is purely phonetic unless we think that the diviner lived in a sort of public inn or shop, and a diviner's house was one of the first kinds of shop. (W. 56 B.) 占 has the same sense as 佔 to usurp or to occupy, hence well used in 店 *tien⁴* inn where one occupies a room for a consideration.

**133** 臉 肉,肉

*lien³*, Face.

*jou⁴*, Flesh, meat, made up of 勹 *pao¹*, a bundle,

and 仌 strips of dried meat; the 130th radical and the radical of this character. (W. 17 G. and 54.)

僉 *ch'ien*[1] All, unanimous, meeting, together. From 亼 *chî*[2], together, 从 several men and 吅 *hsüan*[1], clamor. A crowd cannot keep silent. Suggestive phonetic, for the *faces* are the conspicuous feature of a crowd. (W. 14 E.)

134 壺, 壺　　*hu*[2], A pot, a jug.

士 *shih*[4], a scholar, is the radical, the 33rd, but has nothing to do with the meaning, as it is simply the picture of the cover 土 on a vase 亞. Compare *ch'ü*[4], 去 No. 67. (W. 38 G.)

135 脚　　　*chiao*[3], A foot, a base.
　　脚

肉 *jou*[4], flesh, is the radical, No. 130. See No. 133.

却 *ch'üeh*[4], To throw aside, referring to the leg
却, 谷　being thrust back when sitting flat on the ground. It is composed of 卩 *chieh*[2], the radical, No. 26 (see No. 42), and 去 *ch'ü*[4], to go, reduced from 谷 *ch'iao*[4], the upper lip or 仌 flesh above the 口 mouth. To restrain 卩 the desires 谷. The character is still written 脚. (W. 17 H.)

136 輕　　　*ch'ing*[1], Light, not heavy. To think lightly of; to slight.

車, 車 *ch'e*[1], is the radica , classic *chü*[1]), a cart; the axle 丨 two whee s, 二 and the body 曰; it is set upright in writing to give more room; in composition it means to roll, to crush. It is the 159th radical of characters relating to vehicles. (W. 167 A.)

巠, 巠 *ching¹* is a pure phonetic here. It represents the streams 巛 flowing under the surface of the ground 一, and the 工 is not *kung¹*, but 壬 *t'ing³*, and is of phonetic force only, as seen in the seal writing.　(W. 12 H.)

**137** 乾, 乾

*kan¹*, The drying effect of the sun, dry, exhausted, to dry, clean. Adopted as a son by contract.　Read *ch'ien²*, the cloudy sky, heaven, the powers of nature, father.

乙 *i¹*, one, a stem, curved, vapor, is the radical, the 5th.　A redundancy, however.

倝, 倝 *kan⁴* is the sun 日 penetrating the jungle 朩 and drying up the vapors that were lying low on the ground 乁 万.　The lower part of the 朩 is suppressed to give place to the 万 vapors.　It has the idea of evaporation, fogs lifting, sun rising, etc.　With the adding of 乙 to form 乾 *ch'ien²*, the idea of rising vapors is intensified, and the character means cloudy sky, not the blue firmament.　It is used for *kan¹*, dry, by a license instead of 乾 in which 早 represents the drying effect 乙 of the sun upon dampness.　(W. 117 D.)

**138** 冷

*leng³*, Cold, chilly.

冫, 仌 *ping¹*, To freeze, ice. It represents the crystals that form on the surface of freezing water. It is the 15th radical of characters referring to cold and ice.　(W. 17 A.)

令 *ling⁴*, A law, an order, to command, your honored.　Pure phonetic in 冷.　(W. 14 I. See No. 61.)

**139** 熱     *jo⁴*, Hot, to warm, fever.

火 *huo³*, fire, is the radical, No. 86. (See No. 47). Here written ⺣ to save space.

執 翺 *chih²*, to grasp, to seize, to hold, to attend to. It is composed of

幸 *nieh⁴* a man 大 (changed to 土) who committed an offence 干 twice ⱽ or repeatedly, i.e., a criminal; (辛 *jen³*, is a second offence.) (W. 102 F.) and

丸 *chi⁴* to hold, to keep. A picture of a hand 丮 grasping something ㇇. It is changed in composition frequently to 丸 and 丮 凡. (W. 11 E.) Hence the meaning of 執 *chih²*, is to sieze 丸 a criminal 幸, or to grasp anything. (W. 102 G.) *Jo⁴* 熱 is the sensation when you grasp 執 fire 火.

**140** 深     *shen¹*, Deep, profound, ardent, intense; deep tinted.

水 *shui³*, is the radical, the 85th. (See No. 79.)

罙 窞 *shen¹* is the Chinese hearth or stove, or small cave-like hole 穴 under the kettle, (or in the *k'ang⁴*) in which the hand ⺕ pokes the fire 火. It looks dark and deep, therefore the meanings deep, profound. The fire and hand 㸚 have been transformed into 木 and the dot on the 穴 *hsüeh²* has been arbitrarily omitted by the scribes. Combined with ⺡ water it means deep; combined with 扌 hand, it means to fathom, or probe 探 *t'an¹⁴*. (W. 126 B.)

**141** 濕     *shih¹*, Moist, wet, damp, **low lying** ground, dejected.

水 shui[3], water, is the radical, the 85th. (See No. 79.)

顯 hsien[3], Two silk threads 絲 exposed to the sun
顯 日 where they become visible ; so, to be
visible, to appear, remarkable, evident,
bright. The bottom of the character is
contracted from 烗 to 灬. (W. 92 E.)
The water 水 appears 㬎 in a wet place 濕.
In another writing 溼 the 灬 is replaced by
— and the 灬 by 土 t'u[3], giving the meaning of the earth 土 where water 水 appears 㬎. (W. 92 E.)

142 高,高 kao[1], Lofty, high, eminent, noble, high priced,
excellent.
The 189th radical. In composition it
is variously contracted, overturned and
mingled with other elements. It represents a high pavilion 宀 on a lofty
foundation 冂, and with a hall 口 where
the people sit. (W. 75 B.) See No. 98.

143 帶,帶 tai[4], A girdle, a sash, belt, zone ; to take along
with one as if worn at the girdle, to bring,
to take, to lead, together with. It represents a belt — with trinkets hanging from
it 灬, and the robes falling below 帀 one
over the other. The lower part is made
巾 up of two chin 巾 characters one outside
the other. Chin[1] 巾 is a handkerchief suspended from a girdle, the two ends hanging down, the 丨 also meaning suspension.
It is radical No. 50, relating to cloth.
(W. 35 A, and W. 24 Q.) 巾 chin[1] is the
radical of this character.

**144** 寬,寬    *k'uan*[1], Large, broad; gentle, to forbear, slow, to enlarge.

宀 *mien*[2], roof, is the radical, No. 40. (See No. 1.)

莧,莧    *huan*[1] A chamois with slender horns, 卝 = 丫 *kuai*[1], (W. 103 C.) 見 represents the head, legs, and tail, (often omitted). 寬 may mean broad because a spacious enclosure is needed for the breeding of these wild animals. (W. 106 D.)

**145** 窄,窄    *chai*[3], Narrow, contracted, the opposite of *k'uan*[1]; narrow-minded.

穴 *hsueh*[2] cave, is the radical, No. 116. (See No. 97.)

乍 *cha*[4], To enter a hiding place and be hindered, i.e., crouching. Therefore we have 乍乞, crouching down in a 穴 cave, 窄 narrow. (W. 37 G, and 10 F.) (See No. 123 for *cha*[4].)

**146** 走 走    *tsou*[3], To walk, to travel, to hasten, to depart. The 156th radical. The seal character above represents a man bending over to walk rapidly 夭, and therefore means to bend. The part underneath is 止 *chih*[3], a foot at rest, or to stop; hence the combination may mean to bend the leg and to stop, i.e., to walk. Williams. (W. 112 A, D.)

**147** 放,放    *fang*[4], To put out to pasture, to let go, to put; loosen, liberate, to set free, disorderly.

攴 屶 *p'u*[1] to tap, to strike, oversee, is the radical, No. 66. A hand with a stick. (W. 43 D.)

方,� *fang*[1], A square, an open space, the 70th radical. Hence the combination means 放 to drive out 攴 into an open space or pasture 方. Compare 牧 *mu*[4], to drive 攴 cattle 牛, a shepherd. (W. 117 A.)

**148 講** *chiang*[3], To converse together, to preach, to explain.

言 *yen*[2], is the radical, the 149th.

冓, 冓 *kou*[4] is a graphic representation of the timbers in the roof and framework of a Chinese building ; hence its meaning of a network, a setting in order, a combination. Combined with 言 it means setting words 言 in order 講, i.e., to explain, to converse. Compare 構 wood 木 set in order, the truss of a roof. (W. 104 B.) Tuan shih's Shuo Wen says this character represents a network of irrigating ditches.

**149 作** *tso*[4], To act, to do, to make ; to arise, to appear ; to arouse. It refers to doing things, while 做 refers more to making things.

人 *jen*[2], man, is the radical, the 9th.

乍 *cha*[4], Suddenly, to excite. (See No. 123.) No etymology is given for 作.

**150 救** *chiu*[4], To assist, to rescue, to save from wrong.

攴 *p'u*[1] to tap, is the radical, the 66th. (See No. 147.)

求, 求 *ch'iu*[2], to ask, is the phonetic. Its meaning of to ask, pray, is found in the supposed custom of offering sacrifice and taking the skin of the offering in the hand, to present with the petition. The character repre-

sents the hand 彐 holding the tail or skin
朮. (W. 45 K.)

**151** 舖

*p'u*⁴, A shop. Correctly written 鋪 with 金
*chin*¹ for the radical.

舌, 舌 *she*², tongue, is the radical, the 135th. A picture of the tongue protruding from the
mouth. (W. 102 C.) (See No. 73.) It
is, however, really composed of 舍 *she*²

甫, 甫 (See No. 40), cottage, and 甫 *fu*³ as a pure
phonetic. 甫 is aptitude 用 *yung*⁴ (an arrow
hitting a target) for founding a family,
manhood, and then, the name assumed at
manhood or given by a friend. (W. 109
D.)

**152** 哥

*ko*¹, Older brother.

口 *k'ou*³, mouth, is the radical, No. 30.

可, 可 *k'o*³, To send forth a breathing 丁 of approbation from the mouth. Doubled it means
to sing. It is borrowed for brother.
When the lower stroke 丁 is curved the
other way, it is a cry, or difficult breathing. See No. 258. (W. 58 I.)

**153** 弟, 弟

*ti*⁴, Younger brother.

弓 *kung*¹, bow, is the radical, (the 57th) according
to Kang Hsi's arbitrary classification.
But see No. 86 for the primitive form and
etymology. (W. 87 E.)

**154** 隻, 隻

*chih*¹, A hand 彐 holding a single bird 隹, not a
pair as in 雙 *shuang*¹; hence the meaning
single, one by itself, a numerative of

ships, animals, birds, single individuals of things in pairs or sets, as arm, eye, shoe, etc. (W. 168 G.)

隹, 隹 *chui*[1] short-tailed birds, is the radical, No.
隻 172. The seal forms show it to be a picture of a bird with a short tail, cf. 鳥 *niao*[3],
鳥, 鳥 bird with a long tail. (W. 168 A.) (See No. 41.)

**155 打**

*ta*[3], To strike, to beat ; doing in general.

手 *shou*[3], hand, here called the *t'i*[2] *shou*[3], is the radical, No. 64.

丁, 个 *ting*[1], a nail (a picture) is that which the hand 手 strikes. Therefore the hand and the nail together form the verb to strike (the subject and the object of the verb). (W. 57 A.) Read *ting* it means to nail.

**156 洗**

*hsi*[3], To wash. The radical is 水 *snui*[3], water. (See No. 79.) In order to wash 洗 you must first 先 have water 水. (For *hsien*[1] 先 see No. 27.)

**157 忘**

*wang*[24], To forget. 心 *hsin*[1], heart, is the radical, No. 61.

亡, 亾, 亾 *wang*[2] to enter 入 a hiding place ㄴ to hide ; to perish, to run away, to cease. (W. 10 E.) The mind 心 ceases to act 亡, that is, forgets 忘.

**158 眼**

*yen*[3], Eye, a hole.

目 *mu*[4], eye, is the radical, No. 109. (See No. 102.)

艮, 艮, 艮 *ken*[4] firm, is a suggestive phonetic. It is the 138th R. meaning also, perverse, obstinate, to stop. It is from 目 *mu*[4], eye, and ヒ *hua*

to turn, change suddenly (a man 人 inverted 匕) as the eye changes in anger; therefore anger, defiance, haughtily, etc. (W.
26 L.) It is in the eye that anger may
first be seen in another person, hence the
use of 艮 in the character for eye.

**159** 睛　*ching¹*, The iris of the eye, the pupil; some say
the eyeball.

目　*mu⁴*, is the radical, No. 109. (See No. 102.)

青, 靑　*ch'ing¹*, The first of the five colors, the color of
nature, as the green of sprouting plants,
the blue of the sky, the azure of the ocean,
dark green, and black. (See No. 63.)
The black 靑 part of the eye is the pupil
睛 or the iris.

**160** 條　*t'iao²*, A twig; a bill; a classifier of long,
slender things.

木　*mu⁴*, wood, is the radical, No. 75.

攸, 㑃　*yu¹* to ford, is a man 人 crossing water (reduced to亻), and tapping with a stick 攴 to
sound the depth. It was borrowed to
mean a relative pronoun, and equivalent
in wen li, of 所 *so³*, a place. In 條 the 木
character may have been added because
the pole used in sounding was of wood,
and so the meaning of twig, slender, etc.,
came naturally by extension. (W. 12 C.)
A slender stick 條 of wood 木 is used by a
man who fords 攸 the stream.

**161** 街　*chieh¹*, A street, avenue; place of markets.

行, 彳亍　*hsing²*, to go, is the radical, No. 144. It represents two footprints, one step with the
left 彳 *ch'ih⁴* and one with the right 亍

60

*ch'e*⁴ (the reverse of 彳). 行 *hsing*² is the radical of characters relating to motion, the phonetic being inserted in the middle. (W. 63 C.)

圭 *kuei*¹, Lands, feudal appanages; from 土 *t'u*³, soil, doubled. By extension it is used of the sceptres or batons given the nobles when they were invested with their fief. (W. 81 B.)

162 雙

*shuang*¹, A pair, a match; an equal; to go with, to be matched.

隹 *chui*¹ birds, is the radical, No. 172. (See No. 154.) Two birds 隹 held in one hand 又 make a pair 雙. (W. 168 G.)

163 鞋

*hsieh*², Shoes; also written 鞵.

革,革 *ko*², To skin, to skin an officer, or degrade him from office, leather. It represents the skin of a sheep Ɣ (contracted from 羊) stretched between two bars 二 with two hands ⊖ at work on it to scrape off the wool. Radical No. 177. (W. 105 A.)

圭 *kuei*¹ is the phonetic. (See No. 161.) Leather 革 next to the land 圭 *kuei*¹, is a proper sign for shoes, 鞋.

BALLER, LESSON VI.

164 禮

*li*³, An act, particularly acts of worship, which will bring happiness; ceremony, propriety, good manners; offerings required by usage.

示,示 *shih*⁴, is the radical, No. 113, written 礻 in composition. It means a revelation (auspicious or unlucky) from heaven. The two horizontal lines are the old form of 上 shang⁴, high, superior; and the 小 represents sun, moon and stars, or signs in heaven which reveal transcendent things to men.

豊, 豐 *li*⁴ A vessel used in sacrificing. From 豆 *tou*⁴ (see No. 105), a vessel, and 凵 *k'an*³, a receptacle above it, ornamented with two sprays 丰 *feng*¹, symbol of plenty. (**W. 97 B.**)

Revelation 示 is needed in abundance 豐 to teach how to worship 禮.

**165** 殺

*sha*¹, To mow grass; to cut, shear, slay, kill. 殳 *shu*¹ the right hand making a jerky motion, to strike, a stick, kill, is the radical, No. 79. (See No. 71.) (W. 22 D.)

*sha*¹, to shear off the heads of grain, to kill. *i*⁴ Shears, representing the cutting blades.

*shu*², Millet, the glutinous kind with loose drooping heads, the seal character being a picture of it. (Also another writing is a hand separating three grains, hence glutinous millet, requiring effort to separate.) One dot is omitted in the modern writing 殺. So we have for *sha*¹ 柔, to cut off ㄨ the heads of the millet 术, and for the whole 殺 *sha*¹, the addition of the radical gives the strong motion of striking, intensifying the idea of to kill. (W. 39 B and 45 J.)

**166** 正

*cheng*⁴, Upright, correct, exact. proper, orthodox, etc.

止 *chih*³, is the radical, No. 77. (See Nos. 10 and 12.) To stop 止 at the appointed limit — without going astray is correct 正. (W. 112 A, and I.)

**167** 春, 曹

日 *jih*⁴, is the radical, No. 72. The seal writing has been strangely modified by moderns. It represents the budding and growth 屯 of plants 艸 under the influence of the sun 日. (W. 47 P.)

**168** 夏, 斁

*hsia*⁴, Summer, variegated, large. The first great dynasty.

夊 *sui*¹ to follow, is the radical, No. 35.

頁 *yeh*⁴ A man, head. A man 頁 who walks 夊 with his hands hanging down folded 臼 as farmers do in summer 夏 when the crops grow by themselves. In the modern character 頁 is contracted. (W. 160 D.)

**169** 秋, 燃

禾, 朿 *ho*², grain (growing) (a picture), is the radical, No. 115.

火, 火 *huo*³, fire (picture) is the 86th radical. Therefore autumn 秋 is the season when the grain 禾 standing in the fields, is burned 火, i.e., whitened and ripe (W. 121 C.)

**170** 冬, 𢈢

*tung*¹, The last or winter season; the end; to store up.

冫 *ping*, ice (picture, see No. 138) is the radical, No. 15.

夊 宋 *chung*¹ End, fixed. (To be distinguished from

radicals 34 夊 *chih*⁸, 35 夊 *sui*¹, 36 夕 *hsi*⁴, and 66 夊 *p'u*¹.) It is a skein of thread fastened at the end by a spindle or tie. The frozen 冫 end 夂 of the year is the winter season, 冬. An older form had sun 日 meaning the cessation of the action of the sun; or it might mean the sun confined. (W. 17 F.)

**171** 季

*chi*₄, Tender, the youngest of brothers, the end of a series of months or a season; the four seasons.

子 *tzŭ*⁸, son, is the radical, No. 39.

禾 *ho*² is contracted from 稚 *chih*⁴, the most delicate 稚 among the children 子, i.e., the last; then the last month of a season, and the season itself 季. (W. 94 A.)

**172** 臘

*la*⁴, To dry meat, the 12th month; winter solstice.

月, 肉 *jou*⁴, meat (see No. 133) is the radical, No. 130.

鼠, 巤 *lieh*⁴ Hairy, bristly, disorderly. It is a hairy 巛 head 囟, *hsin*¹ and 鼠 *shu*⁸ rat, contracted into 鼠. It has the legs, head whiskers and tail of a rodent. (W. 40 B, C.)

**173** 夜, 夾

*yeh*⁴, Night.

夕 *hsi*⁴ evening (see No. 14) is the radical, No. 36. The seal form shows that it means what is done by man 大 at evening 夕, that is, to lie down on his side 丿, and sleep; then by extension, night. The modern form is a quaint invention of the scribes, a man 人 under a cover 亠 at evening 夕. (W. 60 I.)

**174** 抬 擡

*t'ai²*, To carry on a pole, to elevate.

手 *shou³*, hand, is the radical, No. 64.

台 *t'ai²*, A mouth 口 exhaling a breath 厶. This is an arbitrary contraction for the form 臺 which is a high place 高 with the topmost point ㇔ changed to 土 and 至 *chih⁴* (underneath in place of 口), birds alighting there. (See No. 88) ; to elevate. (W. 75 B.)

**175** 開, 闇

*k'ai¹*, To open, to begin ; to boil.

門 *men²*, two-leaved door is the radical, No. 169.

廾 *kung³* Two hands folded, the 55th radical. The character represents two hands 廾 taking away the bar — from the door, that is, opening it. cf. 門 *shuan¹*, bolt. (W. 115 C.)

**176** 少

*shao³*, Few ; *shao⁴*, young.

小 *hsiao³*, small, is the radical, No. 42.

丿 *p'ieh¹* A left stroke, to diminish. To diminish 丿 that which is already small 小 ; few, less. (W. 18 M.)

**177** 鐘

*chung¹*, A bell, a clock.

金 *chin¹*, metal, is the R. No. 167. (See No. 13.)

童 *t'ung²*, A boy under 15 and unmarried, a spinster. It was originally a slave boy, like 妾 *ch'ieh¹*, a slave girl. It is from 辛 *hsin⁴*, crime, and 重 *chung⁴*, grave. A grave crime committed by parents caused the children to be reduced to slavery. The slaves were forced to remain unmarried, and so the meaning spinster, bachelor, virgin, and then concubine and catamite, for they were used as such. A slave might be beaten just as a bell. (W. 120 K.)

**178 點**     *tien*³, A black spot, a point, to punctuate, to light, as a lamp ; to count or check off, a minute of time.

黑, 黥   *hei*¹, black, soot, is the radical, the 203rd. The soot 黑 which the fires 灬 leave around the vent 囱 where the smoke escapes. The 灬 is a contraction of 炎 *yen*². (W. 40 D.)

占   *chan*¹, To ask 口 a diviner ト, to divine. It is purely phonetic. (See No. 132.)

**179 動**     *tung*⁴, To move, excite, to begin.

力, 𠚤   *li*⁴, Strength, muscle. A picture of a muscle in its sheath. It is the radical of the character, No. 19. (W. 53 A).

重   *chung*⁴, Heavy. (See No. 22). (W. 120 K.) When force 力 is exerted on heavy things 重, they move 動.

**180 刻**     *k'o*⁴, To cut, to carve ; a quarter of an hour.

刀, 刂   *tao*¹, the Rad., No. 18, a knife.

亥, 𢁅   *hai*⁴ purely phonetic, an horary character, 9—11 P.M. It is a picture of a pig, 豕 *shih*³ with a tail added. (W. 69 K.)

**181 分**     *fen*¹, To divide, distinguish, a minute. *Fen*⁴, duty, share.

刀   *tao*¹, knife, is the radical, the 18th.

八   *pa*¹, To divide.
    A knife 刀 that divides 八 = 分 to divide.

**182 表**     *piao*³, The outside, to make known, to manifest; a watch, indicator.

衣   *i*¹, clothes, is the R., the 145th.

毛   *mao*², Skins, furs, hair. Clothes were originally skins with the hair outside, therefore this character means the outside of clothes, the manifestation of the person, therefore, to manifest 表. A watch manifests the time. (W. 16 K.) The emperor dressed his huntsmen in different kinds of skin 毛 to *indicate* 表 their functions in the chase.

**183** 間

*chien*[1], A space, interval, division of a house.

門 *men*[2], door, is the R., No. 169. 間 has the sun 日 shining through the opening, therefore the meaning, space, interval. See No. 5 and 12.

**184** 多

*to*[1], Many, much, too much, reduplication.

夕,夕 *hsi*[4] evening, is the R., the 36th. Because easy to write it was repeated for the meaning many. Perhaps it means many, like the evenings that follow one another without ceasing. (W. 64 A, E.)

**185** 偺

*tsan*[23] I, we. *To*[1] *tsan* when, sometimes written 喒.

人 *jen*[2], is the radical; 口 *k'ou*[3] is the radical when written 喒.

昝 *tsan*[2] I, we, is an arbitrary abbreviation for 簪 *ts'an*[3] which is 旡 *tsan*[1] doubled, meaning a brooch or hairpin and 曰 *yüeh* added. meaning to murmur, (W. 26 D.)

**186** 後

*hou*[4], After, behind, to postpone; posterity.

彳 *ch'ih*[4] a step, to march, is the R., the 60th.

幺 *yao*[1] A fine thread. (See No. 8 and 24.)

To march 彳 while stretching a fine thread 幺 out behind. The 夂 *chih*[3], to follow is a radical redundancy as it also means to go. (W. 90 A.)

187 地 *ti*⁴, The earth, the ground, a place.

土 *t'u*³, earth, is the R., the 32nd.

也 *ieh*³, Also, see No. 4.

188 拜, 𢪍 *pai*⁴, To worship, pay respect to either man or God.

手 *shou*³, hand, is the R., No. 64. The rest of the character 手 is also *shou*³ 手 and *hsia*⁴, 下.

手 It was formerly written with the *hsia*⁴ 下 under both hands 𢪍 meaning both hands hanging down, in the attitude of respect, or worship. (W. 48 E.)

189 晌 *shang*³, Noontide, midday.

日 *jih*⁴, sun, is the R., the 72nd.

向, 向 *hsiang*⁴, is a picture of a small north window under the eaves of the house 宀; by extension it means, direction, to face; to like, to favor. (W. 36 E.)

When the sun 日 faces 向 the south window it is midday 晌.

190 午 *wu*³, 11 A.M. to 1 P.M., noon; 7th of the 12 stems.

十 *shih*², ten is the R., the 24th.

午, 午 Some say this is the representation of a noon mark on the side or end of a house. In combinations it has the sense of definite, fixed, exact as in 許 *hsü*³, to promise, 忤 *wu*³ obstinate, etc.

191 已 *i*³, Already, past, to cease, to decline.

己, 己 *chï³*, self, is the R., the 49th. The original writing of this character 己 己 is now found in four forms 己 厶 目 以. It is a very ancient symbol, to represent the exhalations of the breath, the virtue that springs from an object, its action, its use, then, use until exhaustion, to end, to pass away. cf. 台 似 官 (W. 85 B.)

192 座

*tso⁴*, A raised seat, throne, numerative of mountains, cities, houses.

广 *yen³* covering, shelter, shed, is the R., the 53rd.

坐, 坐 *tso⁴*, To sit down, to rest, to place; to reign. It is two men 从 seated, facing each other, on the ground 土. (See No. 66.)

The radical 广 indicates larger things, or men sitting in a house, so a seat 座. (W. 27 D.)

193 城

*ch'eng²*, A city, a city wall.

土 *t'u³*, is the R., the 32nd.

成, 厸 *ch'eng²*, is made from a 丁 a nail, a boy and a battle axe 戊 *wu⁴* in which 戈 *ko¹* is the radical. When a boy 丁 is big enough to wield a battle axe he is grown up or completed, a man, i.e. *ch'eng² ting¹*, 成 丁 The character means, completed, to become, to finish. When earth 土 is built into a city wall 城 it has *attained* 成 to its highest usefulness. (W. 71 M.)

194 封, 𡊩

*feng¹*, A fief, a territory; to appoint to office over a fief; to seal up, to blockade, to stamp, an envelope.

寸 *ts'un⁴*, inch, is the R., the 41st. (See No. 69.)

圭 *kuei*[1], is, according to the seal character, the land 土 and crops 㞢 under the rule 寸 of a landlord, that is a fief. Such is the Chinese explanation. Wieger considers it erroneous. He thinks it a tree 朩 on a mound 土 in the center to indicate the feudatory or imperial possession of the land. 寸 added indicates rule. (W. 79 E.)

**195** 信, 㐰 伏 人

*hsin*[4], Faith, sincerity, to believe in; a letter; arsenic.

*jen*[2], is the radical. A man 人 standing beside his word 言, that is, faithful. Some ancient forms are a man and mouth; also a heart and a word; that is words coming from the heart, sincere. (W. 25 H.)

### BALLER, LESSON VII.

**196** 再

*tsai*[4], Repeated, a second time, also.

冂 *chiung*[3] a limit, is the radical according to the dictionaries, the 13th. But etymologically it is

帀 *liang*[3] a weighing instrument or scale in equilibrium and 二 *erh*[4], two, added to indicate a second weighing or repetition, twice, etc. (W. 35 J.)

**197** 歲

*sui*[4], Year, harvest, age; Jupiter, the planet that indicated whether an attack was to be made or not.

止 *chih*[3], stop, is the R. of the dictionaries, the 77th, but the combination 歲 is from 步 *pu*[4] a step, a planet, and

戌, 戌 *hsü*[1] which is a spear 戊 *wu*[4] and its wound —. The lower part of the *pu*[4] 少 is enclosed in the 戌 *hsü*[1], at the bottom. Jupiter's period of twelve years was a cyclical period used by the Chinese and called a great year 大歲. It was later adapted to the twelve months and used commonly for a year. (W. 71 P.)

步, 步 *pu*[4], A step. It is composed of 止 to stop and the same reversed underneath with the opposite meaning, to start. A step 步, is the starting 少, and stopping 止 of the feet in walking. (W. 112 F.)

198 數

*shu*[3], To count, *shu*[4] a number.

攵 *p'u*[1] to tap, to govern, is the radical, the 66th, referring perhaps to the habit of men to check off with the finger as they count.

婁, 婁 *lou*[2] Troublesome, frequent, and so appropriate in the character meaning to count off. It is composed of 女 *nü*[3] women 中 *chung*[1] enclosed in 毋 *wu*[2], no, forbidden, prison, and so has the meaning, idle, useless, troublesome, repetitious, frequent. (W. 67 N.) 數 *shu*[4] meant originally to govern 攵 these women prisoners 婁.

199 等

*teng*[3], To compare, an order, series, class; such, like; to wait.

竹 *chu*[2], bamboo, is the R., the 118th, see No. 7 and cf. 第 *ti*[4] No. 86.

寺 *ssu*[4], Temple, the place where the rule 寸 is constantly applied 土 屮 and people are classed. (See No. 125.)

100 粗

*ts'u*[1], Coarse, rough, vulgar.

米 *mi*[3], rice, is the R., the 119th. (See No. 47.)

且 *tsu³*, moreover (the radical is—i) is a picture of a stool 几 *chi³* with two rungs=to brace the legs and standing on the ground—. It was borrowed for the important conjunction, and, moreover. (W. 20 D.) See No. 228 on 粗 as a character showing contrast.

**201** 細, 紬

*hsi⁴*, Fine, small ; soft ; carefully.

糸 *ssu*, or *mi⁴* a strong thread, is the R., the 120th. (See No. 8.)

田 *t'ien²*, field, was originally written 囟 *hsin¹* or skull open above, meaning the fontanelles of a child, tender ; so appropriate for, fine, tender 細, like the silky 糸 hair around the fontanelles 囟.

**202** 聖

*sheng⁴*, Wise, holy, sacred.

耳 *erh³*, ear, is the R., the 128th, a picture. (W. 146 A.)

呈, 呈 *ch'eng²*, To speak 口 *k'ou³*, while standing in ones place of office 壬 *t'ing²* (a man 人 at his place on the ground 土) therefore 呈 *ch'eng²* means to lay before ones superior, to notify.

聖人 *sheng⁴ jen²*, or wise men, are those who listen 耳 to the 口 information of those under them in office 壬 and so become wise. (W 81 H.) For 壬 see No. 22.

**203** 造

*tsao⁴*, To arrive at, to build, to create.

辶, 辵 *cho⁴* or *tsou³ chih⁴*, to arrive at, is the R., the 162nd. From this meaning, to arrive at, the meaning to accomplish, to build 造 is derived and the 告 *kao⁴* is purely phonetic.

告, 告 *kao*$^4$, To impeach, to indict; that is, to do with the mouth 口 what the ox 牛 does with his horns. By extension it means to tell. (W. 132 B.)

204 還 *huan*$^2$, Also, yet, still more. to give back.

辵 *cho*$^4$ to go is the R., the 162nd.

睘, 睘 *huan*$^2$ The eye 目, horizontal, and 袁 *yüan*$^2$, trailing robes, that hinder ones walk, a hesitating gait and timid look.

袁, 袁 *yüan*$^2$ is made up of 衣 *i*$^1$ a long robe and

叀, 叀 *ch'uan*$^1$ To attach, to trail, being a picture of an ox yoked up and attached by a single trace to a ring. (W. 91 E. H.)

205 貴, 貴 *kuei*$^4$, Honorable, costly, dear.

貝 *pei*$^4$, cowries, precious things, is the R., the 154th. It is a picture of the cowrie shells with feelers out. They were used for money down to 300 B.C. and then brass representations of them were used. (W. 161 A.)

𠀐, 臾 *k'ui*$^4$ a basket, is a picture. (W. 111 A, B.) A basket 𠀐 full of cowries 貝 is a high price, dear.

206 姓 *hsing*$^4$, A surname of a clan.

女 *nü*$^3$, woman, is the R., the 38th and 生 *sheng*$^1$, born. Woman born,—possibly this dates to the time when "mens' mothers were known but not their fathers" and so the woman gave the name to the clan or family. (See No. 15.)

207 黃, 黃 *huang*$^2$, Yellow, the color of loess. 201st R., formed of

田 *t'ien²*, field, 102nd radical, (a picture of furrowed fields) and of an old form of *kuang¹* 光 light, (a man 人 carrying a torch 火). 黃 *huang²* is the yellow light 光 from the fields 田. (W. 171 A and 149 A.)

208 白, 白    *pai²*, White; in vain. Radical No. 106. The seal character represents the sun just appearing above the horizon and so the white light at dawn. (W. 88 A.) (See No. 6.)

209 老, 耂    *lao⁸*, Venerable, old, very. 125th radical. A man 人 whose hair 毛 *mao²* changes 匕 *hua⁴* to white. (See No. 20.) The 毛 and 人 are contracted arbitrarily by the modern scribes. (W. 30 D, E.)

210 主, 坒    *chu⁸*, Lord, master, owner. It is a picture of a lamp and the flame rising above it. So by extension a man who spreads light, a lord. The prince rises above other men and is seen by all as the flame rises above the lamp and shines out to all. (W. 4 B. and 83 D.)

*chu⁸* a dot is the R., the 3rd.

211 敝   *pi⁴*, Rags, unworthy, mean.

攵, 攴 *p'u¹* to tap is the R., the 66th.

㡀 *pi* Broken shreds of cloth.

The whole is a piece of cloth 巾 separated or riddled 八 with holes 八 by the action of tapping 攴. (W. 35 F.)

212 男   *nan²*, Male of the human species; a son

田 *t'ien²*, the land, is the R., the 102nd.

力,为 *li*[4], Muscle, strength, a picture of a muscle and its sheath. The 19th radical.

The man 男 is the one who exerts his strength 力 in the field 田. (W. 53 C.)

213 紀

糸 *chi*[4], To arrange, to narrate, disposition.

糸 *ssu*[1], silk is the R., the 120th, see No. 8.

己 *chi*[3], self, the 49th radical, is a picture of the threads of a weft above and of one thread in the shuttle below; so sorting out and arranging threads; borrowed for self.

紀 *chi*[4], as a whole is to sort 己 threads 糸. (W. 84 A.)

214 發,發,癹

癹,卅 *fa*[1], To shoot an arrow, to send forth, any expansion or manifestation.

癶,卅 *po*[4] Separation; trampling; back to back. It is two 止 *chih*[3] characters back to back. It is the R., the 105th.

弓 *kung*[1], bow, is the 57th radical and the 殳 *shu*[1], to kill, was formerly written 矢 *shih*[3] arrow, so the character meant to separate 癶 the arrow 矢 from the bow 弓 i.e. to shoot. (W. 112 H.)

215 塊

土 *k'uai*[4], A piece, lump.

土 *t'u*[3], earth, is the R., the 32nd; see No. 13.

鬼 *kuei*[3], devil, spirit of a dead man, the 194th rad. The 甶 represents the spirits head, the 儿 is man and the 厶 is a tail or the swirl where the demon vanishes. Purely phonetic here. (W. 40 C.)

A person becomes a spirit 鬼 after the body has stiffened in death and when the earth 土 becomes stiff and hard it breaks up into clods or pieces 塊.

**216** 位

人 *jen²*, man is the R., the 9th.

立, 立 *li⁴*, To establish, to stand. A picture of a man standing firm on the ground.

*wei⁴*, Seat, throne, condition, dignity, a person.

The place, 位 (office, dignity) where a man 人 stands erect 立 ; the place assigned to each official.

**217** 帝, 帝

巾 *chin¹*, is the R., the 50th. It is doubled to represent the skirts hanging from the girdle. Cf. No. 143 帶.

*ti⁴*, The Supreme Ruler, the sovereign.

帝, 帝 The ancient character represented a man clad in many garments and designated by — meaning 上 above. The scribes added two arms. *Li³ Ssu* changed the bottom into 東 *t'zu⁴*, thorns, and then it was contracted into the modern form. (W. 120 H.)

BALLER, LESSON VIII.

**218** 眞, 眞

目 *mu⁴*, eye, is the radical of classification, No. 109, but the character is made up of the following :—

*chen¹*, True, truly, genuine ; rectitude superior to the common ; perfect simplicity.

直 *chih²*, straight, (see No. 99) rectitude ;

匕 *hua⁴* to change, a man tumbled heels over head ;

兀 *wu⁴*, a high platform or base.

In the combination the 十 *shih²* at the top of the character 直 *chih²* is replaced by the 匕 *hua⁴* and the top line of the 兀 *wu⁴* at the bottom is combined with the lower stroke ㇄ of the $chih^2$ 直. The logic of the combination is that moral rectitude 直 $chih^2$ acquired by a change 匕 $hua^4$ and raising 兀 $wu^4$ of the moral nature is true, genuine 眞 $chen^1$. (W. 10 L.)

219 頂 $ting^3$, The top, very; the button on a mandarin's hat.

頁 $yeh^4$, man, the head, is the radical, the 181st, see No. 105.

丁, 个 $ting^1$, A nail, (picture). It is of phonetic force. But the button on a mandarin's hat called 頂戴 $ting^3$ $tai^4$, looks like the head of a Chinese nail and as though it were nailed into the hat or head.

220 賣, 𧶠 $mai^4$, to sell, to betray, to vaunt.

貝 $pei^4$, cowrie, precious, is the radical, the 154th as in 買 $mai^3$, see No. 38.

士=出, 𡳿 $ch'u^1$, The springing of plants, to put forth.

買 $mai^3$, to buy. Therefore 賣 $mai^4$, to sell, is the opposite of 買 in that it consists in putting out 出 goods, and netting or obtaining 网 the cowrie money 貝 $pei^4$. (W. 78 E and 161 D.)

221 家 $chia^1$, Home, family, a profession or class.

宀 $mien^2$ a roof, or house, is the rad., the 40th.

豕 $shih^3$ Pigs, the 152nd, radical.

The seal character of 100 B.C. shows that it is a picture of a pig, the upper line for the head, the left side showing the belly and legs, the right side the back and tail.

In the Oracle Bones this appears as a pig
ready for sacrifice in the home, where
ancestral offerings were made, (J. M.
Menzies). This explanation is not given in
the first edition of this book. An early
form shows three people under a roof,
man, woman and child made a home.
(Chalfant XIX)

**222 錯**

ts'o[4], In disorder, wrong, mistaken ; to polish ;
a polishing stone, a file.

金 chin[1], metal, is the radical, the 167th. (See No.
13.)

昔, 皆 hsi[1] Old, ancient, formerly. Dried meats.
It is formed of 龺 contracted from the seal
form 炊 representing strips of meat hung
up to dry and 日 jih[4] sun. So the meaning is old, dried meat as compared with
fresh meat. (W. 17 J.) Old 昔 metal 金,
scrapped, makes a most disorderly place.

**223 很**

hen[3], Very.

彳 ch'ih[4] a step, is the radical, the 60th. In the
other writing 狠 the radical is 犭 or 犬
ch'üan[3], dog (classical) the 94th radical,
犭 is the form used in combinations.

艮, 臮, 臮 ken[4] is composed of 目 mu[4] eye and 匕 hua[4], to
turn or change ; so 艮 ken[4] is to turn or
change the eye 目, looking in anger, defiance ; stubborn, hard. (W. 26 B & L.)
It seems of phonetic force only in 很 hen[3].
In the second writing one might say "a
dog's 犬 defiance, or obstinacy in holding
on is very 狠 extreme.

**224** 皮,冐 *p'i²*, Skin, leather, bark, wrapping, the case around goods or the tare ; the 107th R. The seal form shows it to be a primitive meaning to skin, representing the skin ⟩ a hand ㋛ and a knife ⊃. (W. 43 H.)

**225** 用,甩 *yung⁴*, To hit the centre, to use, with, by. It is the 101st radical. It is from the same form as 中 *chung¹* which also meant to hit the target and an — *i* showing the part of the arrow that did not go through. By extension the capacity of the archer, the effect, the use, the means. (W. 109 B.)

**226** 更,雪 *keng¹*, To change, *keng⁴*, much.

日 *yüeh*, to speak, is the radical, the 73rd. This is by convention in the dictionaries. It is really formed of the following, according to the *Shuo¹ Wen²:*

丙,丙 *ping³*, Fire, calamity, bright. A fire in a house with flames rising above the roof.

攴 *p'u¹* To tap, to interfere with the hand holding a stick.

Therefore 更 *keng¹*, change, is an intervention of the hand collecting the smouldering embers on the hearth to make a bright fire. (W. 41 A.)

**227** 神 *shen²*, Spirits, animal spirits, gods.

礻,示 *shih⁴*, to reveal, is the R., the 113th, used in characters denoting spiritual things. It is formed of 二 *erh* = 上 *shang⁴* heaven and 小 = the sun, moon and stars, or signs in the heavens which reveal transcendental things to men.

昌, 岬 *shen*[1], To extend, to stretch, to explain. The seal writing shows two hands stretching a rope and so the idea of stretching, expansion. Later the rope was straightened by the scribes and was explained as a man standing and with both hands 臼 girding his body | with a sash. The form 申 is simply an easier way of writing 甲. (W. 50 C.) The combination 神 is probably phonetic but the idea of god may have some connection with an increased or extended 申 spiritual revelation 示. Chalfant, however, finds early forms representing forked lighting. He thinks, probably rightly, that these became the sign for deity from superstitious dread of lightning 電 *tien*[4]. It gradually took the form 申 and 示 was added to distinguish the meaning of God 神, and 雨 *yü*[3] rain, was added to show the meaning lightning 電. (Plates VII and XXVI.)

**228** 肯, 圓

月, 肉, 肉 *k'en*[3], To be flexible, pliant, willing, to assent. *jou*[4], the flesh as opposed to the skeleton 冎 *kua*[3], is the R., the 130th. (See No. 133.) In early writings of 肯 *k'en*[3] the 冎 *kua*[3], skeleton, was at the top of the character. The upper part of 冎 *kua*[3] early dropped out and the scribes replaced the remainder 冂, with 止 *chih*[3] which is nonsense. The flesh is soft and pliable as compared to the bones 冂 (changed to 止) and hence the derived meanings to yield ones self, to be compliant, to assent. (W. 65 A, C.)

In 粗 *t'su*¹, we have another example of two objects of opposite characteristics joined to represent the adjective applying to one of them i.e. 粗 *t'su*¹ coarse is 米 fine grains and a large object, a heavy two runged stool 且. (No. 200.)

**229** 假

*chia*³, False, to borrow, *chia*⁴ leave of absence.

人 *jen*², is the radical, the 9th.

叚叚 *chia*³, False, to borrow. The seal writing shows two 二 skins 皮, that is, double skin, or a borrowed skin over ones true skin, disguise, false. " Wolf in sheep's clothing." (W. 43 I.) The character for shrimp 蝦, *hsia*¹, uses this suggestive phonetic. It sheds one skin gradually while growing another.

**230** 會

*hui*⁴, To meet, to collect, a procession, a society, able.

日 *yüeh*¹ to speak, is the radicai, the 73rd. (See No. 9.)

亼 *chi*² To collect, (see No. 18.)

會,曾 *tseng*¹ To add, still mo e. The words 日 *yüeh*¹, that people say when they meet 亼 *chi*² at the fire under the smoke hole 囧 *ch'uang*¹, in greeting or 八 in parting, i.e. adding more and more. The 八 *pa*¹ at the top is modified in the combination with 亼 *chi*² to form 會 *hui*⁴. (W. 14 D and W. 40 D.)

**231** 使

*shih*³, To cause ; to order, to send, a messenger.

人 *jen*² is the rad., the 9th, with 吏 *li*⁴ an officer.

史, 㝱 *shih³* A hand ㇇ grasping a stylus, see No. 96 ; a historian, scholar.

吏 *li⁴*, Those of the scholars 史 who were set over 一 (= 上) the administration.

The meanings of 使 *shih³* come from the uniting of 人 man and 吏 the superior official of government.  (W. 43 M.)

**232**  強 彊

*ch'iang²*, Strong, firm, determined, good , read *ch'iang³*, to force, to rob.

弓 *kung¹*, a bow, is the radical, the 57th, a picture. As the character 強 *ch'iang²* was originally written 彊, it meant a bow 弓 that shoots over two fields and their boundaries 畺 *chiang¹*, that is, a strong bow, and by extension, good, firm, determined. Being hard to write the 畺 *chiang¹* was replaced by 虽, an insect that bends like a bow and springs into the air when it falls on its back.  ム changed to 口 was the head of the insect.

虫, ⳡ *ch'ung²* an insect, in the seal writing represents a snake, probably the cobra, called *hui¹*, now written 虺.  It is the 142nd radical and used for 蟲 *ch'ung²*, which anciently meant animals with legs, but now means the smaller animals, as frogs, worms, snails, insects.  (W. 110 B.)

**233**  盆

*p'en²*, A tub, bowl, basin.

皿, 㿻 *min³*, a dish, is the R., the 108th, a picture.

分 *fen¹*, to divide, is the phonetic.  (See No. 181.)

**234**  夫

*fu¹*, Husband, man, workman.

大 *ta⁴*, great, (in composition, man) is the R., the

37th. It has a stroke added in 夫 *fu*[1], to represent the pin in the hair used only when, grown to manhood at the age of twenty, the boy took a cap, and received an honorable name as well as used a hair-pin. (W. 60 J.)

**235 餅**

*ping*[3], A cake, pastry.

食 *shih*[2], to eat, food ; *ssu*[4] to feed, to rear, is the R., the 184th, of characters relating to food. (See No. 75.)

并, 并 *ping*[1], The seal represents two men marching
幷     side by side, or on a level 开 *ch'ien*[1], there-
开     fore the meaning even, together, harmony.

开 *ch'ien*[1] is two poised scales, or shields side by side, even, level. *Ping*[1] is phonetic, but cooked grains 皀 united 亼 form cakes 餅, a logical combination. (W. 115 B.)

**236 盒**

*ho*[2], A box or dish, with a cover.

皿 *min*[3], dish, is the R., the 108th.

合 *ho*[2], Shut 亼 the mouth 口; join, unite. (See No. 103.) So 盒 *ho*[2] is a covered dish,—join 合 the dish 皿 and its cover.

**237 孩**

*hai*[2], A child. 子 *tzu*[3], is the R. (See No. 1.)

亥, 荄 *hai*[4] is pure phonetic. It is the 12th of the twelve stems ; 10th of the horary cycle i.e. 9 to 11 P.M. The 10th month. It is said to be a picture of the pig with tail added. (W. 69 K.)

**238 盤**

*p'an*[2], A plate, tray.

皿 *min*[3], dish is the R., the 108th.

般 *pan*[1], To make a boat 舟 move along by a

regular action 殳 of the oars; so the derived meanings of regular way, manner, equally.

舟, 舟 *chou*[1], A boat, (picture showing the high bow the deck, compartments, rudder and an oar.) It is the 137th R. of characters relating to ships. (W. 66 A.)

殳, 殳 *shu*[1] is the right hand 又 making a jerky motion 几 or a rhythmical motion, then, to kill, to strike. The 79th R. (See No. 71.) (W. 22 A. D.)

**239** 板

*pan*[3], A board, flattened bamboo.
木 *mu*[4], wood, is the R., the 75th.
反 *fan*[3], To turn over, inversion. (See No. 75.) A suggestive phonetic, as a board is flat like a hand.

**240** 櫈

*teng*[4], A long bench, a stool.
木 *mu*[4], wood, is the R., the 75th. (See No. 22.)
凳 *teng*[4], A stool or bench. This is composed of
几 *chi*[1], a stool, the 16th radical (picture) and
登 *teng*[1], to ascend, advance, at once. This is from the radical 癶 *po*[4] (See No. 214) to ascend step by step, and a pedestal 豆 *tou*[4]. (See No. 105.) (W. 112 H.)

**241** 但

*tan*[4], But, only. 人 is the radical, the 9th.
旦 *tan*[4], The morning, dawn, daylight. It represents the sun 日 just above the horizon 一. In 但 it is of phonetic force only. It is one of the few indicative characters.

**242** 盞

*chan*[3], A classifier of lamps; a shallow cup.
皿 *min*[3], a dish, is the R., the 108th.

戔 *chien*[r] To destroy, narrow, small. (See No. 13). A small 戔 dish 皿 is a shallow cup 盞. Thus it is a suggestive phonetic.

**243** 燈

*teng*[1], A lamp. 火 *huo*[3], fire, is the R., the 86th. (See No. 169.)

登 *teng*[4], To ascend, to elevate. (See No. 214 and 240.) This is a suggestive phonetic for to elevate 登 fire 火 is a good designation for a lamp 燈.

**244** 帽 帽

*mao*[4], A hat, or head covering, to rush on, rash.

巾 *chin*[1], a napkin, is the R., the 50th.

冒, 冃 *mao*[4], a hat, is the original writing for 帽. It is a 冂 *mao*[3] (to cover 冂 *chiung*[3] something 一) and 一 indicating the head within. The modern writers change 冃 to 曰 and 日 so that it cannot be distinguished from 曰 *yüeh* without reference to the seal character.

冒, 冒 *mao*[4], to rush on, heedless, to act with the eye 目 covered 冃, is a natural meaning for the character. 蒙而前也. (W. 34 J.)

BALLER, LESSON IX.

**245** 賬

*chang*[4], An account, a bill.

貝 *pei*[4], cowrie, precious, is the R., the 154th. (See No. 38.)

長 *chang*[3], to grow, senior, is a phonetic and also the 168th R. (See No. 131.)

A long or growing 長 list of precious things 貝 is a 賬 *chang*[4]. The character is a modern invention to take the place of

帳, the radical 貝 being more appropriate to the meaning than 巾.

**246 找**

手 戈

*chao³*, To seek, to find, to pay a balance.

*shou³*, hand is the R., the 64th.

*ko¹*, A spear or halberd. (See No. 2 我, from which the character must be distinguished.)

The seeking in mind by the inventors of this character must have been a search for an enemy, with spear 戈 in hand 手. It is often used now for seeking a man in the spirit of revenge.

**247 算, 筭**

竹 竹
目

卄, 廾 *kung³*,

*suan⁴*, To reckon, calculate, to plan.

*chü²*, bamboo, is the radical, No. 118. In the Han dynasty bamboo slips, one by six inches were used for calculating. 271 slips made a set. The abacus, 算盤 *suan⁴ p'an²*, seems to have come from Greece about 1450 A.D. The Encyclopedia Sinica, however regards it as indigenous to China. It probably came into general use during the Ming dynasty. In our first edition it was erroneously treated as of ancient Chinese origin. In using the abacus one employs both eyes 目, *mu⁴* and hands, 廾 *kung³*, the 55th Rad. In combination *kung³* is modified in several ways as 寸 in 尊 *tsun¹*; 八 in 兵 *ping¹*; 大 in 具 *chü⁴* and 廾 in 算.

**248 借**

昔

*chieh⁴*, To borrow, to lend. 人 *jen²* is the R., 9th.

*hsi²* Old, purely phonetic here, (See No. 222.)

**249 銅**

*t'ung²*, Brass. 金 *chin¹* is the R., No. 167. (See No. 13.)

同 t'ung², With, together, like. Phonetic. It is 冃 mao³ a cover fitted to the 口 mouth of a vase, thus meaning agreement, union, together etc.   (W. 34 I.)

**250** 角, 肉

chiao³, An animal's horn, a projecting corner, a pod; a dime, a quarter.   It is the 148th radical.   It is a picture of a striated horn and is also said to be a combination of strong 力 li⁴ and flesh 肉 jou⁴.   (W. 142 B.)

**251** 換 換

huan⁴, To change about with the hand, remove, to exchange.   The R. is 扌 t'i² shou³, the 64th.

奐, 奐 huan⁴ To be on the watch for, to examine.   It is from two hands 𦥑 (contracted to 大) and a contraction of 夐 ch'iung², which is a man 人 standing at the door of a cave 穴 hsüeh², peering out 目, with a stick in his hand 夂=攴, that is, to watch, or examine.   Thus 奐 means passing an object from hand 𠂒 to hand 又 while examining it 奐 to avoid deception in the exchange.   It is now written with another hand added as a radical 換, the hand of the other man. (W. 37 F.)

**252** 補 衤, 衣 甫, 甫

pu³, To repair, to mend; to patch, to substitute. i¹, clothes, is the R., the 145th. (See No. 51.) fu³ To begin, great, just now, an honorific name.   It is capacity 用 for founding and governing a family, manhood, the age at which an honorary name was given to a man. Phonetic combination.  (W. 109 D.)

253 洋 氵, 水 *yang*², The ocean, foreign, European, vast.
*shui*³, water, is the radical, the 85th.
羊, 羊 *yang*², A sheep, a goat. It is a picture of a ram seen from above with horns, legs and tail. The tail is often left off in combinations to make room. Phonetic combination. (W. 103 A.)

254 毛,  *mao*², Hair, fur, plumage, (Picture). The 82nd radical. (W. 100 A.)

255 票,  *p'iao*⁴, A signal, a ticket, a warrant, a banknote. For a mnemonic take "a bankbill 票 is a Western 西 revelation 示". This is untrue however.
示 *shih*¹, a revelation, is the R., the 113. (See No. 164.) Etymologically however the 示 is a modification of the seal writing of 火 fire, 火, Chalfant Pl. X shows a beautiful origin of the character in a fire 火 with smoke rising from it and manipulated by four hands 𦥑. This was an ancient method of signalling. The seal writing of 100 A.D. is explained as being an ignis fatuus 鬼火 *kuei*³ *huo*³, below is the fire 火, on top, the head and hands 𦥔 and the line in the middle 一 is the waist. Compare 要 No. 16. (W. 50 O.)

256 市,  *shih*⁴, Market place, a market.
巾 *chin*¹, a handkerchief, is the R., the 50th (See No. 143), a mistake etymologically. The seal shows that it is a broad place 冂 *chiung*³ outside the town, overgrown with

grass 业 *chih*[1], where people go to get 了 what they want. (W. 34 D.)

冂 *chiung*[3], an open space a limit, is the 13th R.

及, 了 *chi*[2], To reach to, to get. (W. 19 D.)

**257 底**

广 *ti*[3], Base, foundation, low, to settle; bottom.

广 *yen*[3] a shed, hut, is the R., the 53rd. (See No. 132.)

氐 氐 *ti*[3], The rest of the character is a development 氐 of 氏 *shih*[4], (See No. 8), a floating plant that branches on the surface of the water and sends a root down to the bottom. A line is added below to represent the bottom of the water. So the meaning to sink, the bottom. (W. 114 A.B.)

氐 *ti*[3] with the 广 *yen*[8] radical means the foundation, base, of a house etc. 底.

**258 號**

*hao*[4], To cry out, an order, a signal; a mark, a label; honorary name.

虍, 肙 *hu*[1] tiger, is the R., the 141st. This is a picture representing the stripes on the tiger's skin. (W. 135 A.)

丂 *ch'iao*[3] Difficult breathing, sobbing. It represents the breath 丩 fighting against an obstacle 一 (cf. 可 No. 152.) The Shuo Wen says. 气欲舒出上礙於一也按丂像形一指事.

号 *hao*[4] is the mouth 口 sending forth cries interrupted by sobs 丂. (W. 58 A, B.) 从口在丂上會意痛聲也.

虎, 虝 *hu*[3], a tiger, is 虍 *hu*[1] with feet like a man's 儿 *jen*[2], added below. This character enters into several compounds meaning cries, clamor. Thus both sides of the 號 *hao*[4] mean outcry.

259 錠

金 ting⁴, An ingot of silver.

金 chin¹, metal, is the R., the 167th. (See No. 13.)

定,向 ting⁴, To fix, to settle, certain, quiet. It is order 正 cheng⁴ (See No. 12) in the house 宀 mien² (see No. 1) i.e. peace, quiet. (W. 112 I.) An ingot of silver 錠 is therefore a fixed or certain 定 lump of metal 金.

260 法

氵,水 fa³, Rule, law, model ; means.

氵,水 shui³, water, is the R., the 85th. (See No. 79.)

去 ch'ü⁴, To go, to remove. (See No. 67.)

The far fetched mnemonic has been suggested "the law, or a model 法 fa³ is intended to raise the moral level, as water 水, by removing 去 vices."

Historically the ancient character for 法 fa³ was written 金 which means 人 chi² to adapt 正 cheng⁴ rightly, that is law, rule.

261 碼

石 ma³, Weights for money or goods, wharf.

石 shih², stone, is the R., the 112th. (See No. 42.)

馬,馬 ma³, horse, is the phonetic. The seal writing shows the head turned backwards, the mane, legs and tail. It is the 187th R. (W. 137 A.)

262 價

亻,人 chia⁴, The value of a thing, the price.

亻,人 jen², man is the R., the 9th.

賈 chia³, ku³ A shopman, as distinguished from a travelling merchant 商 shang¹; from 貝 pei⁴ precious things under a canopy 襾 hsia⁴.

襾,襾 hsia⁴ A cover, a canopy. The 146th R., often confused with 西 hsi¹ West. (W. 41 C.)

263 元

yüan², Head, principal, origin. It is made up of 二, or 上, and 儿 jen² man. That which is upon 上 man 儿, the head. 儿 is the R., the 10th.

264 寶

pao³, A gem, a coin, precious, valuable.

宀 mien², house, is the R., the 40th. (See No. 1.)

缶 fou³ Earthenware vessels in general, the picture of a covered vessel; the 121st R. (W. 130 C.)

寶 pao³, is to have 玉 yü⁴, gems or jade, 缶 fou³ earthenware and 貝 pei⁴ money in the 宀 house. These were the ancient valuables. (W. 130 D.)

265 銀

yin², Silver. 金 chin¹ is the R., the 167th (See No. 13.)

艮 ken⁴ anger, hard, firm, is the phonetic. (See No. 223.) Silver 銀 is hard 艮 metal 金.

266 吊 弔, 口

tiao⁴, To suspend, a string of 1000 cash. k'ou³, mouth, is the R., the 30th.

When written 弔 it means, to condole, and 弓 kung¹ bow is the R., the 57th. It is a man 人 with a bow over his shoulder, coming to help keep the birds and beasts away from the corpse which was exposed to rot. Hence the meaning of to condole. The Mongols still expose, but do not keep away the beasts and birds. The meaning to suspend comes from the fact that the bow was slung over the shoulder. (W. 28 H.)

267 副

fu⁴, To aid; a duplicate, an alternate, a pair.

刀 *tao*[1], knife, is the R., the 18th. (See No. 37.)

畐 *fu*[2], abundance, happiness is from 高 *kao*[1] (contracted) and 田 *t'ien*[2] fields ; the heaping up 高 of the products of the fields 田, i.e. abundance, prosperity 畐.

A knife 刀 cuts off from ones abundant stores 畐 to help 副. (W. 75 D.)

268 平, 亐·

*p'ing*[2], Free expansion on all sides ; plane, even, level ; tranquil.

亐 *kan*[1], arms, crime, is the R., the 51st; (See No. 110.) This is arbitrary classification, for the seal writing shows it to be 亐 *yü*[2], the breath 丂 *hao*[4] overcoming the obstacle — and spreading out freely above —. In 平 the symbol 八 *pa*[1] to divide, adds to the idea of free expansion on both sides. (W. 58 F.)

BALLER, LESSON X.

269 海

*hai*[3], The sea, an arm of the ocean ; lake, an expanse, as a desert, 氵, 水 *shui*[3] is the R., the 85th. (See No. 79.)

每, 𡴋 *mei*[3], Each, every. These are borrowed meanings, as originally it meant swarming, being a combination of 𠂉 or 屮 *ch'e*[4] a sprout, and 母 *mu*[3] mother.

母, 𤔲 *mu*[3], Mother. This is from 女 *nü*[3] female, with the breasts made prominent. (W. 67 O, P.)

270 都

阝, 邑 *i*[4], city, is the R., the 163rd, (See No. 11).

者, 𤲃 *che*[3], Phrase, speech, document ; sign of end of a paragraph ; after other parts of speech it changes them into nouns. This charac-

*tu*[1], *tou*[1], All, the whole ; the capital.

ter was invented to represent a connection between members of a text: above are two crossed branches to represent the preceding members; in the middle a 自=自 *tzu*$^{4}$, from, represents the point already arrived at, the starting point for what follows; and the ㄱ at the reader's right is the continuation of the discourse. (W. 159 A, B.)

**271 喝** *ho*$^{1}$, To drink; to shout.

口 *k'ou*$^{3}$, mouth, is the R., the 30th.

曷, *ho*$^{2}$ A stranger or beggar 匃 *kai*$^{4}$ who speaks, 曰 *yüeh*$^{1}$, to ask the way or beg; to ask, how? where? why? (W. 73 A.)

匃, *kai*$^{4}$, To beg, a beggar. A wanderer 勹 who seeks to enter 入 *ju*$^{4}$ a refuge L. The 勹 formerly stood at the side, now it covers the 亾. (W. 10 G.) cf. No. 145 乍 *cha*$^{4}$.

**272 各,** *ko*$^{4}$, Each, every, all, various; apart.

夂, *chih*$^{3}$ to follow, is the phonetic, it is to reach up to ㇏ a man who walks 夕, to come up behind him. 口 is the R.

各 *ko*$^{4}$ means to go on ones way 夕 without heeding the calls 口 or advice of others following, ㇏, therefore, apart, separate, each. (W. 31 B.)

**273 愛** *ai*$^{4}$, To love, delight in. 心 *hsin*$^{1}$ is the R., the 61st. It is formed of 㤅 *ai*$^{4}$ to love and 夊 *sui*$^{1}$ to go slowly.

[…]=旡 *chi*$^{4}$ The upper part of the character 愛 is strangely contracted from 旡 *chi*$^{4}$, to breathe in, to swallow. The meaning comes from reversing

欠,充 ch'ien⁴, to breathe out, to be lacking, as both are made up of 彡 and 儿 jen², the 充 being a reverse of 充 ch'ien⁴. Both are synonyms of 气 ch'i⁴ breath. 旡 is the 71st R. Joined with 心 it forms

悉,恙
悉 ai⁴. To swallow 旡 down in one's heart 心 ; to take into one's heart, to love, kindness. The radical 夊 sui¹ to walk is added to form 愛 ai⁴, primitively meaning the same as the radical 夊 but now used exclusively in the meaning to love. It suggests that love is an outgoing virtue. (W. 99 E, F.)

**274 辦**

pan⁴, To exert ones strength ; to manage, to arrange.

力 li⁴, strength, is the R., the 19th, (See No. 212.)

辛,辛 hsin¹, Bitter, punishment, criminal, the 160th R. It is made up of 干 kan¹ (see No. 110.) to offend, with two 丷 dots indicating a repeated offence, and 丄=上 shang⁴ a superior; that is an offence against a superior; a crime brings punishment, bitterness.

辡 pien⁴, Two criminals facing and mutually accusing one another ; passionate recrimination. (W. 102 H.)

When the 力 li⁴ strength of the official is interposed between the two parties accusing each other in court we have management, to manage, to arrange, 辦 ; or each criminal in such a recrimination exerts all his strength 力.

275 站      chan⁴, To stand ; a stage in a journey, 60 to 90 li³.

立.企   li⁴, to stand is the R., the 117th. (See No. 216). It is a picture of a man 人 standing on the ground—. (W. 60 H.)

占   chan¹, to consult 口 the diviner 卜, is the phonetic, chan⁴ to seize, invade. (See No. 132.)

276 靠

k'ao⁴, To be close to ; to mutually oppose, lean on ; to trust. It is from 告 kao⁴ to tell, inform and 非 fei¹ not. That is to inform of non-agreement, i.e. to oppose, and so to be opposite to. and then to be next to, to rely on. For 告 see No. 203.

非.非   fei¹, A primitive with two sides opposite to each other and so the abstract notion of opposition, negation, wrong, not. It gives 靠 its meaning of opposition and the idea of nearness is related to that of opposition, (note that the idea of opposition is in 告 also). It is the 175th R. (W. 170 A.)

277 纔

ts'ai², Adverb of time, now, present, just now.

糸   ssŭ, mi⁴, is the R., the 120th, commonly called

爛絞絲   lan⁴ chiao³ ssŭ¹.

毚   ch'an² rodents, or gnawing animals, crafty. It is the pictures of two rodents ; the one

兔.兔   above is 兔 ch'ao⁴ an animal like the hare but larger, (a useless character) ; the one below is

兔.兔   t'u⁴, A hare. It is a picture of the hare squatting, with tail perked up. (W. 106 C.)

278 呢    *ni²*, Interrogative and emphatic particle, twittering sound.

口 *k'ou³*, mouth, is the R., the 30th.

尼, 尽 *ni²*, To stop; a nun; *ni⁴* near, familiar. Phonetic force only.

It is formed of two men in contact, one seated 尸 *shih¹*, the 44th R. and one reversed, ヒ *pi³*. (W. 26 F.)

279 路    *lu⁴*, A road, a way; a kind.

足, 足 *tsu²*, The foot, a picture of a foot at rest, the circle above indicating rest as opposed to motion; enough, full, pure. It is the R., the 157th. (W. 112 B) cf. 止 *chih³* see No. 10. Motion is expressed by ㇗.

各 *ko⁴*, Each. (See No. 272.)

The way 路 *lu⁴*, is that through which each one 各 *ko⁴* goes 足 *tsu²*. (W. 31 B.)

280 光, 苂, 炗 *kuang¹*, Light, bright; honor, naked, smooth; the presence of a distinguished person. Anciently it was twenty 廿 fires 火. The modern form is a man 儿 bearing aloft a fire or torch 火. (W. 24 J.) 儿 is the R., 10th.

281 菜    *ts'ai⁴*, Vegetables, herbs, greens, food, viands.

屮, 艸 *ts'ao³*, is the R., the 140th.

采, 寀 *ts'ai³*, To pick flowers or fruits; variegated; to gather objects. The upper part is 爫 *chao³*, the contracted modern form of 爪 the right hand prone or reaching down, the paws, claws. Normally at the top of a character because of its meaning and here it is above a tree 木 meaning to pick

朵 fruit from a tree 木. It is often written with a hand at the side 探. With grass radical it means the small vegetables, 菜. (W. 49 B.)

**282 起**

*ch'ĭ³*, To rise, to begin ; after a verb an auxiliary denoting the beginning and continuance of the action.

走 *tsou³*, to walk, is the R., the 156th. (See No. 146.)

己 *chĭ³*, self, is the phonetic. (See No. 191.)

**283 樣**

木 *yang⁴*, A pattern, kind, model, manner.

*mu⁴*, wood, is the R., the 75th, as patterns are often made of wood. The character has the same meaning and pronunciation without the R.

羕, 羕 *yang⁴*, A rising or unceasing flow of water (same as 永 *yung³* with 羊 *yang²* added as phonetic) ; uniformity, model, pattern, tediousness.

永, 巛 *yung³*, is unceasing flow of water in veins in the earth, duration, perpetuity. It is a variation of 水 *shuĭ³*, adding foam and ripples. (W. 125 D.)

羊 *yang²*, Sheep, (see No. 253). (W. 103 A.)

**284 魚, 炙, 叟** *yü²*, Fish, the 195th R., relating to names and parts of fish. It is a picture of head, body, fins, scales and tail. The four dots below stand not only for fire 火 but also for tail, and feet in 鳥 *niao³* bird, 馬 *ma³* horse, 羔 *kao¹* lamb 爲 *weī²* monkey. (W. 142 A.)

285 饅　man², Steamed bread or dumplings.

食　shih², food, to eat, to feed, is the R., the
184th. (See No. 75). (W. 26 M.)

曼　man² Wide, long, to draw out. The Chinese
pull dough. (See No. 130.) (W. 34 J.)

286 攏　lung³, To grasp, to collect; to push out, a
comb.

才,手　shou³, hand is the R., the 64th.

龍龍籠　lung², A dragon, imperial, glorious, the 212th
R., contracted from a picture of the
animal. The modern form has on the

飛　right a contraction of 飛 fei¹, to fly, or the
wings (picture of a crane flying W. 11 A.)
and on the left at the bottom is 月=肉 jou⁴
meat or body, and above it 立 li⁴, said
to be a contraction of 童 t'ung², slave boy,
as phonetic. This is probably an artificial
interpretation of a conventional modification of the picture. (W. 140 A.) 攏 is a
hand 手 on a dragon 龍, able to grasp or
gather together legs, wings, tail and all.
Phonetic.

287 總　tsung³, To collect and tie up in a bundle; to
sum up to unite; to comprise, to manage;
before a negative it makes a strong as-
sertion.

糸　mi⁴, called 爛絞絲 lan⁴ chiao³ ssu¹, is the radical,
the 120th.

悤,悤　ts'ung¹ To feel alarm; excited, restless. When
ones mind 心 is excited or restless, one
looks anxiously through the windows 囱
ch'uang², and makes a forecast of pro-

bable outcome; now written 窗. (W. 40 D.) Phonetic combination.

**288** 訴

su⁴, To tell, accuse. 言 yen², words, is the R., the 149th.

斥, 廗, 庎 ch'ih⁴ To attack; a modern abbreviation of 廗 to attack a man 屰 i⁴, in his house 广 yen³; to expel, to scold.

屰, 屮 i⁴ is said by the Shuo Wen to be 干 kan¹, an offence doubled, though not completely, and so having the idea of repeated offence as in 羊 jen³, See No. 139. (W. 102 D.) 訴 su⁴ is to attack 斥 with words 言.

**289** 釘

ting¹, A nail; ting⁴, to nail.

金 chin¹, metal, is the R., the 167th, being the material of which the nail is made. (See No. 13.)

丁, 个 ting¹, A nail with large head, (W. 57 A.)

**290** 徒

t'u², To go on foot; foot soldier; disciple, apprentice; companion; a low fellow; only, futile; to banish.

彳 ch'ih⁴ to walk, called 雙 shuang 立 li⁴ 人 jen², is the R. in the dictionaries, the 60th; but originally it was 辵 cho⁴, the character being written 辻. Later the 止 chih³ was moved over under the 土 t'u³ (See No. 10.) To go 辵 on the ground 土, is the etymology of 徒. (W. 112 E.)

**291** 身, 舟

shen¹, The body, the trunk; ones self; personal; pregnant; the whole life; the 158th R., used in characters relating to the body. The seal form is a human figure with large abdomen and one leg forward to support the body more firmly, or preserve the equilibrium.

Attention is called to other forms of the character 人 *jen*². イ *jen*², erect; ヒ *pi*³, to turn; ノ ト ノ on the top of compounds; 儿 八 the legs, at the bottom of compounds; ⻢ *jen*², leaning or bent over; ヒ ヒ *hua*⁴ heels over head, to change; 尸 ⼫ *shih*¹, a seated man, a corpse; 勹 夗 *pao*¹, a man leaning forward to enfold an object in his apron; 大 *ta*⁴ man with arms; 人 夊 夂 forms of men moving on with hindrances of three forms. (W. Lessons 25-32 54, 60, 61.)

292 體    *t'i*³, The body, the whole person; a class or body of officers etc.; the substance; respectable; a style of writing Chinese characters, of which there are six.

骨 肎 *ku*³, bones is the R., the 188th; a framework. It is made up of skeleton 冎 *kua*³ and flesh 月＝肉 *jou*⁴ opposed to each other, (See 肯 *k'en*³ No. 228.) (W. 118 A.)

豊 豐 *li*⁴³ A vessel used in sacrificing. (See No. 164.) (W. 97 B.)

293 怎    *tsên*³, How? Why? 心 *hsin*¹ is the R. For 乍 *cha*⁴ see No. 145 and 271.

The surprised 乍 heart asks how? why? 怎.

294 鹽　　*yen²*, Salt.

鹵　*lu³* Radical No. 197.　Rock salt ; salt land ; ruds.　Composed of 鹵=西 West and ⅔ four grains of salt, as rock salt comes from the West.　(See No. 26).

監, 鹽　*chien¹*, To watch, prison.　The 監 is a suggestive phonetic (W. 82 F.)—as the Chou Dynasty (1122 to 255 B.C.) appointed officers to have control of salt and salt lands.　The *chien¹* is 臣 *ch'en²* (see No. 120) and reclining man ⼈, which means to recline or bend over, and 血盂 *hsüeh*, a vessel of blood. One explanation of this phonetic is as follows :—in ancient times an oath was taken by having the contracting parties draw blood and an official watch it flow together in a vessel.　When the radical for salt land is added the idea is conveyed that salt is watched over by those who have been appointed to this work.

295 猪　　*chu¹*, Pig.

犭, 犬　*ch'üan³* Radical No. 94, a dog.

This is a modern character and is made up of the above radical and 者 *che³*, (See No. 270) which is here a simple phonetic.

296 狗　　*kou³*, Dog.

犭, 犬　*ch'üan³* Radical No. 94 犭, 犬, a dog.

句　*chü⁴*, or *kou¹*; sentence, (See No. 80) is a suggestive phonetic, as the dog guards by his bark.　This is a modern character.

297 掛　才,手　卦

kua⁴, To suspend; anxious; classifier of bridles.

才,手　shou³, Radical No. 64 ; hand.

卦　kua⁴, The 卦 is a combination of 圭 kuei¹, sceptre, (See No. 161) and 卜 pu³, (See No. 14) and it means to divine ; or a diagram. (W. 56 E.) 圭 is said to represent an hexagram and thus it has no connection with the jade sceptre, but as the writing of the two are identical, it is classed under sceptre 圭. If we suppose that the charts or diagrams of the diviners were hung up then we may regard this as a suggestive phonetic.

298 唱

ch'ang⁴, To sing.

口　k'ou³, Radical No. 30, mouth.

昌　ch'ang¹, The phonetic ; splendid, (W. 73 A). The upper part is the sun and the lower is to speak, emanation. The idea is that the sun sends forth rays as the mouth puts forth words,—a suggestive phonetic. 唱 A more refined quality of voice than ordinary conversation.

299 髒

tsang¹, Dirty.

骨　ku³, Radical No. 188, a bone. (See No. 292).

葬,薵　tsang⁴, to bury, is a suggestive phonetic. What could be more loathsome than a body after mortification is well established and the bones appearing? It is composed of 艹 ts'ao³ grass, (See No. 40) and 死 szu³, to die, which is composed of

死,歺　歹, tai³, calamity and 人 jen², man ; the calamity which comes to all men—

death. (W. 26 H.) The present writing of man in this part of the phonetic is unfortunate as it has but slight resemblance to 人. Beneath is 廾 a contraction of 艸 grass. The dead were tied up in a reed mat 茻. The — is the rope.

300 騎

馬 *ma*,[3] Radical No. 187, a horse. (See No. 261).

奇, 竒 *ch'i*[2], The phonetic; (See No. 54) wonderful, strange. This phonetic is also used in the character for chair. A chair 椅 is used for sitting on; in riding a horse, one sits on the horse as he would sit on a chair, and in the character for riding 騎 radical 木, wood, is replaced by the horse radical. There are not a few characters that have a similarity of action that are formed as the above by a change of radical.

*ch'i*[2], To ride horseback; to sit astride.

301 窮

*ch'iung*[2], Poor, thoroughly exhausted.

穴 *hsüeh*[4], Radical No. 116, a cave. (See No. 97). Caves are used by those who are reduced to the last extremity.

躬, 躳, 躬 *kung*[1], The phonetic, (W. 90 L); to bend the body forward and cause the vertebrae to stand out. The character was formerly written with 呂 *lü*[3] on the right, but 弓 *kung*[1], a bow has been substituted for *lü*[3] the back bone. This is not a bad combination to stand for poor.

302 空, 空

*k'ung*[1], Empty, leisure; the firmament.

穴 *hsüeh*[24], Radical No. 116, a cave (See No. 97).

工 *kung*¹, The phonetic is 工 labor, (See No. 89). This character may have been originally used for caves made by man; a place made empty by 工 labor. (W. 82 A.)

303 綫 *hsien*⁴, Thread.

糸 *mi*⁴, Radical No. 120 but commonly called *lan*⁴ *chiao*³ *ssŭ*¹; silk. (See No. 8).

The phonetic is 戔 *chien*¹ small, narrow. (See No. 13). Thread is made of minute strands of silk.

304 死, 𣦸 *ssŭ*³, To die; death; firm; closed.

歹 *tai*³, Radical No. 78, bones fallen apart; death; bad, perverse.

匕 *jen*², Man inverted.

This is an old character which came into existence before radicals and phonetics were adopted, hence when we say that the radical is 歹 *tai*³ there is no discrepancy, but when we say that the phonetic is 人 *jen*² it is a misnomer as 人 has no phonetic value. (W. 26 H). (See No. 299). Death 死 is the calamity 歹 that comes to man 匕.

305 鍼, 針 *chen*¹, A needle, a pin, a probe.

金 *chin*¹, Radical No. 167, gold, metal. (See No. 13).

鍼 *chen*¹, is the correct writing of this character, but 針 *chen*¹ is shorter and is very often used.

咸, 咸 *hsien*², The phonetic of the correct writing is to bite, to wound with the mouth. 戌 *hsü*¹ is to wound—with a weapon 戌; with the addition of 口 *k'ou*³ to the above, the character means to wound by biting. (W. 71 P.) The needle takes up as it were, little mouthfulls of cloth as if biting its way along. There is no etymology for the short way of writing this character.

**306** 滿

水 氵 *shui*³, Radical No. 85, water. (See No. 79).

滿, 㒼 *man*² The phonetic, is 㒼 equality, equilibrium, (W. 35. M.) The scale pans 兩 are even; when the water is even with the brim of the vessel, then it is full. (See No. 35).

*man*⁸, Full; complete; pride; Manchu people.

The upper part of this phonetic is, by some, supposed to be horns, to indicate equality, as the two horns are apt to be similar. By others it is supposed to be a beam which indicates when the two scale pans are level.

**307** 雞 鷄

*chi*¹, Chicken.

隹 *chui* Radical 172, a short tailed bird. (See No. 21).

鳥 *niao*⁸, Radical 196, a long tailed bird.

The phonetic is 奚 *hsi*¹, a woman condemned to spinning in official prisons. The top is 爪 *chao*³, hand; the center of the character is 糸 silk, contracted, and the lower part is 大 *ta*⁴, an adult. Some think that it was not 大 *ta*⁴ originally but 小 the lower part of 糸, and the 小 was changed to 大 *ta*⁴. 奚 The hand working at spinning, a spinster. These women were condemned to this work, and consequently got no benefit from their labor. The great bulk of the eggs that chickens lay goes to their owners, thus the appropriateness of this phonetic.   (W. 92, C.)

**308** 鐵

*t'ieh*[3], Iron.

金 *chin*[1], Radical 167, gold or metal. (See No. 13).

戥, 戥 *tieh*[4] The phonetic ; to scrape, to pick.

This comes from 呈 *ch'eng*[2], to speak 口 while standing at one's post 壬 ; with the addition of 戈 *ko*[1] it is read *tieh*[4], to notify in a menacing manner ; with the addition of 大 *ta*[4] man, now reduced to 十 *shih*[2] it means to scrape or pick or stab. The metal with which one can scrape or stab best is iron, hence the appropriateness of the phonetic.   (W. 81. H).

**309** 親, 親

*ch'in*[1], near, a relative ; self.

見 *chien*[4], Radical 147 ; to see ; perceive.

亲 *chen*[1], The phonetic, now reduced to 亲 ; hazel. Hazel shrubs grow in clumps, this character is used for those persons which one sees constantly :—those in the same family, relatives.   (W. 102 H.).

**310** 官, 官

*kuan*[1], An official, public.

宀 *mien*[2] Radical 40, a roof.   (See No. 1).

This is an old character which does not conform to rules governing phonetics. The lower part of the character is 𠂤 *tui*[1], terraces, ramparts, city.   The 宀 hall of the 𠂤 city.   It originally referred to the residence of the official who governed a .city. Now it stands for the officer. (W. 86. C.) The top stroke is left off from the 𠂤.

**311** 戴

戈 *ko*[1], Radical 62, a spear. (See No. 2).

*tai*[x], To wear, as hat or spectacles, to bear.

毕

This is an old character and the radical and phonetic are not separable. The foundation of the character is 戋 *ts'ai*[2], to do damage with a spear. The 十 *shih*[2] is a contraction of 才 *t'sai*[2], property or materials; 戋 (W. 71. H.), to plunder with the use of weapons.

異, 粤 *i*[4], To disagree, different. (W. 47. R.). The 田 *t'ien*[2] is a modification of 甶 *fu*[4], devil's head, but here used for the earnest money which is placed on a table 兀 *wu*[4], hands 廾, 臼 are represented as pushing the money away, it is not acceptable. The character 戴 is explained thus. After a place is plundered the marauders divide the spoils according to the number of men, the articles are placed in order, one by one on the several piles; thus the idea of placing on, as the hat is placed on the head is conveyed.

**312** 縫

糸, 枲 *mi*[4], Radical 120, silk. (See No. 8).

*feng*[2], To sew; *feng*[4], a crack, seam.

逢 *feng*[2], The phonetic, means to pick ones way (to walk slowly) 夂 through 丰 *feng*[1], brushwood, to meet. (W. 97. A.). The 辶 *cho*[4] is a redundancy, as 夂 *sui*[1] conveys the idea of walking. When silk is added to this phonetic the idea is that this silk thread, threads its way through the cloth as a man picks his way through brushwood.

**313** 富

*fu*, Rich, abundant, wealth.

宀 *mien²* Radical 40, a roof. (See No. 1).

畐 *fu²*, This phonetic seems to be a contraction of 高 *kao¹* on 田 *t'ien²*. The meaning is that the products of the 田 *t'ien²*, field are piled high, 高 *kao¹*, under cover 宀 *mien*; abundance. (W. 75. D). (See 267.)

**314** 根

*ken¹*, A root, origin, a base, as of a wall.

木 *mu⁴*, Radical 75, wood.

艮 *ken⁴* Phonetic; perverse. (See 223).

Wood added to this phonetic is the character for root. The root is firmly fixed in the ground.

**315** 淨, 淨

*ching⁴*, Clean, pure; to cleanse; only.

氵,水 *shui³*, Radical 85, water.

The phonetic is 爭 *cheng¹*, to pull in different directions, to contend. The upper part is 爪 *chao³* the lower part is a 卂 hand holding a stick, the two hands are pulling the stick in opposite directions. (W. 49. D.). In order to cleanse an article, it must go through what appears to be an active struggle with water.

**316** 河

*ho²*, A river.

氵 *shui³*, Radical 85, water.

可 *k'o,³* The phonetic. (See 54). The idea of this phonetic is that the breath leaves the mouth without meeting obstruction. With the addition of 氵 the idea is that the current is unobstructed, a river flows, but the water of a pond is hemmed in on all sides.

**317** 父, 彐, 月   *fu*⁴, Father.

> This character is the 88th radical. The seal character is a hand holding a rod, the hand which wields authority. The modern writing failed in bringing out this idea (W. 43 G.)

**318** 架

    *chia*⁴, Frame, staging, a rack, to support.

木  *mu*⁴, Radical 75, wood.

加  *chia*⁴, Phonetic ; to add to. To add 加 muscle 力 to persuasion 口, violence. Muscle is 劦 力 *li*⁴, 口 *k'ou*³, indicates a command. (W. 53. D.). When wood 木 is added to this phonetic it indicates that this is a frame on which articles can be added.

**319** 輛

    *liang*⁴, A classifier of carriages,—a pair of wheels, the important part of a cart.

車  *ch'e*¹, Radical 159, a cart, a barrow.

兩  *liang*³, The phonetic, two, (See No. 35.).

> This is an appropriate phonetic as the two wheels of a cart should be a pair, equal in size. With the addition of the cart radical the numerative of carts is completed.

**320** 驢

    *lü*², A donkey.

馬  *ma*³, Radical 187, a horse. (See No. 261).

盧,盧  *lu*² The phonetic ; a hound. This phonetic might have been selected as a donkey is small and not very different in size from a large hound. This phonetic also means a vessel or pan. It is from 虍 *hu*¹ and 甾 *tzŭ*² a vase. This is now made like 田 *t'ien*², a field, but it has nothing in

common with it. 皿 *min*³, added later,
is a redundancy. (W. 135. D.) and
(W. 150 A).

**321** 乘, 乘

*ch'eng*², To ride, to mount, to drive.

*p'ieh*¹, Radical 4, a stroke to the left.

This is a character which does not divide
into radical and phonetic. It is a pictorial representation of a war chariot in
the seal writing (W. 31. E.) 北=舛 *ch'uan*³
represents men sitting back to back. The
chariot has an awning over the men. A
good symbol for riding or mounting.

**322** 轎

*chiao*⁴, A sedan, chair.

車 *ch'e*¹, Radical 159, a cart, a barrow.

喬 *ch'iao*², Phonetic; somethng ihigh, as a tree,
the top of which bends forwards. (W.
75. B.). It is composed of

夭 仌 *yao*¹, and 高 *kao*¹. *Yao*¹ 夭 is a man bending
his head forward getting ready to jump.
(W. 61 B.). 喬 *ch'iao*² is the phonetic in
bridge, 橋 and as a sedan chair when
carried looks like a moving bridge, this
may be the reason for using this phonetic
in sedan chair.

---

BALLER, LESSON XI.

**323** 比, 𠤎

*pi*³, To compare.

This character is radical No. 81.

Two men standing together as if comparing heights. (W. 27. I.).

**324** 及, 𠬺

*chi*², To reach to, to come up to.

又 *yu*⁴, Radical 29, the right hand.

The part of this character which is not the radical is 人 *jen*², man. When the radical is added it indicates that a hand has caught up with the man and has laid hold of him. (W. 19. D.). This character has no connection with 乃 *nai*³, but.

**325** 如

*ju*², Like, as.

女 *nü*³, Radical 38, a woman.

口 *k'ou*³, mouth, is the phonetic. (See No. 10.). (W. 67. D) To speak 口 *k'ou*³, like a woman 女, that is, appropriately to the circumstances.

**326** 嘴

*tsui*³, A bird's bill, the mouth.

口 *k'ou*³, Radical 30, the mouth.

觜 *tsui*³ The phonetic is 觜 *tsui*³, egret of a heron. (W. 142 B.). 此 this 角 horn, with the radical 口 *k'ou*³ is a bill, or mouth.

**327** 泡

*p'ao*⁴, To soak, a blister.

氵,水 *shui*³, Radical 85, water.

包,⍟ *pao*¹, The phonetic; to wrap up; primitive meaning :—gestation. With water added to this we have, water wrapped up, a blister (W. 54. B.).

**328** 擺

*pai*³, To place, to put, to spread out.

手,扌 *shou*³, Radical 64, the hand.

罷 *pa*⁴, Phonetic, an officer; 能 *neng*², able and 网 *wang*³, an officer taken in the net of the law; to discharge. With the addition of hand, which usually indicates that the character is used as a verb, the idea of placing articles in order is conveyed, for in securing the dismissal of an officer one must set forth the evidence ; here the hand is setting articles in their proper position. For 能 See No. 357.

**329** 越

走 *tsou*[3], Radical 156, to walk.

戉 戉 *yüeh*[4] The phonetic; a lance 戈 *ko*[1] with a hook ㇄. (W. 71. L.). 戉 *yüeh* is a halberd with an additional hook thus something extra is inferred. With the addition of the above radical it forms the character for exceed.

*yüeh*[4], to exceed.

**330** 和

*ho*[2], Harmony ; with.

口 *k'ou*[3], Radical 30, the mouth.

禾 *ho*[2], Phonetic ; grain and mouth are adapted one to the other, hence the meaning of harmony.

**331** 罪

*tsui*[4], Sin, crime.

罒,网 *wang*[3], Radical 122, a net.

非 *fei*[1], Phonetic, not right. With the addition of 网 *wang*[3] the idea is conveyed that transgression 非 *fei*[1], is caught in the net of the law and it is called sin. This character was formerly written 皋 *tsui*[4], (W. 102. H.). A malicious scribe substituted the character 皇 *huang*[2] for this character and the Emperor Ch'in-shih-huang forthwith changed the writing of *tsui*[4] by Imperial decree to its present form and tabooed the former writing.

**332 倍**

*pei¹*, To increase, fold, times. Original meaning was to rebel.

人, 亻 *jen²*, Radical 9, a man.

音 *t'ou⁴* Phonetic, to cut a speaker short by interrrupting him in his speech. (W. 133. A). The older writing is 不 *pu¹* above 口 *k'ou³*, mouth and a little stroke on top *chu³*, which is said to represent expression of contempt. The present meaning of the character 倍 seems to have been given it without etymological reason.

**333 着 著**

*cho²*, or *chao²*, Right, to just hit, after a verb the sign of the success of the action.

羊 *yang²*, Radical 123, sheep.

This is a modern character and it is written in several ways. 著 The phonetic which can best be explained is

者, 咼 *chê³*, This symbol was invented to represent the clauses of a sentence which were being connected, the 自 *tzu⁴* is the central part and on either side are branches or arms which take hold of the clauses and bring them together. (W. 159 B.)

**334 像**

*hsiang⁴*, Like, resembling, an image of a man.

人, 亻 *jên²*, Radical 9, man.

象, 豕 *hsiang⁴*, Phonetic, elephant. This is a primitive, representing the animal. On top is the trunk, then are the tusks; the body legs and tail make up the rest of the character. (W. 69. L.). It is difficult to ex-

plain why this symbol should have been
taken for an image.

**335** 蓋

*kai⁴*, To cover, a cover; to build.

卄, 艸 *ts'ao³*, Radical, No. 140, grass.

盍 *ho²* Phonetic; a dish filled and covered; why
not? With the addition of 卄 the character is used for the roof or any cover.
The 艸 *ts'ao³*, indicates that where this
character was coined, houses were
thatched. (W. 38. G.)

**336** 住

*chu⁴*, To dwell, to stop.

亻, 人 *jên²*, Radical No. 9, a man.

主, 坐 *chu³*, Phonetic, a lamp with the flame rising.
(W. 83. D.). By extension, a man who
sheds forth light. (See No. 210). With
the addition of the radical, the character
stands for, to dwell, as if the inference
was:—those who can enlighten others
are those who have a permanent abode.

**337** 屋, 屋

*wu¹*, A room, a house.

尸 *shih¹*, Radical No. 44, a corpse, is the usual
definition of this rad., but a person lying
or sitting down is a better explanation.

至, 坙 *chih⁴*, Phonetic, to arrive at. This is an old
character and what is called phonetic has
no phonetic use. The 至 represents a bird
just alighting on the earth; thus a room
is a place where a person can come and
recline. (W. 32 A, G.). (See No. 88.)

**338** 似, 佁

*szŭ⁴*, Resembling.

人 *jen²*, Radical No. 9, a man.

以 *i*[3] Phonetic. This is a very ancient character and is supposed to represent the breath leaving the mouth without obstruction as from asthma or other impediment. (See No. 121) (W. 85 F). With the addition of 人 the idea is conveyed that the man has the same lung capacity as the normal individual.

**339** 理

*li*[3], Reason, principle.

玉 *yü*[4], Radical No. 96, a gem. (See No. 124).

里 *li*[3], Phonetic, the smallest country village. It is composed of 田 *t'ien*[2] and 土 *t'u*[3], tillable land. (W. 149 D.). This is the 166th radical. (cf. No. 82). With the addition of the 玉 the idea is conveyed that a gem must be cut according to fixed rules just as a field has to be divided into furrows in order that it may be of greatest use.

**340** 布, 市

*pu*[4], Cloth, cotton cloth.

巾 *chin*[1], Radical No. 50, a napkin. (See No. 143).

父 *fu*[4], Phonetic, father. This phonetic is not recognizable in the modern writing, but it is distinct in the seal writing. (W. 35 C.). 父 is probably purely phonetic, but some think that it implies order. In weaving one must proceed according to a fixed order. The material used by the ancients was a kind of linen or flax. Cotton is a modern development. *Fu*[4] 父 is the 88th radical. (See No. 317).

**341** 房

*fang*[2], A house.

戶 *hu*[4], Radical No. 63, a door, a window (No. 5).

方, 圩, 方 fang[1], Phonetic, a square. This is a suggestive phonetic as most houses, or rooms
are nearly square. A thing which is
square and has doors and windows is a
house. For 方 fang[1] see No. 147 (W. 117
A.) ; it is the 70th radical.

342 謝

言 hsieh[4], Thanks, to thank.
言 yên[2], Radical No. 149, word. (See No. 10).
射, 躬, 𣃘 shê[4], Phonetic, to throw out ; to shoot, as an
arrow, against someone 身. See the
oldest form. Combined with the rad., 言,
the idea is to throw out words of thanks.
(W. 131. D).

343 趕

走 kan[3], To drive, to hurry, to strive for.
走 tsou[3], Radical No. 156, to walk. (See No. 146).
旱 han[4], Phonetic, droughth, rainless, dry. This
is composed of 干 kan[1], (supposed to be a
pestle, thus by extension to grind, to
offend), and 日 jih[4]; with the addition of 日
jih[4], the fierce effects 干 of the sun are set
forth. (W. 102 A). When the radical 走
is added, the idea of driving or hurrying is
conveyed. The sun is the signal which
sets the Orient to work.

344 讚

tsan[4], To commend, to praise.
言 yen[2], Radical No. 149, word. (See No. 10).
贊 tsan[4], Phonetic. (W. 79 B.). From 㑄 shen[1],
to advance in order to make a statement
and 貝 pei[4], money ; to come forward with
a present, to aid. When the above radical
is added the idea of commending is given.

345 美

*mei³*, Beautiful, excellent.

羊 *yang²*, Radical, No. 123, a sheep. (See 253).

大 *ta⁴*, Phonetic, large, but originally it meant a man. (W. 103 A). A man who has the disposition of a sheep, mild and gentle.

346 詩

*shih¹*, A song or hymn.

言 *yen²*, Radical No. 149, a word. (See No. 10).

寺 *ssu⁴*, Phonetic, a court or temple. (W. 79 B.). The place where the law 寸 is promulgated. continually 止. (See No. 125). The upper part is 屮 *chih¹*, a small plant issuing from the ground, conveying the idea of development or progress; something which is continual. With the addition of the radical 言 it stands for prolonged words, a song. The words from the throne should be as music in the ears of the people.

---

BALLER, LESSON XII.

347 南, 凷

*nan²*, South.

十 *shih²*, Radical No. 24, ten. (See No. 47). This character cannot be broken up into a radical and a phonetic as it is an old symbol for south or the place of 半 *jen²*, luxuriant vegetation. The 冂 are the boundaries of a place or field and the vegetation forces its way over them by constant growth 十 = 屮. (W. 79 G).

348 北, 林

*pei³*, North.

匕 *pi³*, Radical No. 21, a spoon; inverted man.

This is another character which cannot be reduced to a radical and phonetic. (W. 27 G.). It represents two men standing back to back in the seal writing; compare 从 *ts'ung²* to follow. The custom of the Chinese is to face the south, therefore the back is toward the north.

**349 直**

*chih²*, Straight.

目 *mu⁴*, Radical No. 109, the eye. (See No. 102).

十 *shih²*, Phonetic, ten. (W. 10 K.). What ten eyes declare to be without deviation ∟ must be straight. (See No. 99).

**350 往, 徃**

*wang³*, To go towards, towards.

彳 *ch'ih⁴* Radical No. 60, to step with left foot.

主, 坐 *wang³* Phonetic, luxuriant vegetation which springs from the earth in tufts here and there; rambling, (W. 79 D.). With the addition of the radical it means to stray or roam about.

This phonetic has nothing in common with 主 *chu³* a lord or with 王 *wang²* a prince. In its modern writing it is confusing as it is not always written the same way. 狂 *k'uang²*, a mad dog comes from this phonetic, but the top dot is left off. This is a suggestive phonetic in 狂 as a mad dog wanders about aimlessly. The idea of aimless is suggested as these tufts of vegetation spring up without regard to order.

**351 離**

*li²*, To leave, to separate; from, distant from.

隹 *chui*[1] Radical No. 172, a short-tailed bird. (No. 21).

离, 禽 *li*[3], Phonetic, a yak or elk. (W. 23 E). This phonetic plus the above radical was formerly used for the Chinese oriole, a very beautiful yellow bird now called 黄鸝 *huang*[2] *li*[2]. According to Kuei Shih Shuo Wen, when this bird was heard or seen in the spring, it was the summons for the unmarried daughters to leave the parental roof for the home of their future husbands. Thus the idea of "to leave" attached itself to the character, and another character was adopted for the bird.

352 差, 𤯒 *ch'a*[1], To differ; a discrepancy.

工 *kung*[1], Radical No. 48, work. This is doing violence to the construction of the character to say that 工 *kung*[1] is the rad., as the 工 is only a part of 左 *tso*[3], left hand. (No 89).

垂, 𡍮, 𡋄 *ch'ui*[2], Phonetic, to hang down, (W. 13 E.). (See No. 387).

This character 差 has undergone many changes. The oldest form is 𡗉 (W. 46 C.). The right and left hand are not working in unison, one is directed upward and the other downward. The idea of the present writing is that the left hand is hanging down, not doing its part, thus there is a discrepancy.

353 船 *ch'uan*[2], A boat.

舟 *chou*[1], Radical No. 137, a boat. (See No. 108).

合 *yen*[3], Phonetic, the ravines in the mountains through which the torrents flow. (W. 18 E.). Tuan Shih Shuo Wen gives a better explanation. He says that the phonetic is 沿 *yen*[24], a coast; thus we would have this character taking the place of our English word, coaster, as the Chinese did not build boats for crossing the oceans, a coaster was their largest vessel. Some have tried to prove that this character indicates that the Chinese knew about Noah's ark as it is made up of a boat and eight persons. 八 *Pa*[1] 口 *k'ou*[3]. This is only useful to aid in remembering how to write the character, as it is of modern construction, not much over 2000 years ago—long after the deluge.

354 江

水, 氵

*chiang*[1], A large river.

*shui*[3], Radical No. 85, water. (See No. 79).

*kung*[1], Phonetic, labour. This phonetic may have originally been 貢 *kung*[4] tribute. The Yang Tzu Chiang was the river which bore the tribute from the nine *chou*, 九州 (nine provinces) to the Emperor. Formerly official documents were carved on tortoise shell and the material apparently was limited in quantity, so that occasionally characters were abbreviated on account of lack of space. An abbreviation of a character in an official document was a precedent for all time and some characters have thus been changed so that it is difficult to find an explanation for their present construction.

**355** 裝    *chuang¹*, To pack, to fill, to pretend.

衣 *i¹*, Radical No. 145, clothes. (See No. 51).

壯 *chuang⁴*, Phonetic, a stout man. The idea of stout is obtained from 爿 *ch'iang²*. (See No. 84). The 士 *shih⁴* is man. (See No. 69). (W. 127 B.)

As this character was early used for an officer and as officers wore their robes of office, there are many characters which have the above phonetic whose meaning has to do with appearance. Thus when the radical for clothing is added, the idea is to pretend to be what one is not, or to fill full.

**356** 遠    *yüan³*, Distant.

辶 *cho⁴*, Radical No. 162, to go. (See No. 10).

袁 *yüan²* Phonetic, a long robe. (See No. 51). (W. 16 L.). There is evidence that this character has been changed from the original writing and the present writing is not explained. If one remembers when going on a long journey long clothes are worn it may assist in recalling the make up of the character.

**357** 能,䏻,熊 *neng²*, Able.

肉 *jou⁴*, Radical No. 130, meat. (See No. 133). This character refuses to be broken up into radical and phonetic; it formerly meant the " large brown bear," and because of his great strength he was considered extremely able. This indicates that a slang word has been incorporated into the language as the correct expression for able. (W. 27 J.). The character is explained thus; two 큭 paws, 月 the body, and 厶 the head.

**358** 近

chin⁴, Near, in time or place.

辶 cho⁴ Radical No. 162, to go (See No. 10).

斤, 斥 chin¹, Phonetic, ax, battle ax; catty. A picture of the axhead. It was used for a weight of 16 ounces or catty. (W. 128 A).

The character seems to suggest the proper way for a warrior to advance, (to go to battle), with his battle ax in his hand, i.e near. Both near 近 and 遠 far have this R.

**359** 輪

lun², To revolve; a wheel.

車 ch'e¹, Radical No. 159; a cart, a barrow. (No. 136).

侖, 侖 lun² Phonetic, a bundle 亼 of documents in proper order 冊. (W. 14 G.) With the addition of the above radical the idea of order is retained as a wheel must have the spokes arranged properly. The ancient documents were engraved on bamboo slips and tied together, as shown in the seal writing, consequently the phonetic is suggestive.

**360** 李

li³, Plums; baggage.

木 mu⁴, Radical No. 75, wood. (See No. 22).

子 tzu³, Phonetic, son. Kang Hsi's dictionary affirms that, owing to the plum being very prolific, it was represented bv woode np

son; the character son is here representing the fruit on the tree. When travelling
ones baggage should stick to him as unripe fruit clings to the tree. Pupils are
sometimes referred to as peaches and
plums,—they are unripe fruit receiving
their development from the teacher.

**361** 僱

人, 亻    *jen²*, Radical No. 9 ; man.

*ku⁴*, To hire, to engage.

雇 *ku⁴*, Phonetic, to hire. This character is written
in two ways, with and without the radi-
cal for man and it has the same meaning.
The upper part of the phonetic is 戶 *hu⁴*
the 63 rad., a door, a family, a farmer.
The lower part is 隹 *chui¹*; a short tailed
bird, the 172nd radical. A logical interpretation of the combination of these two
radicals would be, the farmer's bird. In
ancient times there were nine kinds of
birds called 雇 *ku⁴*. The arrival of each of
these 雇 *ku⁴*, on their migratory expedi-
tions was regarded as the sign for commencing certain lines of husbandry. Thus
when the quail was seen in early summer
it set the farmers to harvesting their
wheat ; when wild geese appeared in the
fall, the crops must be gathered in.
Thus the character means to set a person
to work. Shuo Wen. (cf. W. 129 A.).

**362**  經

糸 *mi⁴*, Radical No. 120, silk.

*ching¹*, Classic books ; to pass through ; already.

巠 *ching¹* Phonetic, the watercourses 《 under the

ground 一. (W. 12. H.) These water-courses are of first importance in the mind of the geomancer, hence this phonetic enters into the composition of many characters. (See No. 136). With the addition of the silk radical it stood for the warp, the long threads in a piece of cloth. These threads were very important in Chinese civilization. In 頸 *ching³* the neck, because the courses of the veins were visible, this phonetic was used.

**353 順**

*shun⁴*, Favorable, prosperous.

頁 *yeh⁴*, Radical No. 181 ; head ; leaf of a book. (See No. 105).

川, 巛 *ch'uan¹*, Phonetic, a large river formed by the junction of several others. Perhaps the idea of this combination is :—when affairs flow in a current which is in accordance with ones head or wishes, 頁, it is then favourable. (W. 12 E).

**364 客**

*k'o⁴*, A visitor, a traveler.

宀 *mien²* Radical No. 40 a roof. (See No. 1).

各 *ko²,³,⁴*, Phonetic, each, every, all. (W. 31 B). A place where all can have a roof over their heads. Such an individual is called a 客 *k'o⁴*. (See No. 272).

**365 颳**

*kua¹*, To blow.

風 *feng¹*, Radical No. 182 ; the wind. Insects 虫 are born under the influence of wind or vapor 一 (W. 21 B).

舌, 舌 *she²*, Phonetic, the tongue. (See No. 73). This is a modern character and is not found in the Shuo Wen.   The combination would suggest that the character was coined for a blustering wind which licked up the dust as if by a tongue.

**366** 收

欠, 攴  shou¹, To receive, to gather together.

屮, 弖  p'u¹ Radical No.66; to tap, to rap. (See No. 17).

chiu¹ Phonetic, tendrils.  This is a primitive which was formerly used alone, but in the rearranging of characters a radical had to be written with it, as the primitive is not one of the radicals.  The clinging of tendrils is a very suggestive symbol for the above meaning.  (W. 54 F.).

**367** 拾

扌, 手  shih², to pick up ; ten.

合  shou³, Radical No. 64, the hand.

ho², Phonetic, with. (See No. 103).  The phonetic seems to have no phonetic value in this character, but it indicates that things are picked up when the hand and article come together.

---

BALLER, LESSON XIII.

**368** 丈㝵

一  chang⁴, A measure of ten feet.

i¹, Radical No. 1, one.

This is an old character and it was composed of the right hand 彐又 yu⁴, holding shih², ten, (a ten foot pole).

**369** 電

雨  tien⁴, Lightning, electricity.

申, 电, 乙, 吊  yü³, Radical No. 173, rain.  (See No. 61).

shen¹, Phonetic, Chalfant says that this was a representation of lightning which eventually became the sign for " deity." The combination of the radical for rain and the symbol for lightning is not an inconsistent sign for electricity. (See No. 227).

370 論

言
侖

*lun⁴*, To discuss ; an essay.

*yen²*, Radical No. 149, a word. (See No. 10).

*lun²*, Phonetic, documents assembled in order. (See No. 359). With the addition of the above radical the idea is conveyed of setting statements in order so that the thought is made lucid. (W. 14 G).

371 替 씸

曰

*t'i⁴*, For, instead of.

*yüeh⁴*, Radical No. 73, to speak. The original idea of this radical was to depict a word issuing from the mouth. (See No. 9).

The phonetic of this character has no phonetic value. It was originally two 立 *li⁴* characters side by side, but it was afterwards changed to two 夫 *fu¹* characters, and the lower part was 自 *tzu*, 씁 thus the idea was that the first man 立 *li⁴* could not do something, but the second *li⁴* did it just as if the first man had done it himself 自. Both 立 and 夫 mean man. (W. 60 L.).

372 怕

忄, 心
白

*p'a⁴*, To fear ; lest.

*hsin¹*, Radical No. 61, heart. (See No. 18).

*pai²*, Phonetic, white. White heart—no courage. Fright causes one to turn pale. (See No. 6).

373 量

*liang²*, To measure.

里 *li³*, Radical No. 166, a Chinese mile: (See No. 82).

The phonetic of this character was 良 *liang²*, but it is so modified in the present writing that it is of little aid to refer to it. The etymology of the character is difficult to trace and the Chinese have invented an etymology which after once hearing it is difficult to forget :—the distance to the sun 日 has been measured 量 and it was found to be one *li³* above the Earth. 日 sun 一 one 里 *li³*.

374 殼

　　*kou⁴*, Enough, fully.

弓 *kung¹*, Radical No. 57, a bow. (See No. 55).

殼 *ch'üeh⁴*, *k'e¹*, Phonetic, shell, husk. It is probable that the idea was to strike 殳 *shu¹* something hollow 壳 *k'e¹*. When bow is added to this phonetic the idea of enough is said to be suggested because an archer, in shooting, draws the bow to the full. He makes a large vacant space between the bow and the string. (W. 34 I).

375 尺, 尺

　　*ch'ih⁸*, a foot, a span.

尸 *shih¹*, Radical No. 44, a corpse, a person in the reclining posture, an adult.

乀 乙 *i¹*, Phonetic, germination; here it indicates the opening out of the hand in the act of making a span. The 尸 *shih¹* is said to be the male, adult hand. It is probable that this character has been contracted and thus the part which indicated the hand has been deleted. In the 周 *Chou* dynasty the unit of length measured about twenty centimeters. If one remembers this it will help to understand measurements in the Classics. (W. 32 F.).

**376 報**

*pao⁴*, To announce; to recompense; a newspaper.

土 *t'u³*, Radical No. 32, earth.

幸.夆 *nieh⁴*, a criminal, a man 大 who has committed crime 羊, *jen³*. cf. No. 274 (W. 102 G., D.). It is unfortunate that the scribes have caused the left part of the 報 character to be identical with

幸,夆 *hsing⁴*, fortunate, lucky, as it has a very different meaning.

艮,弖 *fu²* The right part of the character shows a hand holding a seal, and about to stamp the order for punishment. (W. 55 C.) The idea of to announce 報 is obtained owing to an official trying a criminal case 幸 and publishing his decision 艮.

**377 局,局**

*chü²*, an office, a shop.

尸 *shih¹*, Radical No. 44, a corpse. This is another character which cannot be divided up into radical and phonetic as the base of the character is 尺 *ch'ih³*, the expanded hand, a span and 口 *k'ou³*, the mouth. The explanation given is that in fixing up a shop one must not only use the hand but the mouth must also be used to inquire the best mode of procedure. There is another explanation of the character which may be easier to remember. The *ch'ih*[3] 尺 is a foot, (a square foot) and the 口 *k'ou*[3] is one of the positions on a chess board. A chess board a foot square is large enough and the squares are places for stopping or resting. (W. 32 F.).

**378** 福

福 *tu*[2], Happiness, prosperity.

示 *shih*[4], Radical No. 113; to reveal. (See No. 227).

畐, 畗 *fu*[4] Phonetic, abundance. (W. 75 D.). The most satisfactory explanation of this phonetic is that it is a contraction of 高 *kao*[1], high and 田 *t'ien*[2], a field, the products of the field piled high is a good symbol for abundance. With the addition of the radical the idea is that a superhuman influence has decreed abundance, hence the meaning happiness. (cf. No. 267).

**379** 享, 畗

享, 畗 *hsiang*[3], To receive, to enjoy.

亠 *t'ou*[2], Radical No. 8, above.

This character does not divide up into radical and phonetic. The ancient writing was two 高 characters, one upright and the other inverted, they were contracted to 畗. Here is another illustration of the reversing the meaning of a character by inverting it. The upper part 合 is written in the ordinary way and means superior; the lower part is inverted and means inferior. The ⊖ in the seal form is the gift which is being handed up to the superior by the inferior. (W. 75 D.).

**380** 政

政 *cheng*[4], To rule; government.

攴 *p'u*[4] Radical No. 66, to strike or tap. The seal character is a right hand holding a rod. (See No. 17).

正 *cheng*[4], Phonetic, right, exact. A government 政 should act 攴 *p'u*[4] in an orderly and exact 正 manner. (See No. 12). (W. 112 I).

381 貼

*t'ieh*[1], To paste.

貝 *pei*[4], Radical No. 154, precious. (See No. 38).

占 *chan*[4], Phonetic, to usurp, to seize, to divine.

An old definition of the character 貼 is "to leave in pledge." An article left in pledge is marked by pasting a written statement upon it. It is possible that the meaning which is now prevalent originated in this way. The above phonetic also means to divine, but the meaning to usurp seems to be more logical in this combination. (W. 56 B).

382 墨

*mo*[4], Ink.

土 *t'u*[3], Radical No. 32, earth.

黑, 炎 *hei*[1], Phonetic, black. The seal writing of this character is a vent for smoke and the lower part is two fires, one above the other, indicating a succession of fires. Around the vent lampblack accumulates, hence a very appropriate symbol for black. It is the 203rd radical Mixing lampblack with earth 土 is probably the way ink was first made. (W. 40 D).

383 暗

*an*[4], Dark.

日 *jih*[4], Radical No. 72, sun.

音 *yin*[1], Phonetic, sound. This is the 180th, radical. (See No. 39). There are several characters which have this radical as their phonetic and have a meaning of dark or obscure ; it may be that this meaning has been attached to this phonetic owing to sound being invisible. When the sun is invisible it is dark. (W. 73 E).

**384** 恩

ên[1], Grace, to show favor.

心 hsin[1], Radical No. 61, heart.

因, 因 yin[1], Phonetic, because. (W. 60 B). The original meaning of this phonetic was a man confined in a cell. One cannot but feel sorry for a prisoner thus confined. If this feeling of sorrow leads one to liberate him, that is grace and it is represented by placing heart, 心 hsin[1] under 因 yin[1].

**385** 惠, 蕙

hui[4], Kind, grace.

心 hsin[1], Radical No. 61, heart.

重 ch'uan[1] Phonetic. This is supposed to represent an ox with a trace attached to a bar behind the horns ; and at the end of the trace there is a hook for attaching objects which are to be drawn. By extension, when ones heart is drawn into his work he is kind, he allows his better feelings to enter into his actions. (W. 91 E, G).

**386** 典, 興

tien[3], A dictionary, records.

八 pa[1], Radical No. 12, eight.

冊 = 册 ch'ai[2], Phonetic, books. This is an old character and has dropped out of use. It, in the seal writing, represents bamboo books placed in order. The lower part of the character was a table 兀 *wu*⁴, and not 八 *pa*¹, but when radicals were sought to classify all characters, the legs of the table were taken for 八 *pa*¹. (W. 156 C).

387 郵

*yu*², Post house.

邑 *i*⁴, Radical No. 163, a city. (See No. 11).

垂, 坙 *ch'ui*², Phonetic, a bough loaded with leaves and drooping flowers (W. 13 E). Chalfant says that this phonetic is a spray of wistaria. As these flowers hang pendent, this symbol has been adopted for characters which convey the idea of hanging or suspension. Thus 睡 *shui*⁴ to sleep, implies that the eyelids are drooping and are suspended over the eyes. A post house was on the frontier. This was the only place where the Government maintained postal communications, the Emperor especially desiring to know the condition of affairs in the villages or cities which were located on the fringes of his domain. They are looked upon as the "hanging on" cities.

---

BALLER LESSON XIV.

388 府

*fu*³, A prefecture; a palace.

广 *yen*³ Radical No. 53, a covering, a hut.

付 *fu*⁴, Phonetic, to deliver to. With the addition of the radical the meaning of the character is a place 广 where taxes are paid, 付. A man 亻 takes and a hand 寸 gives. (W. 45 C).

**389** 州, 巛

*chou*[1], A political district.

巛 *ch'uan*[1], Radical No. 47, streams. (W. 12 E). This is an old character and does not break up into radical and phonetic. In the old writing it represents tracts of land surrounded by rivers. (W. 12 L).

**390** 縣

*hsien*[4], A district.

糸 *mi*[4] Radical No. 120, silk. (See No. 8).

県, 県 *hsiao*[1] Phonetic, the head of a criminal hanging up, the hair is hanging down. (W. 160 A). With the addition of 系 *hsi*[1], a modification of 糸 *mi*[4] silk, the idea of the head being hung up is emphasized. A *hsien*[4] was a place where an official resided whose rank enabled him to execute criminals. (See Chalmers No. 187).

**391** 省, 眚

*sheng*[3], or *hsing*[3]. *Sheng*[3], a province; *hsing*[3], watchful.

目 *mu*[4], Radical 109, the eye. (See No. 102).

少 *shao*[3], Phonetic, few. This phonetic is devoid of phonetic significance. There are three ways of explaining this character, but only two of them are worth recording. The 少 is said to be the eyebrow frowning as if endeavoring to see more distinctly. The other explanation is that the 少 *shao*[3] indicates a narrowing of the palpebral fissure in order to see better. This is frequently done by nearsighted persons as it gives them clearer vision. (W. 158 D).

**392** 樓

*lou*[2], Loft, a story, a house which is more than one story high.

木 *mu*[4], Radical No. 75, wood. (See No. 22).

婁 *lou*[2] Phonetic, the part of a palace where wo-men are confined. (W. 67 N). Women 女 *nü*[3], enclosed 中 *chung*[1], in the 毋 *wu*[2], prison of the gynecium. With the addition of the wood radical it is the symbol for a house which is higher than the ordinary dwelling.

**393 短**

*tuan*[3], Short, deficient

矢 *shih*[4], Radical No. 111, a dart. (See No. 100).

豆 豆 *tou*[4], Phonetic, a dish. (W. 165 A.) The char-acter for short was formed by putting together two of the shortest utensils of the ancients, namely, a dart and a dish. The character for long 長, was hair that was so long it had to be fastened with a brooch. (For long, see W. 113 A).

**394 新**

*hsin*[1], New, recent.

斤 *chin*[1], Radical No. 69, an ax. (See No. 358).

亲 *chen*[1] Phonetic, the Chinese hazel bush. Rods of this shrub were used for beating crimi-nals and, for this purpose, it was necessary that they be freshly cut. Thus hazel brush 亲 *chen*[1] and ax 斤 *chin*[1] became the symbol for new or fresh, as the ax by the side of the rods implied that they were just cut. (W. 102 H). The present writing of hazel 榛 *chen*[1] is not like the above, which is the old writing.

**395 舊**

*chiu*[4], Old, worn out, formerly.

臼 *chiu*[4], Radical No. 134, a mortar. (See No. 479.)

萑 *huan*[2] or *chui*[2] Phonetic, a horned owl.

匶 *chiu*⁴, was originally used for 柩 *chiu*⁴, a corpse placed in a coffin. In the shops coffins are euphemistically spoken of as 壽村 *shou*⁴ *ts'ai*², material for the aged or old. This usage may have stamped the meaning of old on 舊 *chiu*⁴ as in the above writing it represented the corpse in the coffin. (W. 103 C) (cf. 428.)

**396** 壞

土 *t'u*³, Radical No. 32, earth.

襄 *huai*², Phonetic, to hide in the bosom, covered
   from the eye by putting in the breast.
   (W. 16 J). The upper part of the phonetic is a cover, the part which looks like 罒
   *wang*³ is 目 *mu*⁴ written horizontally in
   order that it may not take up so much
   space, the lower part is the radical for
   clothing with the cords which are used as
   fasteners across the breast of the garment
   represented. Others explain that 罢 *tai*⁴
   means to hide as the eyelashes fall over
   the eye and hide it, and is here placed inside of the 衣 i.e. to hide in the clothing.
   cf. No. 82, 裏.

*huai*⁴, To spoil, ruined.

With the addition of the radical for earth
the idea may have been,—if instead of hiding the article in the breast it was buried
in the earth it would be ruined.

**397** 查
查

木 *mu*⁴, Radical No. 75, wood.  (See No. 22).

且 *ch'ieh*³ Phonetic, a chair without a back.  It is
   used here as a simple phonetic.  This art-

*ch'a*², To examine, to search into.

icle was originally used in sacrificial
ceremonies and it enters into the composition of many characters. With the addition of wood it was originally used as
a proper name and afterwards it was
written instead of 察 *ch'a²*. Thus it has
no etymology. Correctly written 查.

**398 難**

*nan²*, Difficult, to cause distress.

隹 *chui¹* Rad. No. 172, a short tailed bird. (See 21).

莫 嘆 *han⁴* Phonetic, dried in the sun. In the old
seal writing the sun is shining on the loess
with fiery heat and drying out the moisture. With the addition of the radical for
short tailed birds, (most water fowl have
short tails) the idea is that when the pools
where these birds get their food are dried
up they are in distress. (W. 171 B).

**399 草**

*ts'ao³*, Grass, herbs.

艸 屮 *ts'ao³* Radical No. 140, grass.

早 *tsao³*, Phonetic, early. (See No. 111). This
character originally stood for a kind of
grass which was used for dyeing articles
black 皂. With the addition of the radical
it now means any kind of grass or herb.
(W. 143 E).

**400 教**

*chiao¹*, To teach; a religion; to allow.

攴 *p'u¹* Radical No. 66, to strike. (See No. 17).

孝 爹 *hsiao²*, Phonetic, to learn. The seal writing is
two crosses ✕=*i⁴*, above a son 子. (W 39
B). it here indicates question and answer.

爻 ✕ *rao²*, (See No. 165). The character ✕ has the
meaning of influence from the cutting of
shears which it pictures. Here being

doubled it emphasizes the influence of the teacher on the pupil 子. With the addition of the radical 攵 the idea of applying the rod is portrayed. (W. 39 G, H). The modern writing of this phonetic is identical with 孝 *hsiao*[4], filial piety, but it has nothing but 子 in common with it. (W. 30 E).

**401** 煮 煑

*chu*[3], To boil.

火 灬 *huo*[3], Radical No. 86, fire.

者 *che*[3] Phonetic, a final particle, a suffix. (See No. 270). This phonetic can be regarded as the pronoun it; then the etymology is, fire 火 it 者. Boil it by putting fire under it.

**402** 進

*chin*[4], To enter in, to advance.

辶 *cho*[1] Radical No. 162, walking and stopping.

隹 *chui*[1] Phonetic, a short-tailed bird. It has no phonetic significance in this character. 172nd radical. (See No. 21). With the addition of the radical 辶 it stands for to advance; this may be because birds in flying always move forwards, they never fly backwards.

**403** 輛

*t'ang*[4], A time, an occasion.

車 *ch'e*[1], Radical, No. 159, a cart. (See No. 136).

尚 *shang*[4], Phonetic, a roof of a house. (See No. 52). (W. 36 E). With the addition of the cart radical it is used for the number of times a trip has been taken. The cart suggests that the idea may have been, — the number of trips the cart made to a certain house and back.

**404** 益 盆

*i*[4], Advantage, profit.

皿 *min*[3], Radical No. 108, a dish, (See No. 233).

水 *shui³*, Phonetic, water. The character is lying on its side, indicating overflow, or abundance. A dish 皿 overflowing stands for advantage or profit. (W. 125 C). This is an old character and antedated the glazing of pottery. Unglazed pottery if made of sandy clay will not hold water, but pottery made of good clay will retain it. It would not be strange if pottery which held water was taken as the symbol of advantage or profit.

**405** 掃

sao³, To sweep.

手 *shou³*, Radical No. 64 ; the hand.

帚, 肅 *chou³* Phonetic, a dusting brush. (W. 44 K). In the seal writing a hand ㄱ is represented as holding a broom. The addition of the hand radical at the side was made about 200 B.C.

**406** 孝, 耇

hsiao⁴, To honor parents, filial piety.

子 *tzŭ³*, Radical No. 39, a son.

老 *lao³*, Phonetic, old. This phonetic is not brought out in the modern writing. (W. 30 E). The phonetic in 敊 教 *chiao¹* in modern writing is the same as 孝 *hsiao⁴*, but it has nothing in common with it in etymology. (See No. 400). *Lao³* 老 old, stands for parents and the 子 *tzŭ³* son should render that devotion and reverence which is fitting and proper.

**407** 敬

ching⁴, To reverence.

攴 *p'u¹* Radical No. 66, to strike.

苟, 茍 *chi⁴* Phonetic, to restrain ones self. (W. 54 G). This phonetic is made up of 羊 *yang²* sheep, contracted, and 勹 *pao*[1] to cover and 口 *k'ou*[3] the mouth. To stand meek as a sheep and restrain ones words. With the addition of the radical which here can be taken as the one who wields power the idea is to be modest in the presence of those in authority.

**408** 堂

*t'ang*[2], A hall, a meeting place.

土 *t'u*[3], Radical No. 32, earth.

尚 *shang*[4], Phonetic, a house, (See No. 52) ; hence this is a suggestive phonetic. With the addition of the radical for earth we have an inclosure 口 which is roofed over ⺌ but the earth is the floor, a condition which is by no means uncommon at the present time. (W. 36 E).

**409** 處

*ch'u*[4], A place, circumstances.

虍 *hu*[3], Radical No. 141, a tiger. (See No. 258).

処 *ch'u*[4], Phonetic, a place. Suggestive phonetic. The primitive idea of this phonetic was to have walked until tired, 夂 *chih*[3] and come to a seat 几 *chi*[3]. This character had the radical *hu*[3] added to it when the characters were being put under radicals but it contributes nothing save difficulty in writing. To the present day the abbreviated form 処 is without this radical. (W. 20 B).

**410** 常

*ch'ang*[2], Constantly.

巾 *chin*[1], Radical No. 50, a napkin. (See No. 143).

尚 *shang*[4], Phonetic, a house, (See No. 52) (W.

36 E). The radical *chin*[1] is a banner which is constantly 常 floating in front of the headquarters, 尚 *shang*[4], of the general.

**411** 棵

*k'o*[1]. Numerative of trees.

木 *mu*[4], Radical No. 75, wood. (See No. 22).

果 *kuo*[8], Phonetic, fruit. (W. 120 F). The fruit is represented by 田 *t'ien*[2] on the tree. This combination would make an appropriate numerative of fruit trees, but it is used for all kinds of trees.

**412** 樹

*shu*[4], A tree.

木 *Mu*[4], Radical No. 75, wood.

尌, 尌 *chu*[4] or *shu*[4], Phonetic, upright, vertical. (W 165 D). This seems to be a hand 寸 beating a drum 壴 *chou*[4]. The idea of vertical may have been derived from the position in which the drum was held. The left part is a drum 口 on a stand and above is an ornament. With the addition of the wood radical we have vertical or standing wood, trees.

------

BALLER LESSON XV.

**413** 厚

*hou*[4], Thick, generous.

厂 *han*[1] Radical No. 27, a cliff. (See No. 42).

旱 *hou*[4] Phonetic, liberal, generosity. 旱 is the reverse of 㫚=享 i.e. 㝵=旱. The 日 is a gift and the rest of the phonetic is first five strokes of 高 *kao*[1], high, reversed; thus it is a gift 日 come down to an inferior 旱. A superior man or the gods would give lavish gifts, thus the meaning of generous is attached to this phonetic. The 厂 *han*[4] is not cliff but a stroke which indicates descent or the coming down of the gift from above. (W. 75 G).

**414** 傳

伊, 人    專, 叀

*ch'uan*[2], To propagate ; to hand down.

*jen*[2], Radical No. 9, man.

*chuan*[1], Phonetic, singly, particular. (W. 91 F). 叀 *ch'uan*[1] The upper part of this phonetic is an ox harnessed and a trace dragging behind with a ring for attaching loads which are to be drawn. When the lower part of the phonetic 寸 hand, is added, it is the character for a writing tablet which was worn attached 叀 to the 寸 wrist. These tablets were worn by the official scribes. A man 人 proclaims 傳 what is written on his wrist-tablet 專, preaches from notes.

**415** 修, 脩

伊, 人    攸

*hsiu*[1], To repair, to build, to cultivate, adorn.

*jen*[2], Radical No. 9, man.

*yu*[1] Phonetic, to feel ones way across a ford with a stick 攴. (See No. 160). This phonetic has added to it 彡 *shan*[1], feathers, long hair, ornament. This compound phonetic and the radical for man stand for 修 to cultivate, to repair. (W. 12 C).

**416** 薄

艸    溥

*pao*[2], An herb of the mint family ; thin, mean.

*ts'ao*[3], Radical No. 140, grass, is connected with the first meaning of 薄.

*p'u*[3], Phonetic, a wide expanse of shallow water 水. (For 甫 *fu*[3] see No. 151). The phonetic 尃 *fu*[1], the hand 寸 of an adult, 甫,

broad, amplitude. From this meaning the idea of breadth runs through several characters which have this phonetic, (W. 109 D). Here breadth without depth suggests thinness, meanness.

**417** 笑

竹 *chu²*, Radical No. 118, bamboo. (See No. 7).

天, 夭 *yao¹*, Phonetic, a man in the act of bending forward in order to jump, march or laugh more easily. With the addition of bamboo the character is used for, to laugh, because when the wind waves the bamboo it resembles the movements of a man convulsed with laughter. (W. 61 B) (See No. 322).

*hsiao⁴*, To laugh at, to smile.

**418** 圓

□ *wei²*, Radical No. 31, enclosure.

員, 員 *yüan²*, Phonetic, round. (W. 161 B). Originally this phonetic was the full writing of the character, but □ *wei²* was added later. The character now has two □ *wei²* radicals as the small square above the 貝 *pei⁴* is *wei²*. The meaning was something round like a cowrie 貝.

*yuan²*, Round.

**419** 匠, 匠

匚 *fang¹* Radical No. 22, a log hollowed out. (W. 51 A).

斤, 斤 *chin¹*, Phonetic, an ax. No phonetic significance. (W. 128 A). The seal writing is said to be a representation of the instrument. The little stroke to the right is thought to be a chip of wood. This is the 69th

*chiang⁴*, An artisan.

radical. (Cf. No. 358). When the radical for a hollowed out log is added it stands for an artisan or the work of an artisan. The hollowing out of trees to make boats or vessels was probably one of the first mechanical devices employed.

**420** 情

忄, 心    *ch'ing*[2], The affections, the feelings.

青    *hsin*[1], Radical No. 61, the heart.

*ch'ing*[1], Phonetic, the colors of nature, (See No. 63), (W. 115 D). With the addition of the radical for heart the character stands for those feelings which are pure or natural to the heart of man.

**421** 實

宀    *shih*[2], Real, true, really, solid.

貫, 貫    *mien*[2], Radical No. 40, a roof.

*kuan*[4], Phonetic, long strings of cowries or cash. (W. 153 A). The upper part of the phonetic, which by the way has no phonetic value, is two articles 毌 strung together on a string 一, 毌 *kuan*[4], and the lower part shows that these articles are cowries or coins 貝 *pei*[4]. When roof is added the character stands for real wealth stored away where it is available for use, not a false pretense of wealth.

**422** 醒

酉, 酉    *hsing*[3], to become sober after being drunk, to wake up, to startle.

*yu*[3] Radical No. 164; a kind of jar which was used for keeping fermented liquors. The 一 shows that there is something in the jar, (W. 41 G).

星, 星    *hsing*[1], Phonetic, stars. (W. 79 F). The

oldest writing of this character has three stars or suns above 生 *sheng*[1]. The stars are supposed to be formed 生 *sheng*[1] from the quintessence of sublimate matter rising up to heaven. 晶 *ching*[1]=clear, crystal. 醒 *hsing*[3] is to become clear headed after intoxication.

**423** 禍

*huo*[4], Calamity, misfortune.

示, 礻 *shih*[4], Radical No. 113, to reveal. (See No. 227).

咼 *kua*[3] Phonetic, a defect in the conformation of the bones of the mouth a cleft palate. (See No. 119). When the above radical is combined with this phonetic there is the suggestion of divine judgment. If a child is born with a hare lip or a cleft palate 咼 it is regarded as a calamity 禍 sent from heaven 示. (W. 118 A).

**424** 哭

*k'u*[1], To cry.

口 *k'ou*[3], Radical No. 30, the mouth.

犬, 犭 *ch'üan*[3], Phonetic, dog, — without phonetic significance. Confucius remarked that this character is a picture of a dog. The two mouths 吅 *hsüan*[1] indicate a call or outcry, hence 哭 means to howl or cry 吅 after the manner of dogs 犬. (W. 72 C).

**425** 淺

*ch'ien*[3], Shallow.

水, 氵 *shui*[3], Radical No. 85, water.

戔 *chien*[1] Phonetic, to exterminate, to destroy, dangerous. The common work of two or more halberds. (W. 71 R). (See No. 13). This phonetic always gives a bad

or insignificant color to the character.
Shallow water is dangerous to a sailor.

**426** 世, 卋

shih⁴, An age, a generation, thirty years.
— i¹, Radical No. 1, one.
卅 san¹ shih², Phonetic, thirty. No phonetic
significance. (W. 24 O). 卅 is the contraction of three 十 shih² or thirty and the
horizontal line below in 卋, is the radical i¹
— one. Thirty years make one generation.

**427** 文 仌

wên², Strokes, lines, literature, elegant.
Radical No. 67. This is one of the oldest
characters and it is supposed to represent
the grain in wood or ripples on water.
(W. 61 F).

**428** 勸

ch'üan⁴, To exhort, to advise.
力 li⁴, Radical No. 19, strength. (See No. 212).
雚.雈 kuan⁴, Phonetic, a heron. (W. 72 J). A
short-tailed bird 隹 chui¹, with egrets, 丫
or horns, which has a loud call 䖙 hsüan¹.
The horns of a sheep are taken to represent the egrets. The *Shuo Wen* has no
etymology for this phonetic in combination with the above radical. It may be
that this combination was used owing to
the great patience of the heron. Its
Chinese common name is "old waiter",
lao³ teng². It will gaze into the water for
hours without moving, in order to secure
a fish. If we could use the same patience
and vigilance in persuading men much
would be accomplished, hence it is not an
inappropriate symbol for, to exhort.

**429** 罵 ma⁴, To curse, to revile.

㓁,网 wang², Radical No. 122, a net. (See No. 38), (W. 39 C).

馬 ma³, Phonetic, horse. Radical No. 187. (See No. 261), (W. 137 A). The Shuo Wen does not explain this character 罵. It seems to be an arbitrary combination of radical and phonetic. Catch a horse 馬 in a net 网 and you will want to revile 罵.

**430** 惹

jê³, To provoke, to irritate.

心 hsin¹, Radical No. 61, heart. (See No. 18).

若,嚳 jê⁴, Phonetic, the primitive sense is to pick ⇒ herbs 艸 to eat 口 ; to select. (W. 46 G). The ordinary meaning is if. Just why this combination of radical and phonetic should mean to irritate is not very apparent. If the 若 jê⁴ is regarded as selecting,—one who is over particular in selecting is most exasperating, or irritating to the mind 心.

**431** 無, 橆

wu², Without, none.

火 huo³, Radical No. 86, fire. Fire was arbitrarily considered as the radical of this character; in the old writing there is no such element in its composition but 林 forest is the original form for the 灬. Chalfant suggests that this character is made up of 乘 ch'eng², primitive meaning, a warriors car and 亡 wang², lost. This last character, in an old writing, is placed where the horses should be and the idea, according to the above mentioned authority, is that the animals have strayed away in the forest. The forest is represented by 林

*lin²*, in seal writing and the 亡 *wang²* is placed between the two trees. (See Chalfant Plate XXVIII, and W. 10 I).

**432 界**

*chieh⁴*, A boundary, a limit.

田 *t'ien²*, Radical No. 102, a field. (See No. 207).

介, 从 *chieh⁴*, Phonetic, boundaries, the lines that separate 八 *pa¹*, men 人 *jen²*. (W. 18 F). With the addition of the radical for field the idea of field boundaries is very evident.

**433 籃**

*lan²*, A basket.

竹, 竹 *chu²*, Radical No. 118, bamboo. (See No. 7).

監 *chien¹*, Phonetic, to examine, to oversee, a jail. (W. 82 F). (See No. 294). By taking the meaning of this phonetic as a jail or place of confinement, then by the addition of the bamboo radical we have a wicker utensil in which articles may be placed or confined, for safe transportation.

**434 睡**

*shui⁴*, To sleep.

目 *mu⁴*, Radical No. 109, the eye. (See No. 102).

垂 *ch'ui²*, Phonetic, to hang down. (W. 13 E), (See No. 387). With the addition of the radical for eye the idea of the eyelids coming down and covering the eye is set forth, naturally suggesting sleep.

**435 覺**

*chiao³ ⁴*, *chüeh²*, To perceive, to feel.

見 *chien⁴*, Radical No. 147, to see, to perceive. (W. 158 C). (See No. 85).

學 *hsiao²* Phonetic, to learn. (W. 39 I). The two

sides of the phonetic are the two hands of the teacher pressing down on the ⌒ waste space where ignorance reigns in the head of the pupil; the two 乂 $i^4$ between the hands indicate the questioning and answering of teacher and pupil. 彡 = doubling of 乂, cutting shears, idea of influence (see No. 400 and 165). With the addition of the radical, 見 to perceive, the character means, to perceive, to know.

---

BALLER, VOCABULARY III.

436 害,唐    $hai^4$, To injure; to contract a disease.

宀 $mien^2$ Radical No. 40, a roof, (See No. 1).

This being a very old character it does not fall easily into radical and phonetic. The phonetic should be a combination of 丰 $chieh^4$ and 口 $k'ou^3$ but we find no such combination outside of this character. 丰 $chieh^4$ is the first mnemonic invention after the knotting of strings. It represents notches 彡 on a │ stick. The stick was injured by these notches. When the word for mouth, 口 $k'ou^3$, is added the idea is that one injures another by slander and when the above radical is added, the injury is done under cover ⌒ i.e. secretly. (W. 97 E). 丰 $Chieh^4$ is very like, 丰 $feng^1$ a leafy bough, (See No. 312).

437 病    $ping^4$, Disease, defect.

疒 $ni^4$ or $chi^2$ Radical No. 104, disease. This radical is made up of 一 $i^1$ a straight horizontal line, the position of a sick person, and bed

丬 *ch'iang²*. Thus it means, to be sick. The scribes arbitrarily added a dot on top. (W. 127 C).

丙, 夙 *ping³* Phonetic, the third of the ten stems. It is a fire 火 in a house 冂 and thus it is a suggestive phonetic, as a feverish person, a sick person, is hot (W. 41 A). When the radical for disease is added to this phonetic it forms a fitting symbol for disease.

**438** 雪, 屭

*hsüeh³*, Snow.

雨 *yü³*, Radical No. 173, rain. (See No. 61).

彐 *chi⁴* Phonetic, a hand. (W. 44 A). The original phonetic was broom, 彗 *hui⁴* but it has been contracted to *chi⁴* and there is little use in remembering the original phonetic, save to explain why the present phonetic has no phonetic value. (W. 44 J). With the addition of the rain radical we have the rain 雨 which can be taken up in the hand ⇒ or swept away 彗. A good combination for symbolizing snow.

**439** 醫

*i¹*, To heal.

酉 *yu³*, Radical No. 164, wine or a cordial. (See No. 422).

殹 *i¹* Phonetic, to take out 殳 *shu¹* arrows 矢 from the quiver 医 *i¹*. The idea is that these arrows are to be shot at the demon of disease. The cordial radical 酉 is added as it indicates that spirits are to be administered to the patient. (W. 131 C).

**440** 養

*yang³*, To nourish, to rear.

食 *shih²*, Radical No. 184, to eat, (W. 26 M), (See No. 75).

羊 *yang²*, Phonetic, sheep, (See No. 253). This is a suggestive phonetic as the eating 食 of mutton 羊 is one means of securing nourishment, 養 (W. 103 A).

**441** 英, 𦳷

*ying¹*, Brave, heroic; England.

艹 *ts'ao³* Radical No. 140, grass, (See No. 22).

央, 𣎵 *yang¹*, Phonetic, a man 大 in the midst of a large space, 冂; in the seal writing it is a man in the midst of a jungle. (W. 60 K). With the addition of the radical 艹 the idea of jungle is still further elaborated. It requires bravery to enter a jungle where fierce beasts abound.

**442** 德

*tê²*, Virtue, moral excellence.

彳 *ch'ih⁴* Radical No. 60, a step with the left foot. (See No. 128).

悳 *tê²* Phonetic, virtue. 直 *chih²* upright, 心 *hsin¹* heart. This was the original writing of the character 德, but it was finally put under the 60th radical. (See No. 99 for explanation of phonetic). The addition of the radical may impart the idea of action or going out 彳; in order to develope virtue it must be exercised, and go out to others.

**443** 院

*yüan⁴*, A court yard; a public building.

阝, 阜 𠁁 *fu⁴* Radical No. 170, a mound. In the seal writing a mound 厂 is depicted with three steps 彡 leading to the top of a terrace. (W. 86 A).

完 *wan²*, Phonetic, finished, done. (See No. 93). This phonetic often has reference to buildings and with the above radical it indicates a large court surrounded with buildings, or public offices (W. 29 H).

**444 皇**

huang², Imperial; the sovereign.

白 pai², Radical No. 106, white. (See No. 6).

王 wang², Phonetic, king, ruler, royal. (W. 83 C). Chalfant has the most likely explanation of this character. He has found old writings which seem to indicate that it was a string of jade beads ; as jade beads could only be afforded by the royalty, this was the symbol which was adopted to indicate the ruling class. (See Chalfant, Plate XVII). The 白 pai² is contracted from 自 tzŭ⁴ beginning, self, and thus the character 皇 huang² originally meant a king by right of birth.

**445 狼**

lang², A wolf, cruel.

犭, 犬 ch'üan³ Radical No. 94, a dog. (See 424).

良, 皀, 后 liang², Phonetic, good, sagacious. This phonetic has undergone many changes with the varying ideas as to man's original nature. The primary meaning was the nature of man, a gift from heaven, is good. The gift is represented by ⊖. The coming down from heaven was represented by ⼃. The next more modern form is 良. The two convergent strokes at the top are heaven and earth coming together, the middle part of the character is the gift and the bottom part indicates that this gift may be lost 𠤎, (W. 75 F). This seems a most inappropriate phonetic for wolf; the explanation is as follows:—The wolf is extremely sagacious, in knowing where to go to escape danger and where food can be obtained, he is an expert 良 dog, 犭, best of the dog tribe.

446 靈 

*ling²*, Spirit, spiritual, intelligent.

雨 *yü³*, Radical No. 173; rain. (See No. 61).

靈, 霝 *ling²* Phonetic, the falling of rain in large drops, the large drops are indicated by the three circles. These circles have been changed into squares as usual in the modern writing. This phonetic does not conform to the usual rule of phonetics, in that it includes the radical and does not contain all parts of the character except the radical; 巫 *wu¹* was added to the character at a later period. The rain was something very earnestly desired for the crops, and they made supplication for it. The lower part of the character is a symbol which represents witches 从 dancing to obtain rain; the work 工 of witches 从. (W. 72 K and for *wu¹* W. 27 E). Because the spirits were invoked for rain this character has been used to represent spirit or spiritual.

447 魂 

*hun²*, The soul.

鬼, 鬼 *kuei³*, Radical No. 194; the spirits of the dead. (W. 40 C). The old character is a primitive representing a human being vanishing into the air. This character has undergone several changes. The upper part is said to be the head of a demon, the lower part is a human being and the 厶 is a representation of the swirl made by the demon when it moves.

云 *yün²*, Phonetic, clouds, borrowed to mean speak. This phonetic adds the idea of evanescence. The spirit is not visible to the natural eye. (W. 93 B).

**448** 雷, 靁

*lei²*, Thunder.

雨 *yü³*, Radical No. 173 ; rain, (See No. 61).

田 *t'ien²*, Phonetic, field. Without phonetic significance. (See No. 45). This character 雷 was originally written with three or four 田 *t'ien²* and a small symbol in the center which indicated reverberation ; as if the noise of thunder was caused on account of the fields impinging. See Chalfant, Plate VII. (W. 149 F).

**449** 層

*ts'êng²*, A story (of a house), a layer.

尸 *shih¹*, Radical No. 44 ; a person in either the recumbent or the sitting posture. A living person who was, in ancient times, dressed to impersonate the dead, and was worshipped at the funeral. (W. 32 A).

曾 *ts'êng²*, Past, already ; *tsêng¹*, still more, to add. The radical 尸 *shih¹* seems an inappropriate radical, a plausible explanation is as follows :—the character " story " was needed when houses were built more than one story high. This was another room 屋 *wu¹* (See No. 337) added 曾 *tsêng* (See No. 230) above the ordinary room. It may be that the character *ts'eng²* 層 was originally written 廇 i.e. 屋 room 曾 added, but was afterwards contracted to its present form.

**450** 治

*chih*[4], To cure, to heal, to govern.

氵,水 *shui*[3], Radical No. 85 ; water, (See No. 79).

台 *i*[2] Phonetic, I, ones self. No phonetic significance. This was originally the name of a river and it seems to have been adopted to stand for the verb to cure without etymological justification.

**451** 名

*ming*[2], A name, fame, reputation.

口 *k'ou*[3], Radical No. 30, mouth.

夕 *hsi*[1] Phonetic, evening. No phonetic value. In the evening 夕 one should call out 口 his name 名, in order that others may know who approaches. (See No. 14).

**452** 禱

*tao*[3], To pray, prayer.

礻,示 *shih*[4], Radical No. 113, to show, to make known, (See No. 227).

壽,壴 *shou*[4], Phonetic, longevity. (W. 144 B). The upper part of this phonetic is supposed to represent a ploughed field 壴 *ch'ou*[2], and indicates constant repetition, the furrows are turned over one after the other. With the addition of 口 *k'ou*[3] the idea of repeated inquiry is conveyed. The present phonetic has hand, 寸 *ts'un*[4], added by the side of 口 *k'ou*[3], as gestures aid the petition. With the addition of the radical this character fulfills the heathen idea for prayer;—"for they think they shall be heard for their much speaking."

**453** 獅

*shih*[1], A lion.

犭,犬 *ch'üan*[3] Radical No. 94, a dog. (See No. 424).

師 *shih*[1], Phonetic, a leader or master. Composed of 𠂤 *tui*[1] an elevation of two steps, elevated, and 帀 *chin*[1] and 一 *i*[1], one or first. This combination stands for the banner of the commander-in-chief, the first 一 banner 帀 over the fort 𠂤, thus the idea of leader or master is conveyed by this character. With the addition of the dog radical, the idea is set forth that the lion is the king of beasts. (W. 86 B).

454 牆

ch'iang[2], A wall.

爿 *ch'iang*[2], Radical No. 90, a split log, (See No. 84).

嗇 *shê*[4] *se*[4], Phonetic, grain inclosed in a granary, frugal, stingy. The present writing of the phonetic has no phonetic significance, but 牆 *ch'iang*[2], means a wall and it may have been originally used as the phonetic and contracted to the present form. (W. 76 E). 嗇 *Shê*[4] is composed of *lin*[3] 㐭 a place ◎ for putting grain in, 入, 入 *ju*[4], to put in, (contracted) and 來 *lai*[2], grain, also contracted. (W. 13 C), (See No. 64). (This character now means to come). The ᴍ represented bearded grain hanging from the stalk. With the addition of the radical which is a symbol of strength, we have a good combination for wall. Walls were early built around granaries.

455 劑

刂,刀 齊,𧮫

*chi*[4], To adjust, to trim ; A dose of medicine.

*tao*[1], Radical No. 18, a knife. (See No. 37).

*ch'i*[2] Phonetic, even. Doses of medicine should be of uniform size. (W. 174 A). This is the 210th radical. In the seal character there are three stalks of grain. Stalks of grain, standing in the field, are practically all of equal heighth. These three appear to us as quite uneven, but this is because our ideas of the perspective differ from those of the framer of the character. The lower of the two horizontal lines at the bottom, is the foreground and the upper of these two lines is the background, thus because each head of grain is equally high from the ground, the character stands for even. With the addition of the knife radical we have the idea of the apothecary using the spatula in apportioning doses of medicine.

456 藥

艹 樂,𣗥

*yao*[4], Medicine.

*ts'ao*[3], Radical No. 140, grass, (See No. 22).

*yao*[4], *yüeh*[4], Phonetic, an ornamented frame on *le*[4] which drums and a bell are placed. The drums are on the sides and the bell is in the middle. (W. 88 C.) This instrument gives the five sounds of the Chinese scale. It is necessary to observe the seal writing in order to see the intention of the symbol. These five parts of the instrument are all in tune. With the addition of the radical for grass, the idea is any vegetable substance which will restore the proper functioning of the body ; restore harmony. Vegetable substances were first used as medicines.

---

BALLER LESSON XVI.

**457 被**

*pei⁴*, Bed-clothes, a sign of the passive, to suffer.

**礻,衣** *i¹*, Radical No. 145 ; clothes. (See No. 51).

**皮** *p'i²*, Phonetic, skin or covering. (W. 43 H.) (See No. 224). This is the 107th radical. Its use here as a phonetic with the radical for cloth or clothing is logical. The integument not being sufficient to keep the individual warm, blankets were regarded as cloth skin. The use of this character as the sign of the passive and its use meaning to suffer are without etymological warrant.

**458 橋**

*ch'iao²*, A bridge.

**木** *mu⁴*, Radical No. 75, wood, (See No. 36).

**喬** *ch'iao²*, Phonetic, lofty. (See No. 322), (W. 75 B). A bridge is a high 喬 structure, often made of wood 木.

**459 罷**

*pa⁴*, To stop ; finish, resign: sign of the imperative, interrogative particle.

 **,网** *wang²*, Radical No. 122, a net, (See No. 38.)

**能** *nêng²*, Phonetic, able. (W. 27 J). (See No. 357). The explanation of 罷 by the Shuo Wen is ; an officer,能 an able man, taken in the meshes 网 of the law and dismissed.

**460** 蒙

*mêng²*, To cover, to conceal; sign of passive.

屮 *ts'ao³*, Radical No. 140, grass. (See No. 22).

冡 *mêng²*, Phonetic, to cover. (W. 34 I). The upper part of this phonetic is 冂 *mao³*; to cover something. The lower part is 豕 *shih³*, a pig under cover. Another explanation is that it is a representation of the wistaria which forms dense foliage and hides from view any thing beneath it. The 豕 *shih³* is not pig, but the vine twisted and coiled around itself.

豕, 矛

**461** 碰

*p'eng⁴*, To strike against; to happen; to meet with.

石 *shih²*, Radical No. 112, a stone. (See No. 42).

並 *ping¹* Phonetic, together. (W. 115 B). From 开 *ch'ien* two scale pans or shields (?) evenly poised; in *ping¹* 并 幷 a man is placed above each pan, or shield, indicating that the two are going along together. When one comes into collision with a stone 石 he is struck 碰.

幷

**462** 學, 学

*hsüeh²*, To learn, to study.

子 *tzŭ³*, Radical No. 39, son. (See No. 1).

與 *hsiao² hsüeh²* Phonetic, to learn. (W. 39 I). (See No. 435). This phonetic in combination with 子 *tzŭ³* is a good symbol for, to learn.

**463** 受, 敎, 受

*shou⁴*, To receive, to endure.

又 *yu⁴*, Radical No. 29, the right hand, (See No. 43). This character cannot be broken up into radical and phonetic; the upper part is 爪 *chao³*, the right hand and below is the right hand of a second person, (written in another way). Between these two hands, one of which is giving and the other receiving, there is a boat, only seen in the seal writing. This portrays a common occurrence ; articles are brought to a boat and received for shipment, (W. 49 E.)

464 廟

miao⁴, temple.

广 yên³, Radical No. 53, a covering a shelter. (See No. 132).

朝,翰 chao¹, Phonetic, morning ; to have an audience with the Emperor. (W. 117 D). This phonetic is made up of kan⁴ (See No. 137), and 舟 夕 chou¹, a boat, changed to 月 in modern writing. The rising of the mist 丂 through the jungle 伏 as seen from the deck of a boat, in the morning. By extension, morning ; the Imperial court, so called because court was held early in the morning.

A temple is a place 广 where one can have an audience with the gods.

465 想

hsiang³, To think, to ponder, to hope.

心 hsin¹, Radical No. 61, the heart, (See No. 18).

相 hsiang¹, Phonetic, to examine, to inspect. (W. 158 B), (See No. 106). There is another explanation of this phonetic which is not given under the 106th character which suggests one of its meanings, it is as follows :—When about to build, one goes into the wood, 木 and examines 目 mu⁴ the trees until one is found which answers the requirements. With this explanation the idea of appropriate is brought out. In hoping, the heart longs for that which is considered appropriate, or that which is suited to its needs.

**466** 鄉, 鄉

*hsiang¹*, The country.

邑. 阝 *i⁴*, Radical No. 163, a city, (See No. 11).

皀 *hsiang¹* Phonetic, cooked grain. (See No. 75). (W. 26 L). This character is made up of two 邑 阝 *i* radicals, one on the right, written in the usual manner 阝 and one on the left is reversed 阝. The 皀 is written between these for the country is the region between cities, where food is produced.

**467** 弄, 弄

*nung⁴*, To toy with ; to do

廾 *kung³* Radical No. 55, hands joined. (See No. 247.)

玉, 王 *yü⁴*, Phonetic, jade. Without phonetic significance. (See No. 124.) The hands are toying with a string of jade beads,--a very natural procedure.

**4 68** 內

*nei⁴*, Within, inside.

入 *ju⁴*, Radical No. 11, to enter. (W. 15 A.) (See No. 35)

冂, 冂 *chiung³* Phonetic, space, a waste area. (W. 34 A.) The two vertical strokes indicate the limits, and the horizontal stroke indicates the space between. When 入 is added, the idea of going into this area is set forth, so this character is the symbol for inside.

**469** 苦

*k'u³*, Bitter, sorrow, suffering.

艸, 屮 *ts'ao³*, Radical No. 140, grass. (See No. 22).

古 *ku³*, Phonetic, old. (See No. 17.) (W. 24 F.) This phonetic plus 艸, grass, originally stood for a bitter plant which became sweet after freezing. It is now used merely as the character for bitter.

470 遭

*tsao¹*, To meet, to encounter, a turn. Generally used in a bad sense of encountering evil conditions.

辶 *cho⁴* Radical No. 162, to walk. (See No. 10.)

曹, 曹 *ts'ao²* Phonetic, judges (W. 120 K.). In ancient tribunals, two judges sat in the Eastern Hall, represented by two 東 characters, to pronounce judgment 曰 on cases brought before them. When 辶 is added, we have the picture of a man who goes before the judges to endure an unpleasant ordeal. Thus the character implies meeting with undesirable conditions. The modern arbitrary contraction makes the character lose much of its original significance.

471 議

*i⁴*, To discuss, to talk over.

言 *yen²*, Radical No. 149, words. (See No. 10.)

義 *i⁴*, Phonetic, harmony, righteous, public, (W. 71 Q.) This phonetic is made up of 我 *wo³* (See No. 2) and 羊 *yang²*, sheep. (See No. 253). (W. 103 A.) When the above two characters are combined, the 我 *wo³* has its original meaning, namely, a conflict,—two spears attacking each other. With the addition of 羊 *yang²*, the two combatants have changed and become

lamblike :—neither one is aggressive, con-
cord is restored. With the addition of 言
*yen*², this combination stands for dis-
cussing affairs in the spirit just described.
Discussion 言 in a righteous 義 way.

472 領

*ling*³, To lead, to guide ; to receive.

頁 *yeh*⁴, Radical No. 181, a man—head and body ;
but the meaning often is restricted to the
head. (See No. 105.)

令 *ling*⁴, Phonetic, an order. (See No. 61.) With
the addition of 頁, a man, the idea is that
this man or leader gives the order of procedure.

473 村

*ts'un*¹, A village, a hamlet.

木 *mu*⁴, Radical No. 75, wood. (See No. 36.)

寸 *ts'un*⁴, Phonetic, hand ; modern meaning—an
inch. (See No. 69.) Originally the character for village was 邨, *ts'un*¹ ; but 村 has
supplanted the former entirely. As there
is no etymological reason for using the
present character, therefore there is no
logical explanation. In looking over the
North China plains in winter, the
villages seem to be nothing but little
clumps or handfuls 寸 of trees 木, and by
keeping this in mind one can remember
how to write the character.

474 另, 冎

*ling*⁴, Separate, besides, extra.

口 *k'ou*³, Radical No. 30, mouth.

This does not break up into phonetic and
radical, as it is a primitive. In the seal
character it represents a knuckle bone,

(joint) extending out from a piece of meat. In the seal writing it very closely resembles 咼 *kua*³; but it is not the same. The knuckle or bone extending beyond the meat is taken as the symbol for that which is extra, or something left over. (W. 118 B.)

475 商, 喬

*shang*¹, To consult, to give advice, to deliberate.

口 *k'ou*³, Radical No. 30, mouth.

This is a character whose modern radical does not agree with the original composition of the character. The 冂 is a house, and 言 is words (See No. 10). Between the lower two elements of *yen*² the symbol 入 *ju*⁴, to enter, is inserted. This gives the idea of being away from others, where two persons can consult in private. In the oldest writing two 日 *jih*⁴ (sun, day) characters are added, thus implying that the consultation took place between two days, at night. To trade or to do business is a secondary meaning; but as bargaining requires much consultation it is logical.

476 綢

*ch'ou*², Silk.

糸 *ssŭ*¹, Radical No. 120, silk.

周 *chou*¹, Phonetic, complete, (W. 109 C.). This is a combination of 用 *yung*⁴, useful, and 又 *chi*², the old writing of 及. The idea of 用 is an arrow piercing the target, ability, and when 及 or 又 (which is now changed arbitrarily to 口 *k'ou*³) is added, the idea is ability to hit every target hence, universally. With the addition of the radical for silk, it is a simple phonetic in the character for silk fabric. It may be that originally silk threads were sometimes mixed with other fibre, and this was to indicate that it was pure silk.

477 尊, 𤔔 *tsun*[1], Honorable, noble.   (W. 47 C.)

寸 *ts'un*[1], Radical No. 41, a hand or measure. (See No. 69.)

酋 *chiu*[1] Phonetic, liquor 酉 *yu*[3], when the fermentation is over and the dregs are entirely separated 八 *pa*[1]. Thus spirits that have settled and are kept in a wine vessel, only used on sacrificial occasions. With the addition of 寸, which in the seal character is two hands 廾, we have the idea of offering good spirits with both hands, reverently to a distinguished guest. Compare 卑 𤰔 *pei*[4] ordinary, vulgar. (W. 46 E; W. 47 C.) (See No. 526). It is a common wine glass, presented with the left hand only.

---

## BALLER LESSON XVII.

478 當 *tang*[1], To value, appraise, to compensate.

*tang*[4], To be equal to, to pawn, ought.   (W. 36 E.)

田 *t'ien*[2], Radical No. 102, a field.   (See No. 82.)

尚 *shang*[4], Phonetic, a house.   (See No. 52.) This character shows that the Chinese have long been in the habit of pawning.   House and field being of most value, all other articles are included; and because in pawning the value of the article or thing is that of most importance, therefore the character stands for " to be equal to," to value.

**479** 與, 鬨

yü³, To give, with.

臼 chiu⁴, Radical No. 134, a mortar. The character is supposed to picture a mortar; but the representation is not striking. This radical was arbitrarily given, and has nothing in common with the original idea.

与, 与 yü³ Phonetic, giving food from a spoon; to give, with. 与 indicates a full spoon with—in it. —(at the top) shows that something is being given away, i.e., removed from the bowl of the spoon. This character 與, was originally written in this way 与, and is still so abbreviated. But it has suffered great changes. The hands of the giver 臼 and the receiver 廾 have been added.

**480** 所, 所

so, A place, that which, whatsoever.

戶 hu⁴, Radical No. 63, one leaf of a door; by extension, a house. (W. 129 A.) In the seal writing 戶 is one half of 門 mên². (See No. 5.)

斤, 斤 chin¹, Phonetic, an axe; catty. It has no phonetic significance, because the character 所 was made before radicals and phonetics were adopted. The Shuo Wen says that this character 所 represents the sound of chopping. It would be more logical to say it represents the place where the fuel is prepared. As this was done near the door or house 戶, it has come to mean a place or building, 所. (W. 128 A.)

**481** 管

竹 *chu²*, Radical No. 118, bamboo.

官 *kuan¹*, Phonetic, an official. (W. 86 C.) (See No. 310.)

*kuan³*, To care, to control; a tube.

With the addition or 竹 *chu²*, it forms the character for tube; and it is reasonable to suppose that this was the original meaning, and that the meaning to control or to care for was added by extension, as a tube controls the flow of water.

**482** 燒

火, 火 *huo³*, Radical No. 86, fire. A pictorial representation of a flame of fire, in the seal writing.

堯 *yao²* Phonetic; eminent, great. (See No. 77.)

*shao¹*, To burn, to heat, to roast; fever.

(W. 81 C.) The phonetic is made up of 垚 *yao²*, earth heaped up, and 兀 *wu⁴*, a stool or platform. (W. 29 K.) Thus the idea of very high is set forth. When the radical for fire is added, the character stands for a big blaze or great heat.

**483** 哄

口 *k'ou³*, Radical No. 30, the mouth.

共, 𦥑 *kung⁴*, Phonetic, all, together. (W. 24 I.) In one old writing four hands are represented as working in unison. With the addition of 口 *k'ou³*, the idea of unison is transferred from hands to words. If several persons assist by saying the same

*hung³*, To cheat, to deceive.

thing, deception is easier of accomplishment. (The seal writing is twenty ᵾ Pairs of hands. 舟.)

**484** 跟

*kên¹*, To follow, the heel, and, with.

足, 𤴓 *tsu²*, Radical No. 157, the foot. (W. 112 B.) The Shuo Wen says that the upper part of this radical is ⊙; the circle indicates that the foot is at rest. When motion is indicated 𤴓, 疋 is used. The lower part is 止 *chih³*, to stop. 足 is now used for the foot in general. 𤴓, 疋 *p'i³²* (*shu²*), the 103rd radical, was the counterpart of 足. The seal writing shows the 𤴓 on top of 止, a foot in motion. The use of 止 seems unfortunate ; but in walking the foot is constantly starting 𤴓 and stopping 止. The present use of 疋 *p'i³²* (*shu²*) is a bolt of cloth. This is undone by turning it over and over,—a repetition of stopping and starting 疋. The character 步 *pu⁴*, to walk, also represents stopping 止 and starting 歨. The 歨 is 止 *chih³*, reversed so meaning to start. Thus walking is a repetition of stopping and starting of the feet. (W. 112 C, G.)

艮 *kên⁴* Phonetic, perverse, obstinate. (See No. 223.) (W. 26 L.) In following there must be persistence of action, or it is not accomplished. The fixed or hard part 艮 of the foot 足 is the heel 跟. "To heel" is the order to a dog to follow.

**485** 贖

*shu²*, To redeem, to atone, to ransom.

貝 *pei⁴*, Radical No. 154, precious. (See No. 38.)

賣, 鬻 *yu*⁴ Phonetic, to hawk, to peddle, (W. 79 J.)

The modern writing of this character is identical with 賣 *mai*⁴, to sell; but it is from a different root, and this explains why so many characters with this phonetic have a final *u* instead of *ai*. The phonetics 買 *mai*³ and 賣 *mai*⁴ are used in only a few characters as phonetic. The upper part of this phonetic is 朱 夫 *lu*⁴, a mushroom, a plant 中 that stands as a man 大. Below the 夫 there is a 目 *mu*⁴, eye, written horizontally.— ㎜ *mu*⁴, a loving eye. With the addition of the radical 貝 the idea of hawking is set forth. Hawkers look on their wares with great regard, and in this way they induce purchasers to give the highest price.

With the addition of a second 貝 *pei*⁴ this is the symbol for to ransom; in ransoming the full value must be paid.

**486** 面, 圖 面

*mien*⁴, The face, a surface, a side.

Radical No. 176, the face. (W. 160 B.)

This radical is made up of 百 *shou*³, the head, and a primitive 凵 which is the outline of a face. The 百, while said to be the face, is nose 自, all save the—dash above. The nose is the most prominent part of the face.

**487** 該

*kai*¹, Should, ought, to owe.

言 *yen*² Radical No. 149, words. (See No. 10.)

亥 *hai*⁴ Phonetic, nine to eleven P.M.,—a symbol in the horary cycle. (W. 69 K.) (See

No. 180)   When combined with 言 yen²
it has only simple phonetic force.

**488 花**

hua¹, Flowers ; to spend.

卄 ts'ao³ Radical No. 140, grass.  (See No. 22.)

化 hua⁴, Phonetic, to change.  (W. 30, D.)

Originally 化 was ㇈ ㇇, man tumbled
heels over head ; i.e. changed and later the
radical 人 jên² was added.  The character
enters into the composition of 老 lao³, old.
(See No. 209).  When ts'ao³, is added to
化 hua⁴, it forms the symbol for flower.
A flower is that part of a plant which is
strikingly different or changed from the
other parts.

**489 彼**

pi³, That, the other, there.

彳 ch'ih⁴ Radical No. 60 ; a step, to go.

皮 p'i², Phonetic, skin.  (W. 43 H.)  (See No.
224.)  This is the 107th radical.  It is
here used as a simple phonetic.
The radical 彳, going, is chosen for the
demonstrative pronoun " that," because
it is distant and one must go 彳 to it.
此 t'su³ here, has 止 stop, as the radical—
one stops and that object now becomes
" this."  (cf 491.)

**490 割**

kê¹, To cut, to hack, to reap.

刂, 刀 tao¹, Radical No. 18, a knife.  (See No. 37.)

害 hai⁴, Phonetic, to injure.  (F. 97 E.)  (See
No. 436.)
This when combined with 刀 tao¹ is a
suggestive phonetic, as in reaping violence
has to be done to the standing grain.  To

reap was probably the first meaning of this character.

**491** 此, 屵

止   *t'zu*³, This, here. (W. 112 A.)

*chih*³, Radical No. 77, to stop. (Chalfant, Plate VIII.) Chalfant has an old writing which represents a plant withered from lack of moisture.

ヒ, ᅥ   *pi*³ Phonetic, to˙turn one's self around ; the 21st radical. (W. 26 B.) The modern writing of this radical is identical with ヒ 与 *hua*⁴, change, (W. 30 D) ; but they are quite different in the seal writing. "*This* 此 is the place to stop 止 and turn ヒ" is a convenient mnemonic for 此, and 止 *chih*³ is a logical radical, as one going to a distant object, (彼 designated as that, there,) stops on arrival and may now say this, here 此. (cf. 489).

**492** 便

亻, 人   *pien*⁴, Convenient, advantageous.

更, 雪   *jên*², Radical No. 9, man.

*kêng*¹, Phonetic, to change, to improve. (W. 41 A). This comes from 网 *ping*³, a fire burning a house, calamity. When 攴 *p'u*, a right hand using a rod, a sign of control, is added, the fire, instead of being a destroyer, is a convenience, an advantage. (See No. 226).

When the radical for man is added the idea is set forth that affairs are adjusted so that men are satisfied, get advantage.

**493** 隨

*sui*², To follow, to accompany.

阜, 阝, 𠂤 *tu*⁴ Radical No, 170, a mound. (W. 86 A.) In the seal writing it represents a terraced embankment; by extension earthworks, embankments, etc.

遀 *sui*², Phonetic, to follow (W. 46 D.). This phonetic has its root in 陸 *to*⁴, to build earthworks about a city in order to besiege it. The 左 left hand repeated indicates that the enemy is in great numbers, and that the action is contrary to the action of the besieged. In 隋 (meat cut up) one of the 左 *tso*³, is replaced by 月 *jou*⁴. This may have been suggested on account of the mutilation of the vanquished! With the addition of 辶 *cho*⁴, the character indicates following around the ramparts, perhaps in order to avoid being wounded, (mutilated).

**494 加**

*chia*¹, To add to, to increase. (W. 53 D.)

力 *li*⁴, Rad. No. 19, strength, muscle. (See No. 212.)

While 口 *k'ou*³, occupies the place of the phonetic, it has no phonetic value. The idea is: first give the order, 口 and if it is not heeded follow it up with chastisement (muscular punishment) 力.

**495 跑**

*p ao*³, To run.

足 *tsu*², Radical No. 157, the foot.

包 *pao*¹, Phonetic, to wrap up. (W. 54 B.)

This is made up of 勹 ⼓ *pao*¹, a person bending over to enfold an object (See No. 80). With the addition of 巳 ⼰ it means to wrap up. The primitive meaning was gestation. In 跑 the 包 is a simple phonetic, but when one runs the feet 足 may be wrapped 包 in a cloud of dust.

**496** 費

*fei*[4], To waste, to expend.

貝 *pei*[4], Radical No. 154, shell, precious. (See No. 38.)

弗, 弗 *fu*[24] Phonetic, not. Two rods, bound together which bend in opposite directions, therefore opposition, negation. In the character 費 it is a suggestive phonetic,—to look on valuables (money) as if they were of no value ; thus to waste them.

**497** 通

*t'ung*[1], Through, universal.

辶 *cho*[4] Radical No. 162, to walk. (See No. 10.)

甬, 肙 *yung*[3] Phonetic, blossoming. 𠮛 *han*[3], a bud, opening flower (W. 55 K). The phonetic of this phonetic is 用 with the addition of 辶 *cho*[4], to go, the idea is that it is open in all directions. This character was on all " cash " to indicate that it was current coin, passing everywhere, 通行.

**498** 閣

*kê*[2], A door screen, an ante-room, feminine apartments.

門 *mên*[2], Radical No. 169, a door. (See No. 5.)

各 *kê*[4], Phonetic, each, to be separate. (See No. 272.) (W. 31 B.) This phonetic implied separation ; and when the radical 門 *mên*[2], (door) is added, the idea of separate apartments is obtained.

---

BALLER, LESSON XVIII

**499** 連

*lien*[2], To connect. (W. 167 B).

辶 *cho⁴* Radical No. 162, to walk. (See No. 10.)

車 *ch'ê¹*, Phonetic, cart or carriage. (See No. 136.)

Without phonetic force. The Shuo Wen says that the character represents a string of carriages moving along as if connected. Thus the idea of to connect is obtained. Carts 車 moving leave a continuous track, not broken like the track of a man.

**500** 犯

*fan⁴*, To transgress, to offend.

犭, 犬, 犮 *ch'üan³* Radical No. 94, a dog. The seal character is a pictorial representation of a dog. (W. 134 A.) (See No. 424.)

卩 *han³* Phonetic; to blossom, expansion, eruption. (W. 55 K). (See No. 497.) This combination of radical and phonetic is very apt. What could be more suggestive of heedlessness than a dog in a flower garden ?—unless it were a bull in a china shop.

**501** 倒

*tao³*, To fall over.

亻, 人 *jên²*, Radical No. 9, man.

到 *tao⁴*, Phonetic, to arrive at. (See No. 88.) The original meaning of this phonetic may have been similar to the expression " The hangman's noose will be his end " ; as a sword was used for executions, the man is prostrate when the knife descends. The present meaning may have been acquired by extension.

When the executioner's axe 刀 arrives 至 the man 人 falls 倒.

502 感

> *kan³*, To influence, to affect. (W. 71 F.)
>
> 心 *hsin¹*, Radical No. 61, heart.
>
> 咸 *hsien²* Phonetic, to bite (modern meaning—all). A wound 戌 made by the mouth 口. (W. 71 P.) 戌 *wu⁴*, a halberd. 戌 *hsü¹*, is a wound inflicted by a halberd, the -dash, being the wound. Where 口 *k'ou³* is added, the character is used for a wound inflicted by teeth. This kind of wound is most painful; therefore when 心 is added it forms an appropriate symbol for moving the emotions. This is the character which is used for physiological stimulation.

503 旁, 旁

方, 方, 囗

> *p'ang²*, By the side of, others, border, lateral.
>
> *fang¹*, Radical No. 70, square. (W. 117 A.) It is supposed to be two boats lashed together so that they form a square pontoon.
>
> 产, 宂 *p'ang²* Phonetic. A space with three boundaries. The 亠 *shang⁴*, is the top, and the two lower lines are the side limits. The radical 方 *fang¹*, was added later, and it conveys no additional meaning, as the sides are the parts of the character on which emphasis is laid. cf. 宂.

504 必, 帲

> *pi⁴*, Must, certainly. (W. 18 G.)
>
> 心 *hsin¹*, Radical No. 61, heart. (See No. 18.) This character has been so mutilated in its modern writing that all of its etymology is lost; but a glance at the seal writing enables one to understand the meaning. 八 *pa¹* eight, forms the two sides, and

means to divide; between these two strokes is a dart. The arrow must strike the target in a certain spot, like the arrow shot by William Tell. It seems primarily to have been an interjection pointing out a strict order. The placing of this character under the radical for heart is a mistake.

505 雖

*sui*[1], Though, even if.

隹 *chui*[1] Radical No. 172, a short-tailed bird. (See No. 21.)

虽 The phonetic of this character is not common, and is not found in the dictionaries. Williams says the character is composed of 唯 *wei*[2], only, and 虫 *ch'ung*[2], a worm, and that it was a lizard. Others say it is an insect 虫 with a special head 口. This meaning has long since been lost, and the character now means though.

506 然

*jan*[2], Yes; still, nevertheless, on the other hand. (W. 65 G.)

火 巛 *huo*[3], Radical No. 86, fire. (See No. 482.)

肰 *jan*[2] Phonetic, dog meat. From 肉 *jou*[4], and 犬 *ch'üan*[3], dog. With the addition of the radical for fire the character originally was used for roasted dog meat; but it is now used as a conjunction, and consequently there is no logical warrant for its present use.

507 旡

*chi*[4], Since; a sign of the past.

无 *wu*[2] Radical No. 71, without. (W. 61 C.) A lame man 尢 *wang*[1], who makes an effort, but meets with an obstacle — which he is unable to overcome. While the above is the radical under which Kang Hsi places this character, it has nothing to do with it. It is 㐬 *chi⁴* (W. 99 E), to breathe in, or to swallow which is the reverse of 欠 *ch'ien⁴*, to breathe out ; but as this is not a radical it was placed under *wu²*. Cf. 273.

皀, 皀 *hsiang¹* Phonetic, boiled rice. (W. 26 L.) ㅂ is a kettle, and the dash — is its contents ; ヒ is the spoon with which it is eaten. (See No. 75.)

This is an endeavor to put into pictorial form an intangible condition, and therefore belongs to a class of characters which is often disappointing ; but here we have an exception. The 㐬 is to swallow. The remainder of the character is boiled rice, a mouthful or a meal swallowed is something finished or ended, hence it is taken as the sign of the past.

**508** 喜, 喜

*hsi³*, Pleasure, joy. (W. 165 B.)

口 *k'ou³*, Radical No. 30, mouth.

壴, 壴 *chou¹* Phonetic, a drum on a stand, the 口 representing the head of the drum. Above are the ornaments. This phonetic has no phonetic value. When 口 *k'ou³* is added it stands for singing. Thus the character represents vocal and instrumental music, and by extension, joy.

**509** 卻

*ch'üeh⁴*, Yet, still, to reject. (W. 17 H.)

卩 *chieh²* Radical No. 26, a joint. (See No. 42.) It has the idea of restraint, as it is part of a seal,—a seal prevents forgery. The meaning of joint may have originated owing to this being only a section of the seal.

谷,谷 *ch'iao*[4] Phonetic, the upper lip; the flesh 仌 above the mouth 口 *k'ou*[3]. This phonetic when 卪 *chieh*[2] is added means to restrain one's desires; to reject, because nothing more is desired. We speak of "keeping a stiff upper lip" when undergoing that which requires determination.

510 尾,尾  *i*[3]; *wei*[3], The tail of animals. (W. 100 B.)

尸 *shih*[1], Radical No. 44; a person in the recumbent posture. (See No. 449.)

The phonetic in the seal character is 毛 *mao*[2] inverted; but the scribes have written it in the regular way in the modern character. Inverted it indicated that the hair was growing downward.

511 歡  *huan*[1], Pleased, rejoiced, happy.

欠 *ch'ien*[4], Radical No. 76, to exhale; to owe. (See No. 273.)

雚,雚 *kuan*[4] Phonetic, the heron. (See No. 428). When a heron has just swallowed a fish it frequently emits a scream of satisfaction; and this may be why heron 雚 and to exhale 欠 are used to express rejoicing.

512 辮  *pien*[4], A queue; to plait.

糸 *ssŭ*[1] Radical No. 120, silk. (See No. 8.)

辡 *pien*[4] Phonetic. Two 辛 *hsin*[1], criminals (W. 102 H.) 辛 *hsin*[1] is composed of 干 *jen*[3], a serious offence, and 上 shang⁴ (⊥ old writing) ; to offend one's superior. In the phonetic two criminals are supposed to be mutually incriminating one another ; each accusation is met with a retort of the other's deeper guilt. With the addition of the radical for silk the character is used for, to plait, as the two outer strands are repeatedly thrown across to the opposite side. In all compounds it has the idea of reciprocal action.

---

## BALLER, LESSON XIX.

**513 遍**

pien⁴, Everywhere, the whole.

辶 cho⁴ Radical No. 162, walking. (See No. 10.)

扁 pien³, Phonetic, a tablet, or signboard ; thin and flat ; an inscription hung over a door. (W. 156 D.) With the addition of 辶 cho⁴, the idea of universal is conveyed, as go where you will, the tablets are seen over doors.

**514 饒**

jao², To forgive, to pardon, to overlook.

食 shih², Radical No. 184, food. (See No. 75.)

堯 yao², Phonetic, eminent, great ; earth heaped on a high base. (See No. 77,) With the addition of 食 shih², the first meaning was the abundance of food. Thus by extension to forgive. If one has plenty 堯 of food 食 (the first article used in barter) he should forgive 饒 a debt to one in want.

**515 埋**

mai², To bury ; to lie in wait.

土 *t'u³*, Radical No. 32, earth. (See No. 13.)

里 *li³*, Phonetic, a Chinese mile; old meaning, farm land, village, (W. 149 D.) (See No. 339). Because 土 *t'u³*, is added, it is reasonable to suppose that the first use was trenches for military purposes. These cut up the land as if for farming, only the trenches were deeper and longer.

**516** 準, 准

凢, 冫 *chun³*, To allow, to permit; exactly, certainly.

*ping¹*, Radical No. 15, ice. The seal writing represents the ice crystals that form when water is freezing. (W. 17 A.)

水 氵 *shui³*, Radical No. 85, water. (See No. 79.)

隹 *shun³* Phonetic, a falcon, which always comes to roost on one branch and is sure in its movements, swooping on its prey. (W. 168 B.) 准 is a contraction of 準. Thus 隹 *shun³*, is taken as a sign of certainty. Water 水 or ice "is the most level substance in the world." Formerly 準 *chun³*. was used as a symbol for weighing: the scale pans were always (隹 *shun³*) even or level (水 *shui³* or 冫 *ping¹*). This old meaning is obsolete, and the present meaning is certainly, or to allow. The meaning to allow came about thus: when one applies for permission to do a certain thing, he must assemble reasons sufficient to equal the reasons opposing this mode of action before he can obtain the desired permission.

**517** 談

*t'an²*, To chat, to converse.

言 *yen²*, Radical No. 149, words. (See No. 10.)

炎 *yen*² Phonetic, flames rising. (W. 126 D.)
Flames that rise high. This is indicated,
as there is one fire above another. When
the radical 言 *yen*² is added, the idea is
that in conversing words follow each
other, or pile up like flames, and one becomes interested (warm) in the process.
(See No. 178.)

**518** 恐

*k'ung*³, Lest, fearful.

心 *hsin*¹, Radical No. 61, the heart.

巩 *k'ung*³ Phonetic, to take hold of, to undertake.
(W. 11 F.) From 珙 巩 (abbreviated);
to take an instrument in the hand 丮 in
order to do work 工 *kung*¹. When heart
心 *hsin*¹, is added, the one who has under-
taken a piece of work 巩 *k'ung*³ has
trepidation 心 *hsin*¹ lest he will be unable
to accomplish it.

**519** 貨

*huo*⁴, Goods, wares.

貝 *pei*⁴, Radical No. 154, money, valuables. (See
No. 38.)

化 *hua*⁴, Phonetic, to change; 人 man changed to
匕. When 貝 *pei*⁴, is added, the etymology
is goods which are to be exchanged for
money. Articles not for sale are not 貨.

**520** 惜

*hsi*¹, To regard, to love, to be sparing of.

忄, 心 *hsin*¹, Radical No. 61, heart. (See No. 18.)

昔, 㫺 *hsi*² Phonetic, strips of meat dried in the sun.
(See No. 222.) These strips of meat ap-
pear shriveled and worthless, but they
are nutritious. With the radical for heart,

心 *hsin*[1] added the idea is : one should be sparing in the use of the prepared meat. (W. 17 J.).

521 恕

*shu*[4], To forgive, to excuse.

心 *hsin*[1], Radical No. 61, the heart. (See No. 18.)

如 *ju*[2], Phonetic, like. (See No. 325.) To speak with womanly skill in conformity to the circumstances, and the disposition of the man (husband) she desires to wheedle. When 心 *hsin*[1], is added, the idea is to act in accordance with the higher impulses of one's nature, or in harmony with the desires of the suppliant, i.e., forgive.

522 復, 復

*fu*[4], To return, to repeat. (W. 75 I.)

彳 *ch'ih*[4] Radical No. 60, a step. (See No. 10.)

复, 夏 *fu*[4] Phonetic, to return to quarters. This phonetic is derived from 享 倉 *kuo*[1], walls, fortifications. The seal writing ○ in the center is the city, and the two smaller circles,—one above and one below,—are the gates, each surmounted by a tower. In 夏 the lower gate and tower are replaced by 夂 *chih*[4], to walk single file. With the addition of 彳, nothing is added to the meaning; thus the 60th radical is here a redundancy. To return to quarters was the original meaning.

523 墓

*mu*[4], A grave.

土 *t'u*[3], Radical No. 32, earth. (See No. 13.)

莫, 墓 *mu*[4] Phonetic, the sun setting ; to disappear. (W. 78 G.) The sun is seen through the vegetation, 艹 *mang*[3] setting in the west.

When *t'u*³, is added, the idea is that the corpse disappears in the earth,—is buried in the grave.

**524** 未, 米

*wei*⁴, Not yet, not. (W. 120 C.)

木 *mu*⁴, Radical No. 75, wood. (See No. 36.)

The phonetic is a curved line in the seal writing; and contrasting this character with 末 朿 *mo*⁴, the highest branches or twigs of a tree, it may be that in 未 the tree had not yet attained its full growth In 末 the top or end is emphasized —. In 未 it is small, hidden, not yet grown.

**525** 墳

*fên*², A grave, a tomb.

土 *t'u*³, Radical No. 32, earth.

賁, 賁 *fen*⁴ Phonetic, ornaments. (W. 78 F.) 卉 *hui*³, vegetation, and 貝 *pei*⁴, shells. Plants and shells were the first articles used in decorating. When 土 *t'u*³, is added, it means a grave. When burying the dead the grave is more or less elaborately decorated.

**526** 碑

*pei*¹, A stone tablet, a tombstone.

石 *shih*², Radical No. 112, a stone. (See No. 42.)

卑, 宿 *pei*¹, Phonetic, ordinary, mean. (W. 46 E.)

Originally this phonetic was a drinking vessel which had a handle on the left side, and which was held with the left hand 𠂇. There was another drinking vessel, the 萬 尊 *tsun*¹, this was used only for the sacrifices, hence its meaning, honorable. (W. 47 C). The 卑 *pei*¹, was a common, permanent thing, not something only seen on sacrificial occasions. Hence its use with

石 to represent a permanent tablet. cf. No. 477.

527 許    *hsü³*, To promise, to allow, perhaps.

言 *yen²*, Radical No. 149, words. (See No. 10.)

午, 夲 *wu³*, Phonetic, noon. (W. 130 A.) Chalfant and Wieger give different explanations of this symbol. Chalfant appears to conform more nearly to the meaning imparted by this phonetic. The seal writing represents a noon mark drawn from the ridge pole down through the gable. When the shadow coincides with this mark it is noon. When word 言 is added, the meaning is that ones words are exact 午, and will be fulfilled,—a promise which one cannot depend on is no promise.

528 概    *kai⁴*, Generally, for the most part. Original meaning—a striker to level off the grain from the top of the measure.

木 *mu⁴*, Radical No. 75, wood. (See No. 36.)

既 *chi⁴*, Phonetic, to swallow; (modern meaning —since, already). (See No. 507.) The striker pushed off all the grain which was higher than the top of the measure,—all that cannot be held inside of the measure; thus the idea of sum, general, average.

529 規    *kuei¹*, Rule, custom. (W. 131 F.)

見 *chien⁴*, Radical No. 147, to see, to perceive. (See No. 85.)

夫, 夿 *fu¹*, Phonetic, an adult. This should be 矢 *shih³*, an arrow (See No. 100); but owing

to the seal writing of 夫 *fu*[1] and 矢 *shih*
being very similar (木 *fu*[1] 失 *shih*[1]) 夫 was
substituted for 矢. Neither of these phonetics has any phonetic significance, as
the character is old, having been in
use before the system of phonetics was
well established. The significance of the
original combination was: in order to
conform to rule one must act as when
practicing archery,—observe 見 the target,
and adjust the arrow     according to requirements. To watch 見 the workmen
夫, and keep them to the rules 規.

**530 活**

水, 氵
昏, 昏

*huo*[2], Living, lively ; movable
*shui*[3], Radical No. 85, water.  (See No. 79.)
*kuo*[2] Phonetic, to hold in one's mouth ; (W.
114 C.), abbreviated to 舌 *she*[2]. This
phonetic comes from a different writing of
氏 *ti*[3] 氒 pronounced *kuo*[2] fixed ; (see No.
257).  In 昏 *kuo*[2] the 十 *shih*[2] is deleted.
The idea is that something is permanent
in the mouth.  When water was added
this formed the character for living. This
character showed that the physical conditions were early studied : they observed
that moisture in the mouth was a sign of
health and life.  A moist 水 tongue 舌 is
lively 活 is an easy mnemonic.

**531 略**

*lüeh*[4], Slightly, a little, in general, a summary.  Original   meaning — boundaries
that separate every 各 *ko*[4], field 田 *t'ien*[2].
(W. 31 B.)
田 *t'ien*[2], Radical No. 102, a field,  (See No. 82.)

各 *ko⁴*, Phonetic, each, every. (See No. 272.) The original meaning of 略 *lüeh⁴*, was logical ; but owing to the tendency of the farmers to encroach little by little on the land of their neighbors, it has obtained a new meaning, of few, slightly.

**532 哎**

*ai¹*, Exclamation of disgust, Alas !

口 *k'ou³*, Radical No. 30, the mouth.

艾 *ai⁴*, Phonetic, artemisia, a plant. This phonetic is made up of the two blades of shears 乂 *i⁴* (W. 39 B) and 艹 *ts'ao³*, grass. It is used here with *k'ou³* as a simple phonetic.

**533 呀**

*ya¹*, An interjection.

口 *k'ou³*, Radical No. 30, the mouth.

牙 *ya²*, Phonetic, the teeth. (See No. 97.) It is the 92nd radical. It is used here with *k'ou³* as a simple phonetic.

---

BALLER, LESSON XX.

**534 脱**

*t'o¹*, To cast off, to abandon ; to undress.

肉,月 *jou⁴*, Radical No. 130, flesh ; (See No. 133.)

兑 *yüeh, tui⁴*, Phonetic, to exchange, to barter. Original meaning, to dispel grief and give pleasure, (See No, 72) (W. 29 D). The Shuo Wen does not explain this combination, but if one recalls how pleasant it is to throw off clothing when over warm it may aid in the writing of the character.

**535 約**

*yüeh⁴*, To bind, a covenant, an agreement.

糸 *ssu¹*, Radical No. 120, silk. (See No. 8.)

勺 shao², Phonetic, a spoon. (W. 54 H.) (See
No. 6.)

The Shuo Wen is silent on this character.
In order to aid the memory as to its construction one should remember that at
the conclusion of a treaty or contract
there are presents of 糸 silk and a feast.
勺 shao², spoon, stands for the feast.

**536** 隔

chieh¹ or ke², To separate ; divided by ; a parti-
tion.

阜, 阝 tu⁴, Radical No. 170, a mound. (See No. 493.)

鬲, 鬲 ke⁴ Phonetic, a large three-legged caldron ; a
statesman ; radical No. 193. (W. 155
A.) This being large, it differed from ordinary utensils ; and with the addition of
a radical which indicates lofty, it forms a
character which suggests separation or a
removal from the common class.

**537** 善, 譱

shan⁴, Good, moral. (W. 73 D.)

口 k'ou³, Radical No. 30, mouth.

This character, in its modern form, will
not break up into radical and phonetic.
Kang Hsi has used 口 k'ou³ instead of 言
yen², word, for the radical. It had its
root in a character composed of two 言
yen² characters. i.e. 誩 ching⁴, to dispute.
It is now often written 競 : and when 羊
yang² was written above 譱 it implied
that harmony or good feeling was restored after a quarrel. (See 義 i⁴, righteous-
ness, No. 471.) As this character was
complicated it was abbreviated to its
present form by the scribes. One 言 yen²

has been discarded, and the seal writing is partially followed in the one retained.

**538** 惡

*o⁴*, Evil, wicked.   Read *wu⁴*, it means to hate·

心 *hsin¹*, Radical No. 61, the heart.

亞 *ya³*, Phonetic, ugly.  (W. 82 H.)  It is supposed to be two hunchback men talking to each other.  When heart is added, the person's heart takes the ugly characteristics, i.e., evil, wicked.

**539** 其, 箕

*ch'i²*, He, she, it.  (W. 70 C.)

八 *pa¹*, Radical No. 12, eight.

其, 甘 *ch'i* Phonetic, a sieve.  (W. 70 A.)  The phonetic is a pictorial representation of the object.  In the seal character the bottom part of this character is 兀 *wu⁴*, a stand, and not 八 *pa¹*.  This character lost its original meaning, and is borrowed for a personal pronoun.

**540** 悲

*pei¹*, Grieved, sorry, sad.

心 *hsin¹*, Radical No. 61, heart.

非 *fei¹*, Phonetic, not.  (W. 170 A.)  Radical No. 175.

This combination is not explained in the Shuo Wen, but the etymology is not difficult to trace.  It is something which is not 非 *fei¹*, according to one's desire 心 *hsin¹* ; therefore it causes sorrow.

**541** 傷

*shang¹*, To wound, to injure, distress.

亻,人 *jen²*, Radical No. 9. a man.

𩇠 *shang¹*, Phonetic, to wound.  (W. 101 B.)

𥏨 To wound with a spear. 𥏨 *shang¹* was the original writing.  The 易 *yang²*, 一

which means to expand, glorious, the rays 勿 of the sun, rising above the horizon 旦 旦, 一 was phonetic.

Now all that remains of the 矢 *shih*³, are the two strokes, 厶 above 昜 *yang*², the radical 人 *jen*², takes its place on the left.

**542 赦**

*she*⁴, To forgive, to pardon.

赤 *ch'ih*⁴, Radical No. 155, a reddish carnation color. (W. 60 N.)

It is composed of 大 *ta*⁴, a man, and 火 *huo*³, fire. It may mean the blush of shame, or it may mean the flush of anger.

攴 *p'u*¹ Phonetic, to rap, to tap (W. 43 D.) The right hand holding a rod. It is the 66th radical. It has here no phonetic significance. It generally indicates action. Here it may indicate the red, which an official marks on a petition for pardon when the petition is granted, to strike 攴 red 赤,—to pardon 赦.

**543 免**

*mien*³, To avoid, to escape, to remit, to forgive. (W. 106 A.) (See No. 107.)

儿 *jen*², Radical No. 10 man.

This character does not break up into radical and phonetic. It is old, and according to Chalmers it represents a man trying to hide himself by drawing himself into his clothing, thus avoiding being seen.

**544 豈, 昰**

*ch'i*³, An interrogative particle. (W. 165 E,)

It is a drum (not 豆 *tou*⁴, a dish, although

the writing is identical) which was beaten with the left hand. The drum which was beaten with the right hand was written thus 尌. The upper stroke is the drum head, the ○ is the drum, and the 山 the stand. Observe the character 默 *tai*[1], foolish. A dog 犬 is beside himself when a drum is beaten. As this character has long since lost its original meaning, owing to this kind of a drum being discarded, the character has been adopted for the above meaning.

**545 敢**

*kan*[3], To dare, to venture.  (W. 146 H.)

支 *p'u*[1] Radical No. 66, to strike.

The phonetic is a bear 熊 耳. 能 *neng*[2], able, is a bear, and the right part of the character represents the paws. (See No. 357). But in 敢 the paws are suppressed to make room for the radical; a person who has the courage to strike a bear, therefore brave.

**546 基**

*chi*[1], A foundation ; property.

土 *t'u*[3], Radical No. 32, the earth.

其 *ch'i*[2], Phonetic, it.  (See No. 539.)

The Shuo Wen does not treat of this combination. As 土 *t'u*[3], earth, is below 其 *ch'i*[2], it may be that the inventor of the character intended to show that the earth beneath it (a structure) is the foundation, or the place where the foundation must be laid ; its 其 earth 土.

**547 督**

*tu*[1], To oversee, to superintend.

目,囧 *mu⁴*, Radical No. 109, the eye.  (W. 158 A.)

⑪　In the oldest writing two eyelids and the pupil are represented ; later the pupil was suppressed.

叔,杸 *shu²*, Phonetic, to collect ⺊ beans 未.  The character is supposed to represent a stalk 未 of beans with two pods attached.  This meaning is now obsolete.  With the addition of 目 *mu⁴* it implies that there is a person who oversees the bean picking ; and the character now is used to mean overseer, and is borrowed for uncle, a father's younger brother.

**548 怪**

　　　*kuai⁴*, Strange, to blame.

心, 忄 *hsin¹*, Radical No. 61, the heart.

圣, 彐 *kuai⁴* Phonetic, to till the ground, a hand 又 over the earth 土.  (W. 81 A.)

The produce of the ground when tilled struck the ancient Chinese as remarkable, and when the radical heart 心 is added, the character is used to convey the idea of strange or abnormal.

**549 梳**

　　　*shu¹*, A comb.

木 *mu⁴*, Radical No. 75, wood.

㐬 *t'u²* Phonetic, a child being born, with long hair.  (W. 94 F.)  From 㐬 (W. 94 E); the birth of a child, head presenting: the most favorable position.  In the above, hair is added, and it is the striking part of the character.  With the addition of the radical for wood 木 *mu⁴*, it forms the character for comb, as combs in China are made of wood.  㐬 = 子 inverted.

550 捨 she³, To give alms, to bestow, to part with, to reject.

手 扌 shou³, Radical No. 64, the hand. (See No. 53.)

舍 she⁴, Phonetic, a cottage. (See No. 40.)

When the radical for hand is added, it forms the character to give. Beggars go to houses in order to get food.

551 命, 𠎤 ming⁴, Life ; fate ; destiny ; a command. (W. 14 I.)

口 k'ou³, Radical No. 30, the mouth.

令 ling⁴, Phonetic, an order, a law. (See No. 61.)

When the order is stamped 令 it is published or made known 口 ; an order or command by word of mouth.

552 全 ch'üan², Entire, perfect, all, the whole. (W. 15 B.)

入 ju⁴, Radical No. 11, to enter. (See No. 35.)

As this character has been placed under 入 ju⁴, it is not now possible to break it up into radical and phonetic. The more plausible explanation is that it is composed of 亼 chi and 工 kung¹. It is also written 全 and 𠆌 the work 工 has been completed 亼. In making a chair or other article, when all the parts were finished and put together 亼 the article is finished.

553 應, 𧡪 ying¹˒⁴, Ought, proper, respond, fulfill.

心 hsin¹, Radical No. 61, heart.

雁 ying¹, Phonetic, the falcon, now written 鷹 (W. 168 J.) It is made up of 广 yen³, a house - here indicating domesticated - and 隹 chui¹ and 人 jen²: a tame bird which

serves man. These birds have long been
used for hunting small game. With the
addition of heart the character means;—
to answer, or obey, to do what one feels
心 is proper. This meaning is placed on
the character as the falcon fulfills the desire 心 of its master in seizing game.

**554 佛**

人

弗

fŏ², Buddha.

*jen²*, Radical No. 9, man.

*fu²* Phonetic, not. (W. 87 D). Two bent
rods or bows so tied together that their
force is neutralized ; therefore they stand
for not. This combination not 弗 man 人
may have been selected by the Buddhists
in order to emphasize that Buddha was
a supernatural being. Another writing is
儞 — 西國人 Western man.

**555 耶**

耳

邑, 阝

*yeh²*, A final particle. (W. 146 E).

*er³*, Radical No. 128, the ear. (See No. 71).

*i⁴*, Phonetic, a city. (See No. 11). No phonetic value. This character is said to be 邪
*hsieh²* arbitrarily changed. It originally
was the name of a city in the eastern part
of Shantung. It now means depraved,
erroneous. At present these two characters are entirely distinct 耶 is only used as
a final particle.

**556 穌**

禾, 朮

*su¹*, To glean, to revive. (W. 121 D).

*ho²*, Radical No. 115, growing grain. In the
seal writing the ear or head of grain is,
owing to its weight, hanging to one side.
(W. 121 A.)

魚 *yü²*, Phonetic, a fish. This is radical 195. (See No. 284). There is no explanation of this character which throws any light on its etymology. To the present day gleaning after the field is reaped is an important affair in the rural districts. It is possible that formerly the fishermen left the small fish after they had removed from their nets the larger ones, but the present custom is to remove every thing for themselves. Both fish 魚 and crops 禾 when dying for lack of moisture may be revived 穌 by water.

**557** 切

*ch'ieh¹*, To cut, to slice. (W. 33 A).

刀 *tao¹*, Radical No. 18, a knife.

七 *ch'i¹*, Phonetic, seven. (See No. 32). This may have been selected as the phonetic as the permanent, incisor teeth appear about the seventh year and these are the cutting teeth.

---

BALLER, VOCABULARY NO. IV.

**558** 瓶

*p'ing²*, A vase, a jug, a bottle.

瓦, 呙 *wa³*, Radical No. 98, earthen ware. (W. 145 A). Chalfant on Plate XIV, has a very plausible explanation of the origin of this radical. He believes it to be a pictorial representation of the tiles on the roof. Originally written ⌒ and afterward changed to ⻚.

幷, 并 *ping⁴*, Phonetic, two men with shields, marching side by side, even, united. Simple phonetic. (W. 115 B.) (See No. 235).

**559** 亮,亯

*liang⁴*, Clear, luminous, bright. (W. 75 C).

亠 *t'ou²* Radical No. 8, a cover or roof.

This character has been given a radica which prevents its being divided into radical and phonetic. There is an old writing 倞, 倞 and it is thus explained :— The men 人 at the capital, 京 ; those who are advisers to the Emperor, are more enlightened than other men. The present writing of the character is relatively modern, the upper part is from 高 *kao¹*, high, referring to the capital and man is substituted for the lower 口 in *kao¹*. The etymology is the same as that of the older writing.

**560** 兵,㲋

*ping¹*, Soldier, military. (W. 47 D).

八 *pa¹*, Radical No. 12, eight.

斤 *chin¹*, Phonetic, an ax or battle-ax. (W. 128 A). The lower part of 兵 is not *pa¹* but a contraction of 𦥑 廾 *kung³* thus in the seal writing two hands are wielding a battle-ax.

**561** 推

*t'ui¹*, To push ; to shirk ; to refuse.

手,扌 *shou³*, Radical No. 64, the hand.

隹 *chui¹* Phonetic, a short tailed bird. Radical No. 172. (See No. 21). The Shuo Wen is silent as to the etymology of this character ; but it may be that it was suggested by poultry raising. When the feed trough is surrounded by those first on the spot, the tardy bird pushes and shoves until it reaches the desired place.

562 材, 粉
木, 朮
才, 才

ts'ai², Material, stuff.

mu⁴, Radical No. 75, wood. (See No. 36).

ts'ai², Phonetic, talents, power, genius. This phonetic originally was used for material suitable for building, but gradually it was adopted for its present meaning. The upper horizontal stroke in the seal writing, indicates the large branches of a tree: the second horizontal stroke is the ground (W. 96 A). A tree when of proper size for building purposes is spoken of as 材 t'sai², before it attains to that distinction it is referred to as 劈紫 p'i³ ch'ai², fire wood. Financial power is 財 t'sai². Wood 木 was one of the first substances 才 worked upon by man.

563 熟, 飘

shou², Ripe; experienced; versed in; cooked; intimate.

火, 火 huo³, Radical No. 86, fire. (See No. 47).

孰, 窻 shu² Phonetic, who, which, what; but originally, a lamb of proper size and condition for roasting. (W. 75 E). The right side of the phonetic 丸, 夘 chi⁴, implies holding the animal. (See No. 139) 夐, 亨, Ch'un² is a lamb large enough to be offered as a present 曰, to a superior 古. The writing has been contracted to the present form. (W. 75, E). With the addition of ⑴⑴ fire, the idea of cooked is set forth.

564 姑

ku¹, A girl.

女, 庄 nü³, Radical No. 38, a woman. (See No. 16).

古, 古 ku⁸, Phonetic, old. (See No. 17). This is a

simple phonetic. (W. 24, F). It is not a fortunate combination for "girl" in a country where, formerly, a girl twenty years of age and unmarried was almost unheard of.

565 娘

*niang²*, A girl, a woman, a mother.

女, 虍 *nü³*, Radical No. 38, a woman. (See No. 16).

艮, 盲, 皀 *liang²*, Phonetic, good. (See No. 445). Because this phonetic sets forth respect, dignity and sagacity its combinations also partake of same. Mother 娘 is a good 良 woman 女.

566 失, 光

*shih¹*, To lose ; to slip ; to err.

大, 大 *ta⁴*, Radical No. 37, great. (See No. 113). This radical was arbitrarily given to the character and has no further use than to aid in looking it up in the native diction- aries. In the ancient writing a hand is seen with the 乀 *i⁴*, which indicates slip- ping away or shooting. There is no re- semblance, in the ancient writing, to an arrow 矢 as there is in the modern form. This is an old character and it has no phonetic. (W. 48 B).

567 仗

*chang⁴*, To rely on ; to fight.

亻, 人 *jên²*, Radical No. 9, man.

丈, 弓 *chang⁴*, Phonetic, ten feet. Under the Chou Dynasty this was about six and a half English feet. When a man 人 is accom- panied by a person of over six feet 丈 in height (revised measurement), it gives assurance of not being molested. (W. 32 F). One can rely on 仗 a ten foot 丈 man 人 to fight 仗. (W. 24 E).

**568** 料　*liao*[4], Material; ingredients; to estimate.

斗, 乇　*tou*[3], Radical No. 68, a peck measure, a dipper. (See No. 117).

米, 米　*mi*[3], Phonetic, rice, used of other grains. (See No. 47). The phonetic has no phonetic significance. Grain is measured with a 斗 *tou*[3], but chaff and straw, on account of their being of less value are not thus measured. According to the make up of this character materials of worth are 料 *liao*[4]. (W. 98 B).

**569** 公, 尚　*kung*[1], Public; fair, just; male.

八, 八　*pa*[1], Radical No. 12, eight. Because the two parts of this radical, in the old writing, are similar in construction and are not united, it was early adopted as the symbol for separation.

厶, ὁ　*ssŭ*[1] Phonetic, private. The ancient writing represented a silkworm which has shut itself into its cocoon. By extension it was used for private, selfish. (W. 89 A). This symbol has no phonetic value. The character 公 implies the right division 八 of private 厶 property for the benefit of the public.

**570** 吐　*t'u*[3 4 1], To spit, to vomit.

口, 口　*k'ou*[3], Radical No. 30, the mouth.

土　*t'u*[3], Phonetic, the soil, earth, place, local. From mouth 口 to the earth 土, to spit.

**571** 砍　*k'an*[3], To hack, to chop; to throw stones at.

石　*shih*[2], Radical No. 112, a stone. (See No. 42).

欠,充 *ch'ien¹*, Phonetic, to breathe out. (See No. 273).
This character may date back to the
stone age when axes were made of stone.
If so the combination of radical and
phonetic is appropriate ; with the steel ax
choppers often make audible expiration
with every stroke ; how much more difficult would chopping be if a stone ax were
used !

**572 夢**

*mêng⁴*, To dream ; a dream.

夕,夕 *hsi¹ ⁴*, Radical No. 36, evening. (See No. 14).

瞢,瞢 *mêng⁴* Phonetic, dimness of vision. The 目 *mu⁴*
at the bottom of this phonetic is replaced
by 夕 *hsi¹*, evening, as dreams belong to the
hours of sleep or the night. (W. 158 F).
Dreams are frequently hazy and indefinite,
consequently this combination of elements
is not inappropriate.

**573 財**

*ts'ai²*, Property.

貝,貝 *pei⁴*, Radical No. 154, precious. (See No. 38).

才,才 *ts'ai²*, Phonetic, talents, powers, genius. (See
No. 562). This is a happy combination
of radical and phonetic as it portrays the
idea of ability in the financial line.

**574 貪,貪**

*t'an¹*, To covet ; avaricious.

貝 *pei⁴*, Radical No. 154, precious. (See No. 38).

今 *chin¹*, Phonetic, now. (See No. 18).

The emotion of greed which is excited in
the presence 今 of valuable 貝 articles.
(W. 14, M). The phonetic in this character is the same as in No. 18, 念 *nien⁴*,
and its rather unusual meaning of present,
is the same in both instances.

575 麵 麫

麥, 夌    *mien*[4], Flour.

*mai*[4], Radical No. 199, wheat, barley. This radical is made up of 來 *lai*[2], which originally was the character for barley, (See No. 64), and 夂 *sui*[1], a man who persists in advancing in spite of trammels and obstacles. This may have been added to indicate the gradual development of the grain.

面    *mien*[4], Phonetic, the face. (See 486). Its use here is as a simple phonetic.

丏, 丏    *mien*[4] Phonetic, to conceal. (See 122).

576 式, 玎

弋, 弋    *shih*[4], A form, a pattern.

*i*[1] Radical No. 56, a dart. This radical is not looked on alike by all scholars. Some are of opinion that it represents a nail or peg in a wall on which articles may be hung. Still another theory is that it is a tally for counting or ordering; when this tally was placed upon an article, this article was the pattern. Each of these explanation has its advantages, but no one comes up to all requirements. It seems wise to adhere to the first explanation and regard it as a dart, as these must have been very plentiful, owing to the state of civilization, and it is not improbable that they were used as tallies and as pegs. (W. 71, A).

工    *kung*[1], Phonetic, work. No phonetic significance. (See No. 89). Here the most plausible explanation is:—a dart, used for a peg on which is suspended a pattern of the article ordered.

**577** 陽

yang², The sun ; open, front.

阜, 阝 *fu⁴* Radical No. 170, a mound. (See No. 493).

易, 昜 *yang²* Phonetic, glorious, open out, a flag ; the sun above the horizon 日 *tan.⁴* 勿 *wu¹*, rays of light. This is a suggestive phonetic. (W. 101, B).

**578** 娶

*ch'ü³*, To marry.

女, 虎 *nü³*, Radical No. 38, a woman. (See No. 16).

取, 肙 *ch'ü³*, Phonetic, to take. A hand 乀 holding an ear 耳. To hold by the ear, to hold securely. A betrothal in China has been regarded as more binding than the marriage ceremony in many lands. (W. 146 F).

**579** 容, 㝐

*jung²*, Appearance ; to allow ; to endure.

宀 *mien²* Radical No. 40, a roof.

谷, 㕣 *ku³ ⁴ ²*, Phonetic, a deep gorge, a valley. This is the 150th radical. The old writing depicts two strata or ridges of rock, one above the other and at the bottom a mouth, a place where water flowed. This valley is open and one can see all within, but in 容 *jung²* there is a cover over the valley. Here the valley is said to refer to the depths of the heart, the emotions which are concealed from others. Thus the idea of to contain and to allow is given the character. (W. 18 E).

**580** 臺

*t'ai²*, A terrace ; a title of respect.

至 至 *chih⁴*, Radical No. 133, to arrive. (See No. 337). The phonetic part of this character is 高 *kao¹* and 之 土 𡳿 *chih¹*. The former

is changed both at the top and bottom,
on the top the *chih*[1] 止 is placed, which
indicates the summit, and 至 *chih*[4] replaces
the 口 at the bottom. This character was
constructed before they had definitely
settled on the scheme of radicals and
phonetics, 高 *kao*[1] and 之 止 *chih*[1] both
suggest height but neither aid in pronunciation.

**581** 朶, 朵

木, 米
乃, 㲋

*to*[3], A cluster, a head, pendent things.

*mu*[4], Radical No. 75, wood. (See No. 36).

*shu*[2] Phonetic, a wing, which on account of
its being short, vibrates rapidly while in
flight. (W. 22. A). This is without
phonetic significance but it suggests the
movement and appearance of pendent
flowers in the wind. The modern writing
is identical with 乃 *nai*[3].

**582** 妻

*ch'i*[1], A wife.

女 *nü*[3], Radical No. 38, a woman. (See No. 16).
The phonetic part of this character is not
used alone 龶 and it is not given a pronunciation. It is a hand holding a duster.
It is not an old character. The hand that
manages the household affairs is the wife.
The present form is a contraction of an
older writing.

**583** 扇

*shan*[4], A fan; the leaf of a door.

戶 *hu*[4], Radical No. 63, a door, a window. (See
No. 480).

羽 *yü*[3], Phonetic, wings, plumes. It is a representation of a pair of wings or two wing

quills. (W. 62. E). In appearance it is suggestive, but without phonetic significance. A fan or the leaf of a door resembles a wing in that its attachment is at one extremity or side and has a vibrating movement.

584 窗

ch'uang¹, A window.

穴 hsüeh⁴, Radical No. 116, a cave. (See No. 97).

囱, 囪 ch'uang¹ Phonetic, a window. There are two
囮 forms of the ancient writing, one seems to be partly covered by a curtain or shutter and the other has lattice work within. The make up of this character indicates that it dates back to the time when caves and dugouts were in general use.

585 慈

tz'u², Compassionate.

心 hsin¹, Radical No. 61, the heart. (See No. 18).

茲, 兹 tzü¹ Phonetic, the fine velvety appearance of luxuriant vegetation. All this disappears if covered by dust or if there is a shortage of rain. With the addition of heart the above beautiful qualities are transferred to the disposition. Compassion is that quality of heart which is admired by all, but is easily lost owing to the cares and worries of life.

586 聰

ts'ung¹, Wisdom, quick of apprehension, clever.

耳 er³, Radical No. 128, the ear. (See No. 71).

悤, 怱 ts'ung¹, Phonetic, the feelings stirred. When one is fearful of being apprehended he is constantly looking out of the window 囱 to

see if the officers are coming. (W. 40, D).
With the addition of the radical 耳 *er*[3], the
idea is to listen with the same vigilance
that a criminal uses in trying to elude
arrest. The combination is fortunate but
difficult of application at all times.

---

### BALLER LESSON XXI.

587 香, 甬, 香    *hsiang*[1], Incense, fragrance. Radical No.
186. There are two seal writings of
this radical. The oldest is explained as
representing the sweet odor of millet when
undergoing fermentation. The other represents millet held in the mouth because
the flavor is agreeable.

588

*lien*[2], To pity.

忄, 心    *hsin*[1], Radical No. 61, the heart. (See No. 18).

舛, 粦    *lin*[2], Phonetic, an ignis fatuus. This phonetic
has been unfortunately changed so that
the original idea is not portrayed by the
present writing. It should be 粦. The
light is supposed to be seen on old battle-
fields and is the result of the mingling of
the blood of men and horses. The light is
indicated by 炎 炎 *yen*[2], one fire above
another. The battle is indicated by 舛
*ch'uan*[3], to contend, as two persons are at
variance. With the addition of 心 heart,
the character represents the emotion of
pity that one would experience on seeing
an ignis fatuus if he believed it was caused as above stated. (W. 126 D).

589 酒　*chiu³*, Wine, spirits.

氵,水 *shui³*, Radical No. 85, water. (See No. 79).

酉,酉 *yu³* Phonetic, a jar for holding liquors. The old writing is not a bad picture of these jars. When 氵 water is added to the phonetic the character is used for all spirituous beverages. (W. 41 G).

590 湖 *hu²*, A lake.

氵,水 *shui³*, Radical No. 85, water. (See No. 79).

胡 *hu²* Phonetic, dewlap. This phonetic is made up of old 古 *ku³*, and 月 *jou⁴*, meat. The dewlap is made up of a fold in the skin and is tough, hence the idea of old or tough is fitting. Its use as a phonetic in this character is rather far fetched, but when the dew on the grass is heavy the dewlap of the ox plows through it and is wet like the prow of a vessel in a lake.

591 瞎 *hsia¹*, Blind.

目 *mu⁴*, Radical No. 109, the eye. (See No. 102)·

害 *hai⁴*, Phonetic, to injure. (See No. 436). This phonetic has no phonetic signification, but it indicates why the eye is blind, that is, it had been injured.

592 聾 *lung²*, Deaf.

耳 *er³*, Radical No. 128, the ear. (See No. 71).

龍,龍 *lung²*, Phonetic, the dragon. (See No. 286). The dragon is supposed to be deaf and with the addition of the radical we have a dragon's ear, or a deaf ear.

593 疼 *t'êng²*, Pain, to pain, to ache.

疒,疒 *ni*[4] Radical No. 104, disease. This is in the ancient writing the representation of a bed with a horizontal line at the top to indicate the posture of a person when ill. The dot on the top of this line has been arbitrarily added by the scribes.

冬,夂 *tung*[1], Phonetic, winter. (See No. 170). This is a suggestive and very appropriate phonetic as the pain which is experienced from cold is very intense and there are few persons who have not experienced it. Pain being a pathological manifestation the above radical is also a happy selection.

**594 瘸**

*ch'üeh*[2], Lame.

疒 *ni*[4], Radical No. 104, disease. (See No. 593).

㓀 *chia*[1], Phonetic, scabs and ulcers. This phonetic is not found in most modern dictionaries. The idea of a swelling is set forth by an addition 加 *chia*[1] of flesh 肉 *jou*[4]. Most lame joints are swollen and enlarged.

**595 腿**

*t'ui*[3], The leg, the thigh.

月,肉 *jou*[4], Radical No. 130, the flesh. (See No. 133).

𧢲,退 *t'ui*[4], Phonetic, to retreat, to decline. The idea of to retreat seems to be derived from the apparent movement of the sun, 昆 each morning it slowly 㚒 ascends until midday and then slowly recedes. This is not like Wieger's description (W. 31. C). The 162 radical added to the phonetic is a redundancy as it contributes nothing. The limbs in walking go through the same movement, each one is one half of the time advancing and one half the time apparently, receding.

**596 賞**

shang³, To reward, to grant; a reward.

貝 pei⁴, Radical No. 154, precious. (See No. 38).

尙 shang⁴ Phonetic, a house. (Archaic meaning). (See No. 52). Houses, which includes real estate, and money 貝 pei⁴ are here used to represent all that is of value or what would be appreciated as a reward.

**597 賜**

tz'ŭ⁴, To bestow, to confer on an inferior, to give.

貝 pei⁴, Radical No. 154, precious. (See No. 38).

易, 昜 i⁴, Phonetic, to exchange. It is supposed to represent the house lizard, a creature which is agile and moves with great rapidity. Some think that the idea of " to change " is dependent on the creature's changing its colour to that of the object on which it rests. The lizards in North China have this power to a certain extent, but it is not noticed when the animal is in the house. With the addition of the radical we have the idea of giving, that is exchanging articles of value. If the giving is always on one side it sooner or later ceases. (W. 101 C).

**598 災**

tsai¹, Calamity, divine judgment.

火, 灺 huo³, Radical No. 86, fire. A representation of a flame in the old writing.

巛, 川, 巛 ch'uan¹, Phonetic, streams. It represents a stream which is formed by the union of other streams 〈 〉 chuan³ is a small stream; 《 𡿨 *kuai*⁴ is a stream which is formed by the union with another stream. The overflow of rivers is one of the great calamities of China.

Fires are not very common in North China but at times they cause great loss of property; and 巛 floods and 火 fire make up the character which stands for divine judgment; as these are regarded as calamities sent from Heaven.

**599** 閒

*hsien*², Leisure, idle.

門 *mên*², Radical, No. 169, a door. (See No. 5).

月 *yüeh*⁴, Phonetic, the moon. (See No. 43).

The moonlight coming in through the cracks of the door and doing nothing is taken as a symbol of idleness or leisure.

**600** 課

*k'o*⁴, A lesson, a task.

言 *yen*², Radical No. 149, a word. (See No. 10).

果 果 *kuo*³, Phonetic, fruit. (See No. 411). To so use ones opportunities that the instruction 言 *yen*² received may bring forth results, 果 *kuo*³.

**601** 耕

*ching*¹, To plough, to till.

耒, 耒 *lei*³ Radical No. 127, a plough. The old writing resembles a harrow more nearly than it does a plough. It probably was a tree with branches so cut as to scratch furroughs in the earth. (W. 120 E).

井 *ching*³, Phonetic, a well. A very necessary part of a farmer's equipment in North China where irrigation is required for many kinds of agriculture. Breaking the ground and watering is the symbol for cultivating or tilling the soil.

**602 喊**

*han*[3], To call, to halloo.

口 *k'ou*[3], Radical No. 30, the mouth.

咸 *hsien*[2] Phonetic, to wound by biting, all. (Archaic). (See No. 305). With the addition of another mouth the meaning is changed from biting to calling.

**603 除**

*ch'u*[2], To remove, to do away with, to subtract, to discount.

阜, 阝 *fu*[4] Radical No. 170, a mound. (See No. 493).

余, 余 *yü*[2] Phonetic, I, me. (See No. 40). With the addition of the radical which means lofty the meaning of the character can be remembered by the following :—If one extols or elevates himself he is sure to be discounted.

**604 種**

*chung*[3], Seed ; a class or kind.

禾 *ho*[2], Radical No. 115, grain, grain on the stalk. (See No. 556).

重 *chung*[4], Phonetic, heavy. (See No. 22). The heavy end of the stalk 禾 *ho*[2] is where the grain 種 is found.

**605 莊**

*chuang*[1], Serious; a farm.

艸 *ts'ao*[3] Radical No. 140, grass. (See No. 22).

壯 '*chuang*[4], Phonetic, strong. (See No. 355). With the addition of the grass radical the character is used for a farm or serious. The latter meaning is difficult of explanation, but the first might be explained as

the strong 壯, luxuriant vegetation, 艸
ts'ao³, of a well ordered farm.

**606** 稼

chia⁴, Growing grain.

禾 ho², Radical No. 115, grain, growing grain.
(See No. 556).

家 chia¹, Phonetic, a family. (See No, 221).
With the addition of the radical it implies,
crops for the family or household.

**607** 升, 汞

sheng¹, A measure equivalent to one tenth of a
斗 汞 tou³ a peck, to promote. The old
writing of this character is similar to the
writing of the character for peck save that
it has an oblique line across the handle.
This line ノ ／ p'ieh, is supposed to indicate that one tenth part of the tou³ has
been taken out. (W. 98 B).

十 shih², Radical No. 24, ten. This by some is
regarded as a contraction of two contracted fives 乂.

汞 tou³, Phonetic, a peck. This has no phonetic
significance, it only aids in explaining the
meaning of the character in the old writing. Why shêng¹ has the meaning of to
promote is not easy to understand, unless
this measure, being the smallest in common use, any change is necessarily an
increase or promotion. (W. 98 B).

**608** 犂

li², A plough, to plough.

牛 niu², Radical No. 93, an ox. (See No. 50).

利 li⁴, Phonetic, to cut grain, (archaic); profit.
Standing grain and sickle was adopted as
the symbol for, to reap. The addition of

ox forms the character for plough as that
animal was used for pulling the plough,
the use of which was a necessary step
before reaping. (W. 52 F).

---

**609** 賸

*sheng*[4], Remainder.

貝 *pei*, Radical No. 154, precious. (See No. 38).

朕,朕 *cheng*[4] Phonetic, to curve with fire the planks
for a boat 月. In this process the plank
was partially destroyed by the fire before
it could be bent into the desired shape, but
that part of the plank which remained
was now adapted to the requirements.
By adding the radical 貝, precious, the
idea is set forth that remnants 賸 are of
value. The 舟 *chou*[1] boat has been contracted to 月 in the modern writing.

**610** 勝

*sheng*[4], To conquer, to excel.

力 *li*[4], Radical No. 19, strength. (See No. 212).

朕 *cheng*[4] Phonetic, to curve with fire the planks
for a boat. (See No. 609). In the pro-
cess of bending the planks the strength
of the fire plus the strength 力 of the workmen's hands 月 overcomes the resistance
of the plank, thus with the addition
of the radical for strength, the character,
to conquer is formed. (W. 47 D.

**611** 科

*k'e*[1]. A class, a series.

禾 *ho*[2], Radical No. 115, grain, standing grain.
(See No. 556).

斗,斗 *tou*[3], Phonetic, a peck measure. (See No. 117).

It is without phonetic value, but suggests the idea of the coiner of the character. In measuring 斗 *tou*³ grain 禾 *ho*² each kind was stored in separate bins, and thus the idea of class is set forth.

612 飛, 飛   *fei*¹, To fly. Radical No. 183. This radical is the representation of a crane in flight; the neck is folded on itself and the long bill rests on this fold. The pinions are seen on either side. The body and tail are represented by the straight line in the center. (W. 11 A).

613 交, 亣   *chiao*¹, To commit to, to hand to, friendship, intercourse. (W. 61 D).

亠 *t'ou*² Radical No. 8, above. Kanghsi says that the meaning of this radical is lost. The meaning "above" has been given it because it is always used at the top of a character. The original or old writing did not have this radical; in the modern writing it is arbitrarily introduced.

父 *fu*⁴, Phonetic, father. This phonetic is also a modern innovation, having no connection with the original writing, which represented a man sitting with crossed legs, thus each limb is occupying the place of its fellow. From this the idea of "to commit to or to hand over is obtained.

614 之, 㞢, 屮   *chih*¹ He, she, it; sign of the possessive.

丿 *p'ieh*¹ Radical No. 4, a stroke to the left. (See No. 176). This radical having been arbitrarily given it destroys the original

idea of the symbol; which was a small
plant Ψ issuing from the ground —. The
need of a character for the above process
not being great, and owing to its being
easy to write, it was adopted to represent
the meaning given above.

**615** 結

*chieh*², To make a contract; to produce, as
fruit; a knot.

糸 *ssu*¹, *mi*⁴, Radical No. 120, silk. (See No. 8).

吉, 吉 *chi*², Phonetic, fortunate, lucky. This phonetic
is made up of 士 *shih*⁴, which often is used
for 串 *shih*⁴ in the archaic writing, and 口
*k'ou*³ the mouth. To announce a fortunate affair or condition. It seems reasonable to believe that this phonetic has been
abbreviated from 頡 *chieh*⁷, to be level headed. 纈 *chieh*² is another writing of knot.
The abbreviated phonetic has as happy a
meaning as the older form but does not
aid in determining the pronunciation :--
When a thing is fortunate make it secure.
The addition of the radical 糸 often implies tying or making secure. (W. 24 C).

**616** 夥

*huo*³, Numerous, a company, an associate.

夕 *hsi*⁴ Radical No. 36, evening. (See No. 14).
The radical should be doubled 多 *to*¹ many,
as its use here has no reference to the
evening or new moon but to many or
much. (See No. 184).

果 *kuo*³, Phonetic, fruit. (See No. 411). When
多 *to*¹ is combined with this phonetic the
idea of much or many is brought out; as
numerous as the fruit on the tree.

617 計    *chi*[4], A plan, a device, all told, to reckon.

言   *yen*[2], Radical No. 149, a word. (See No. 10).

十   *shih*[2], Phonetic, ten. The oldest form of ten seems to be a contraction of two contracted forms of five 乂 ; this was afterwards contracted to ╂ and as this was difficult to make it was finally written in the shape of a cross. This is an old character and the phonetic only explains an idea without aiding in pronunciation. If a person can count 言 *yen*[2] up to ten ╋ they are able to reckon, to plan.

618 嘗    *ch'ang*[2], To taste, to experience.

口   *k'ou*[3], Radical No. 30, the mouth. (See No. 17). This selection of the radical is unfortunate as it is taken from the phonetic.

尚   *shang*[4], Phonetic, a house. (See No. 52). This should complete the character, but in the present instance the important or distinctive part is not yet touched. 旨, 旨 *chih*[3], something pleasant to the taste, that which is pleasant to hear, as the edict of the Emperor. The 匕 *pi*[3], may be regarded as a spoon and the lower part in the old writing is 甘 *kan*[1], something agreeable to the taste held in the mouth, hence to taste. It is fortunate that few characters in their transition from the old, to the new writing, have undergone such destructive alterations. (W. 26 K).

619 揀    *chien*[3], To select, to pick up.

扌,手   *shou*[3], Radical No. 64, the hand. (See No. 53).

束, 柬 *chien³*, Phonetic, to select, to choose. This phonetic is made up of 束, 柬 *shu⁴*, a bundle tied to or hung on a tree ; to this is added 八 *pa¹*, eight, written, one stroke on either side of the bundle, to indicate that it is opened or divided. (See No. 569). (W. 75 A). With the addition of the radical for hand the act of selecting is more emphatically brought out.

620 敗

*pai⁴*, To ruin.

文, 攴, 与 *p'u¹* Radical No. 66, to tap, to rap. (See No. 17).

貝 *pei⁴*, Phonetic, precious. (See No. 38). The object of this combination is evident viz., the result of hammering sea-shells is their destruction.

621 降

*chiang⁴*, To descend.
*hsiang²*, To submit, to surrender.

阝 *fu⁴*, Radical No. 170, a mound. (See No. 493).

夅, 夅 *chiang⁴*, Phonetic, to subject. (W. 31 F). This is the 34th, radical 夂 *chih⁴*, a man overtaking another, written in two ways, above it is upright, the usual writing, and below it is inverted. The idea of the combination is, a suppliant overtakes a man and prostrates himself in token of subjection. The meaning of to descend is set forth in prostration or inversion of the suppliant. The meaning of to submit is the above idea carried a little farther, prostration implies submission or surrender. Wieger puts this character under the 35th, radical. The radical 阝 *fu⁴* added to this phonetic simply complicates the writing and as to etymology, it is a redundancy.

**622 俗**

亻, 人    *su²*, Vulgar, common.

   *jen²*, Radical No. 9, a man.

谷, 尙    *ku³*, Phonetic, a valley, a ravine. This is composed of two 八 *pa¹* characters superimposed one above the other which indicates a gorge of great depth, below is 口 *k'ou* which stands for a water-course. (W. 18 E). The addition of the radical implies that the man is a rustic from the ravines or mountains, uncouth.

**623 猶**

犭, 犬, 尨    *yu²*, Like; undecided; still.

   *ch'üan³* Radical No. 94, a dog. (See No. 424.) In modern writing, when used at the left of a phonetic, the present form is used in order to occupy less space.

酉, 酋    *chiu¹* Phonetic, liquor. A liquor after fermentation is completed and the dregs have settled, divided 八 *pa¹*. If the Chinese, colorless liquor were placed before a thirsty dog 犬 the resemblance to water is striking, but the odor would cause him to hesitate 猶 about drinking. (W. 41 G).

**624 托**

扌, 手    *t'o¹*, To support with the hand; to commission.

毛, 乇    *shou³*, Radical No. 64, the hand. (See No. 53).

   *t'o* Phonetic, a plant just appearing above the ground bearing the cotyledons. The stalk seems often too delicate to support these first leaves and on this account they attract attention ; thus the idea of to support is set forth by this phonetic. When the radical for hand is added the meaning of to support is changed from the plant to the hand. (W. 33 B).

**625** 矩

chü³, A rule, a pattern, a custom. (W. 82 D).

矢 shih³, Radical No. 111, a dart, an arrow. (See No. 100).

巨 chü⁴ Phonetic, a square. This is an instrument larger than the 工 kung¹, the ordinary square. The square was the guide when building or laying out a plot of ground. When 矢 shih³ is added it indicates, appointed, determined, irrevocable. This meaning is derived from archery ; after the arrow is shot one knows the skill of the archer, as its position on the target cannot be changed. Thus this combination is used for established custom.

**626** 髮

fa³, The hair of the human head.

髟,髟 piao¹ Radical No. 190, hair, shaggy hair or locks. In the old writing it is the same as 長 ch'ang², long, save three strokes 彡 are added on the right, these represent the long locks. (Cf. No. 131.)

犮,犮 pa² Phonetic, a dog led by a leash, by a strap behind the shoulders and in front of one fore leg. During the Manchu rule, prisoners were led by their cues. This practise may have been handed down from the dim past as the Chinese have long worn long hair, dressed in different styles as the dynasty determined. The long braided hair looks like a leash and thus the phonetic was adopted. (W. 134 A).

**627 雀**

佳 *chui*[1] Radical No. 172, a short-tailed bird. (See No. 21).

*ch'iao*[2], A sparrow or small bird.

小, 川 *hsiao*[3], Phonetic, small. It is made up of 八 *pa*[1] eight, to divide. The idea of to divide is given to this numeral because in the seal writing the two parts are identical and they do not touch, thus they suggest division. Between these two parts there is a vertical line. This is an object which is to be divided and as that will make it smaller, this combination is used for small. Add to this the radical for short tailed bird and the sparrow family has an appropriate appellation. (W. 18 N).

**628 鳥, 鳥**

*niao*[3], A bird. Radical No. 196. A pictorial representation of a long tailed bird.

---

BALLER, LESSON XXIII.

**629 流**

氵, 水 *shui*[3], Radical No. 85, water. (See No. 79).

*liu*[2], To flow, to drift.

㐬, 㐬 *t'u*[2] Phonetic, a fetus in the easiest position for delivery, viz., a head presentation. This is similar to 𠫓 *t'u*[2], the delivery of a child, save the present phonetic depicts a child with long flowing hair. With the addition of the above radical the character is used for, the current or the flow of a river. (W. 94 F).

**630** 慣　　kuan⁴, Accustomed to, practised in.

忄, 心　hsin¹, Radical No. 61, the heart. (See No. 18).

貫, 貫　kuan⁴, Phonetic, long strings 毌 huan⁴ of cowries, 貝 pei⁴, to pierce, to tie, to string. The sea-shells were kept on a string and only opened when it was necessary to do so to make change. Thus with the addition of heart a character is formed which means, usage, custom or experience. It having become as familiar or common to one as the condition of being strung was to the cowries. (W. 153 A).

**631** 掉　　tiao⁴, To fall down, to lose.

扌, 手　shou³, Radical No. 64, the hand. (See No. 53).

卓, 桌　cho¹ Phonetic, high, elevated. (See No. 56). It represents a kind of mast with a hopper shaped box half way from the ground to the top. Many characters with this phonetic have an ending like the character under consideration, and it is probable that the phonetic has been abbreviated from one of these. The addition of the radical 手 shou³ signifies, to fall. In climbing such a mast 卓 if ones hold 手 is not good a fall 掉 is inevitable.

**632** 鑼　　lo², A gong.

金　chin¹, Radical No. 167, gold or metal. (See No. 13).

羅, 𦋐　lo², Phonetic, a net, a sieve. A net 网 wang³ made of silk 糸 mi⁴, ssu¹ for catching birds 隹 chui¹. These nets, in shape, resemble a gong and when the radical which is used for all kinds of metal is added the character for gong is formed. (W. 39 D).

**633 破**

石
皮

p'o⁴, Broken, to break.

shih², Radical No. 112, a stone. (See No. 42).

p'i², Phonetic, the skin. (See No. 224). The present form of 破 p'o⁴ is quite different from the old writing and this accounts for the variance of the phonetic. (For old form see K'ang Hsi). Although the combination of this character has been arbitrarily changed its present form is not inappropriate:—if one comes in contact with a rock or stone, the skin is apt to be broken.

**634 跪**

足
危

kuei⁴, To kneel, to bow down to.

tsu², Radical No. 157, the foot. (See No. 484).

wei², Phonetic, peril, hazard. This is made up from 尸 wei², a man standing on a rock in order to get a better view. When 巳 卩 chieh² is added, (See No. 42), it means he restrains his movements owing to the height of his position and danger of falling. With the above radical the emotions of one on a rock with a precarious footing is given to the suppliant, he regards himself with apprehension. (W. 59 H).

**635 而. 禾**

er², Radical No. 126, and, yet, still, but. The archaic meaning is the beard. The horizontal stroke is the mouth. (W. 164 A).

The use of this radical as above set forth is said to have originated from the fact that the beard is suspended from the chin and the above connectives act as appendages for connecting together the various parts of the sentence.

**636 園**

yüan², A garden, an orchard.

口 wei², Radical No. 31, an inclosure.

袁,衾 yüan² Phonetic, trailing robes. This is a combination of 衣 i¹, clothing and 重 卷 chuan¹, to attach, to drag, (See No. 385) at the end of a trace. This is contracted to 亠, which is placed at the top of the character, and 口 which is placed between the upper and lower parts of 衣 i¹, making 袁 and with the additional top 袁 yüan². With the radical which often means a fence, placed around the phonetic we have the character for garden. A garden with its tall stalks and long vines gives one the impression that the inclosed plot of earth has donned its long garments.

**637 答**

ta², to reply, to respond to.

竹 chu², Radical No. 118, bamboo. (See No. 7).

合 ho², Phonetic, union, agreement, harmony. (See No. 103). The joints of 竹 chu², bamboo, harmonize 合 ho², or answer to each other, in their positions on the stalk, as to size and shape. From this the idea of to answer or respond to is obtained.

**638 撒**

sa¹, To scatter, to sow, to let loose.

扌,手 shou³, Radical No. 64, the hand. (See No. 53)

散,𢿐 *san⁴* Phonetic, to pound 攴 *p'u¹* meat 月 until the fibres separate, like shredded hemp, 林 *p'ai⁴*. (See No. 24). When the hand is added to this phonetic the idea of, to scatter or disperse is conveyed. The modern writing is quite arbitrary and it is only by consulting the seal character that the etymology can be traced.

**639 謊**

言 *huang³*, To talk wildly, to lie, lies.

言 *yen²*, Radical No. 149, word. (See No. 10).

荒,𣺤 *huang¹*, Phonetic, wild overgrowth. This is derived from 兦 *wang²* (See No. 123) an entering in of the rivers, 巛 *ch'uan¹*, an overflow. When 艸 *ts'ao³* is added it indicates an overgrowth of weeds or worthless vegetation on wild lands. When word 言 is added it indicates wild, worthless talk or lies. (W. 12 J).

**640 武**

止 *wu³*, Military, warlike.

止 *chih³*, Radical No. 77, to stop. (See No. 10).

戈,夫 *ko¹*, Phonetic, halberd. (See No. 2). For some unaccountable reason the stroke across the handle of the halberd has been placed above the horizontal stroke on the left. (W. 71 K).

The lancers 戈 who stop 止 the hostile incursion, thus allowing the people to proceed with their peaceful occupation.

**641 剃**

刂,刀 *t'i⁴*, To shave.

刂,刀 *tao¹*, Radical No. 18, a knife. (See No. 37).

弟 *ti⁴*, Phonetic, a thread wound on a spool. (See No. 86). The hair grows as if it were being unwound from a hidden spindle and the idea of to shave was set forth by placing a razor 刀 *tao*[1] by the side of this phonetic.

**642 清**

氵,水 *shui*[3], Radical No. 85, water. (See No. 79).

青,青 *ch'ing*[1], Phonetic, light green, the color of sprouting vegetation. (See No. 63). As the tips of recent sprouts are translucent, they are regarded as being pure and with the addition of water, which is transparent, the character for clear is obtained.

*ch'ing*[1], Clear, pure, correct, as an account.

**643 藍**

艹 艸 *ts'ao*[3], Radical No. 140, grass. (See No. 22).

監 *chien*[1], Phonetic, to watch. (See No. 294).
This is a simple phonetic and consequently 藍 has no logical explanation.

*lan*[2], Blue, indigo.

**644 性**

忄,心 *hsin*[1], Radical No. 61, the heart. (See No. 18).

生,生 *sheng*[1], Phonetic; to grow, bear, produce. Radical 100. A plant that grows more and more. A whorl was added to 屮 之 showing increasing growth (W. 79, B, F). When 忄 *hsin*[1], heart, is added the character is used for the natural inclinations or desires of the heart.

*hsing*[4], Nature, disposition, a quality.

**645 傢**

亻,人 *jên*[2], Radical No. 9, a man.

家 *chia*[1], Phonetic, a family. (See No. 221). This 傢 is an unauthorized character and is not found in the old dictionaries. The only explanation is:—what a man 亻 *jên*[2], sup-

*chia*[1], Tools, furniture.

ports his family 家 *chia*[1] with ; tools and furniture are necessary in the home.

**646** 伙

*huo*[3], Tools, furniture.

亻,人 *jên*[2], Radical No. 9, a man.

火,火 *huo*[3], Phonetic, fire. A pictorial representation of a flame of fire. This, 伙 like No. 645, is an unauthorized character. It is supposed to have originated from the expression 十人爲一火 ten men make one mess or fire. The mess includes the utensils for cooking.

**647** 袱

*fu*[2], A square cloth for tying up bundles.

礻衣 *i*[1], Radical No. 145, clothes. (See No. 51).

伏 *fu*[2], Phonetic, to hide, to stoop. This is composed of man 人 and dog, 犬. It was first used as the character for, to ambush, a man 亻 assuming the posture of the dog 犬 in order not to be seen. With the addition of 礻 *i*[1], cloth, it becomes a suggestive phonetic, because it surrounds the articles inclosed,—hides them.

---

BALLER, LESSON XXIV.

**648** 盡

*chin*[4], All, entirely, exhaust.

皿,皿 *min*[3], Radical No. 108, a dish. This is a pictorial representation of a dish with a pedestal such as the Chinese often use at feasts.

妻,妻 *chin*[4] Phonetic, ashes which remain after the fire. This phonetic, in modern writing, has one less horizontal stroke than in the ancient writing. It is difficult to account for the use of 妻 *chin*[4] as a phonetic in this character. 桂氏 Kuei Shih Shuo Wen has the most plausible explanation :—he says that 灰 is a contraction of 薪 *hsin*[1] fuel, and 火 *huo*[3], fire. Thus when the fire has consumed the fuel, its force is expend-ed ; nothing remains save the ashes. The radical 皿 *min*[3] indicates the stove. It might have been a brazier for holding coals for warming the hands of scribes 聿.

**649 渴**

*k'o*[3], To thirst, thirsty.

氵,水 *shui*[3], Radical No. 85, water. (See No. 79).

曷,曷 *ho*[2] Phonetic, to ask. (See No. 271). With the addition of the radical the idea is :
To ask 曷 for water 水 because one is thirsty 渴.

**650 邪**

*hsieh*[2], Vicious, depraved, heterodox.

阝,邑 *i*[4], Radical No. 163, a city. (See No. 11).

牙 *ya*[2], Phonetic, tooth. (See No. 97). This is a contraction of the original phonetic 衺 *hsien*[2], a garment like a buskin which wraps around the legs, awry. The con-traction has deprived the character of a proper phonetic. The radical added to this was the name of an ancient city in Eastern Shantung. The city may have had a bad reputation. Owing to the original meaning of the phonetic being, awry, 衺 this character has been used for depraved or hetrodox.

**651 停**

*t'ing*[2], To stop, to delay ; suitable.

亻,人 *jên*[2], Radical No. 9, a man. (See No. 5).

亭 亭 *t'ing*[2], Phonetic, a pavilion, terrace. This is

formed of 高 *kao*[1], high, and 丁 *ting*[1], a person. In the combination, the lower 口. of the *kao*[1] is deleted. With the addition of the radical 人 the idea is:—When a 亻 man comes to a pavilion 亭 while on a journey, he will stop, 停 to rest.

**652**

肩.肙.肙.肙 *chien*[1], The shoulder.

肉.月 *jou*[4], Radical No. 130 ; meat. (See No. 133).

戸 *hu*[4], Phonetic, a door. (See No. 5). A glance at the development of this character will reveal why 戸 *hu*[4], a door has been added ; it has gradually been substituted for a curved line which represented the arm. Because this line was only used for this one character, its form was not easy to remember ; first 尸 *shih*[1], a person in the sitting or reclining posture, was substituted, and afterwards it was changed to 戸 *hu*[4]. This shows that early in the development of the written language, unusual symbols were gradually replaced by those in common use and this too at the expense, in many instances, of logical etymology. The facility of remembering oft recurring elements brought about these changes. The 月 represents the muscles about the shoulder joint. In No. 361, 戸 *hu*[4] is referred to as "a farmer" ; in farming the shoulder of man and beast must be strong, the former for carrying burdens and the latter for pulling the plow. This may aid in remembering the combination.

**653**

*yüan*[4], To be willing, to be desirous of, a vow.

頁 *yêh*⁴, Radical No. 181, a leaf of a book, the archaic meaning is, the head. (See No. 105).

原, 厡 *yūan*², Phonetic, a spring. It is represented as gushing out from a hillside 厂 *han*⁴, or a projecting cliff. The little dot at the top of 㕕 *ch'üan*², and the short horizontal line are the springs and the other lines are the rills which are fed by them, (See W. 125 F). 頁 *yêh*⁴ is here used to represent the brain or the soul ; that which issues from the soul are desires and aspirations.

**654** 將

*chiang*¹·⁴, To take, to hold.

寸 彐 *ts'un*⁴, Radical No. 41, an inch ; archaic meaning, a hand.

㸚, 牆, 牆 *chiang*⁴, Phonetic, three archaic forms of the character under consideration show its development. The first one is a meat-block and meat. The second is the same plus salt and the last is the first plus the pickle or brine 酉 for preserving the meat. The modern character is the first of this series plus 寸 *ts'un*⁴, the hand which takes the meat and places it upon the meat-block. (W. 127, B).

**655** 待

*tai*⁴, To treat, to wait for.

彳 *ch'ih*⁴, Radical No. 60, a step. (See No. 78).

寺, 峕 *ssŭ*⁴, Phonetic, a court, a place where the law 寸 rule is constantly 㞢 (continually as the growth of a plant), applied. (See No. 125). This phonetic has no phonetic value, but it sets forth the way one should treat others, viz ; constantly according to propriety. The radical is not particularly appropriate, but it serves to distinguish the character from others which have the same phonetic. Characters which have this radical generally indicate action.

**656** 刑,荆     *hsing²*, To punish, punishment.

刂,刀,𠃌     *tao¹*, Radical No. 18, a knife. A pictorial representation of the instrument.

幵,开     *ch'ien¹* Phonetic, balanced scale pans. The seal writing represents the two objects as being even. This was not the original phonetic, 井 *ching³*, a well is the archaic writing and this accounts for the pronunciation. The well, was in the centre of a plot of ground divided into nine squares and farmed by eight families, the central square was farmed for the state by the joint labor of the eight families. The well being in the centre, was where all public functions were attended to. The knife indicates that punishment, generally decapitation, was inflicted.

**657** 罰     *fa²*, To fine, to punish, punishment.

罒,网     w*ang³*, Radical No. 122, a net. (See No. 38). There was a mistake made in putting this character under 网 *wang³*, as it destroys the phonetic which was 詈 *li⁴*, to blame or accuse one 言 with a fault and thus, entangle 网 *wang³*, them. To this is added the knife which is an instrument of torture.

658 迷    *mi²*, To deceive, to delude, to lead or go astray.

辶 *cho¹* Radical No. 162, stopping and starting. (See No. 10).

米 *mi³*, Phonetic, rice. (See No. 47). There is a still older writing than that referred to in No. 47. This depicts nine grains of rice ⁖ without any lines dividing them; as they are identical in appearance it would be impossible to keep track of any one grain if their position were disturbed. It may be that this was the reason why rice was adopted as the phonetic of this character.

659 惑

*huo⁴*, To doubt, to mislead.

心 *hsin¹*, Radical No. 61, the heart. (See No. 18).

或 *huo⁴*, Phonetic, an appanage, or feudal holding (archaic meaning). (See No. 70). As these appanages had no boundary there must have been continual strife between barons of contiguous regions, as one could never be sure on whose territory he was when nearing the imaginary boundaries. Add heart to this phonetic and we have a good symbol for " to doubt."

660 望, 望

*wang⁴*, The full moon; to expect, to hope, to look toward.

月 *yüeh⁴*, Radical No. 74, the moon. (See No. 43).

望, 望 *wang⁴* Phonetic, (abbreviated), a solemn imperial audience. The explanation of this phonetic is that the minister 臣 *ch'en²*, when in the presence 壬 of the sovereign, received light from him as the moon 卪

receives light from the sun. The 臣 *ch'en*[2] is deleted and 亡 **wang**[2], destroyed or ruined, is substituted. This is a very old character and the absence of the radical does not leave a definite phonetic; this is because the character was in use before the principle of radical and phonetic was adopted. (W. 81 G).

**661** 悆, 忌    *chi*[2], Anxious, hurried, urgent.

心 *hsin*[1], Radical No. 61, the heart. (See No. 18).

及, 戽 *chi.*[2], Phonetic, to catch up with. (See No. 324).

This phonetic indicates a person running after another and laying hold of him; a situation requiring haste; and with the addition of the radical for heart we have the feelings of the pursuer set forth, he is fearful lest he will not be able to overtake his man.

**662** 歇    *hsieh*[1], To rest, to stop.

欠 *ch'ien*[4], Radical No. 76, to owe, to lack; archaic meaning, to exhale, to breathe. (See No. 273).

曷 *ho*[2] Phonetic, why? (See No. 271). There is an old reading of this character 歇 as "*ho*[2]," but that is now obsolete. The etymology is: — why not stop for a breathing spell?

**663** 甜    *t'ien*[2], Sweet, pleasant.

甘 *kan*[1], Radical No. 99, sweet. (See No. 23).

舌 *she*[2], Phonetic, the tongue. (See No. 73

This phonetic has no phonetic significance. The old writing of this character was 甛. The present writing conveys the idea of sweet owing to the adoption of the above radical, viz., that which is sweet 甘 to the tongue, 舌.

**664** 酸, 醆    *suan¹*, Sour, acid, grieved.

酉   *yu³*, Radical No. 164, wine. (See No. 589).

夋, �   *tsun¹*, Phonetic, to walk slowly. This is composed of 以 厶 *i³*, the exhalation of the breath and 儿 尺 *jên²*, man = 允 㽞 *yun³*, to consent; and 夂 又 *sui¹*, to walk slowly. It is probable that the acid was obtained by a process of fermentation and as this is a slow, steadily advancing condition, the present phonetic is appropriate.

**665** 抹    *mo³*, To smear, to rub over, to wipe.

扌, 手   *shou³*, Radical No. 64, the hand. (See No. 53).

末, 朮   *mo⁴*, Phonetic, the tips of the branches of a tree. The horizontal line indicates the part of the tree referred to just as in the character 本 *pên³*, root; the lower horizontal line does the same. With the addition of hand, which generally indicates motion, the character for rubbing 抹 is formed.

**666** 搶    *ch'iang³*, To take openly by force, to snatch or grab.

扌, 手   *shou³*, Radical No. 64, the hand. (See No. 53).

倉, 倉   *ts'ang¹*, Phonetic, a granary. This is a contraction of 食 *shih²*, food. (See No. 75).

The lower part is deleted to make room for 口 *wei²*, the store-room for grain. The granary was the most important asset which the farmer possessed, it was his money, it was his very life, therefore he used all diligence in guarding it. When the radical for hand is added it implies the hand of a forager or robber removing the grain by force.

667 接     *ch'eh¹*, To receive, to meet, to accept.

扌,手   *shou³*, Radical No. 64, the hand. (See No. 53).

妾,薵   *ch'ieh⁴*, Phonetic, the daughter of a culprit. (Archaic). The modern meaning of this phonetic is, a concubine. This is composed of 干 *kan¹*, fault, crime, against a superior 上 二 *shang⁴*, and 女 虔 *nü³* a girl or daughter. Children of offenders were appropriated by officials. With the addition of hand this was first used for the taking of a concubine from among the daughters of the vanquished but it now has no restrictions and simply means, to take, or receive.

668 簾     *lien²*, A screen.

   *chu²*, Radical No. 118, bamboo. (See No. 7).

廉,廫   *lien²*, Phonetic, the roof and wall of a house, frugal. (W. 121 K). From 广 广 *yen³*, a roof or shelter, and 兼 蒹 *chien¹*, stalks of grain held together by a hand, corn stalks bound together to form a wall. When the radical for bamboo is added to this phonetic it indicates the screens which are made of bamboo, split into strips about the size of straw and woven together.

**669** 忽, 㣺

*hu¹*, Suddenly, all at once.

心 *hsin*, Radical No. 61, the heart. (See No. 18).

勿, 勿 *wu⁴*, Phonetic, a flag of three pennons attached to a staff. Used to signal a negative reply. When the heart is added it indicates that the action was not intentional but instinctive, sudden. (W. 101 A).

**670** Y, Y

*ya¹*, A slave girl.

亅 *kou¹* Radical No. 6, a barb.

There is no phonetic to this character owing to its being an old symbol which cannot be broken up. Some take it to be a forked stick ; others think it was an abbreviation of 木 朩 *mu⁴*, wood. Slave girls wear their hair in two tufts, wrapped with a cord, which stand up from the head and, with the body, resemble the character Y *ya¹*, therefore a slave girl is called Y頭 *ya¹ t'ou²*.

**671** 吩

*fên¹*, To mete out words, to give a command.

口 *k'ou³*, Radical No. 30, the mouth.

分, 𠛐 *fên¹*, Phonetic, to divide. (See No. 181).

As this Phonetic is frequently used with 給 *kei³*, to give, the phonetic itself seems to infer giving, after the division is made ; therefore 口 *k'ou³*, the mouth, in combination with 分 *fên¹* implies the separation of an order from ordinary speech and giving the same to the person addressed.

**672** 咐

*fu⁴*, To give a command.

口 *k'ou³*, Radical No. 30, the mouth.

付,阝 *fu⁴*, Phonetic, to give. This represents two men, the one on the right is only the hand of a man 寸 giving something, (the article is not pictured), to the man 人 on the left. When 口 *k'ou³*, the mouth, is added it indicates the giving of a command.

---

### BALLER, LESSON XXV.

⁶⁷³印, 𥃲, 㠯 *yin⁴*, To print; to stamp, an official seal, a stamp.

卩 *chieh²*, Radical No. 26, a joint or seal. (See No. 42).

爪, 爫 *chao³*, Phonetic, the right hand. This is a pictorial representation of the right hand, palm down and resting on the tips of the fingers. This is an old character and the phonetic has no value as such, but it indicates a hand pressing a seal. It also may indicate the use of the imprint of finger-marks as a seal. The Chinese have long used finger-prints on bank notes. With the addition of a joint, or seal we have the character for the latter.

⁶⁷⁴灰 *hui¹*, Ashes, dust, lime.

火, 灬 *huo³*, Radical No. 86, fire. A pictorial representation of a flame of fire in the old writing.

ナ, 又, 彐 *yu⁴*, Phonetic, the right hand, (Archaic). It has no phonetic significance. This combination was first used for ashes; the product of fire which can be handled. Limestone is burned and converted into lime and this can be handled, but it is said to contain fire which is apparent when brought in contact with water.

**675** 幫帮　*pang*[1], To help, a class, a guild.

巾,巾　*chin*[1], Radical No. 50, a cloth, a kerchief. (See No. 143).

邦,㗗　*pang*[1], Phonetic, a fief, a region, a country. The 丰 *feng*[1], is a primitive representing a leafy bough. The 阝 邑 *i*[4] a city, the upper part is the official residence and the lower part is the seal which is kept in the official residence. The 丰 represents the wooded tracts surrounding the official residence. The oldest writing of this character was with 帛 *po*[4], silk, wealth. From 白 *pai*[2], white and 巾 *chin*[1], a cloth, a kerchief, or rolls of silk which are still used as legal tender in Mongolia. Thus the help which the emperor recognized was the financial aid received from his nobles.

**676** 忙　*mang*[2], Hurried, in haste, busy.

忄,心　*hsin*[1], Radical No. 61, the heart, (See No. 18).

亡,亾　*wang*[2], Phonetic, to hide, lost, to die. (See No. 123).

To lose ones senses because of pressure of duties is the etymology. This would be sufficient to enable one to remember the composition of the character were it not for 忘 *wang*[4], to forget, being made up of the same radical and phonetic; in the case of "hurried," 忙 the heart is at the side and it may aid in recalling the position of the radical if we recall the expression :—

" Hurried until he is beside himself." In case of to forget :—忘 " That has dropped entirely out of mind." The heart has dropped to the bottom of the character.

**677** 助

力, 另 　chu⁴, To aid, to help.

且, 且 　li⁴, Radical No. 19, strength. (See No. 212).

tsu³ ch'ieh³ Phonetic, a small stand used at sacrifices (archaic) ; moreover, also.

The lower stroke is the ground, the two parallel strokes above are rungs. In the sacrifices for the dead the apparent idea is to do a favor to the departed, to aid them, but this requires utensils 且 tsu³ and 力 li⁴ strength in order to perform the ceremonies according to prescribed rules.

**678** 畫

田 　hua⁴, A drawing, a picture.

t'ien², Radical No. 102, a field. A pictorial representation of a field.

聿, 聿 　yü⁴ Phonetic, to trace lines, to draw. (See No. 7). The radical and phonetic do not compose the whole character in this instance as formerly the 田 t'ien² was inclosed with a 囗 wei², but this has been reduced to one stroke and that is at the bottom of the character. This phonetic has no phonetic value, it indicates how drawing is accomplished, by showing a pencil tracing the boundaries of a field.

**679** 賤

貝 　chien⁴, Cheap, mean, worthless.

戔 　pei⁴, Radical No. 154, precious. (See No. 38). chien¹, Phonetic, to destroy, narrow, small. (See No. 13). This phonetic is generally

attached to characters which have the idea
of small or mean; in this instance the
meaning is cheap, mean, worthless. The
radical, here, with the phonetic can be
interpreted :—the value is insignificant.

**680 鎖**

so³, A lock, to lock.

金 chin¹, Radical No. 167, gold, metal. (See No.
13).

貨, 貧 so³ Phonetic, a small 小 object not larger than
a cowrie, 貝 pei⁴. These small shells were
also used as money. With the addition
of the radical, metal,. the combination is
used to represent a lock, a small metal object, round like a cowrie. It is a safe pre-
caution to keep money under lock and key.

**681 飽**

pao³, To eat to the full, satiated.

食 shih², Radical No. 184, to eat, food. (See No.
75).

包 pao¹, Phonetic, to wrap up. (See No. 327).
When one has over eaten he realizes the
aptness of this combination, the stomach
feels as if it had difficulty in surrounding .
its contents.

**682 功**

kung¹, Merit, efficacy, good results.

力 li⁴, Radical No. 19, strength. (See No. 212).

工 kung¹, Phonetic, labor. (See No. 89).
This is not a bad combination to fulfill the
idea of efficiency; one must work and
exercise all the energy available in order
to be efficient.

**683 勞**

lao², To toil, to suffer, weary.

力 li⁴, Radical No. 19, strength. (See No. 212).

熒 *ying²*, Phonetic, the light of many lamps in a ⌐ *mi²*, a house. (W. 126 F). There is but little phonetic value in this symbol, but there is much significance as to the meaning of 勞 to toil; to labor through the night with artificial light. This phonetic loses the 火 at the bottom to give place to the radical.

684 鼓, 尌 *ku⁴*, A drum, to drum, to arouse; it is radical No. 207; bulging. A drum 壴 *chou¹*, beaten by a hand holding a stick 攴 *p'u¹*. The lower part of *chou¹* is not 豆 *tou⁴*, as one might think, it is a drum placed on a stand. The straight line above the drum is the skin and all above this line is supposed to be ornaments. (W. 165 C). Written 皷 the radical is 皮 skin.

685 傘, 䈉, 傘 *san³*, An umbrella, a parasol.
人 *jên²*, Radical No. 9, a man. This radical was arbitrarily given as it has nothing to do with the original character, which was a pictorial representation of an umbrella. The archaic writing sets this forth very satisfactorily. See Chalfant, Plate XIV.

686 腫 *chung³*, To swell, a swelling.
月, 肉 *jou⁴*, Radical No. 130, meat. (See No. 133).
重 *chung⁴*, Phonetic, heavy. (See No. 22). This phonetic also conveys the idea of being large and consequently is a satisfactory combination for a swelling.

687 吵 *ch'ao³*, To quarrel, to dispute.
口 *k'ou³*, Radical No. 30, the mouth.

少 *shao³*, Phonetic, small. (See No. 176). Small, mean talk is a very proper definition of to quarrel.

**688** 鬧

門,㘞 *nao⁴*, To make a disturbance, bustle, noise.
*tou⁴*, Radical No. 191, to fight, to grapple with an antagonist. This radical is made up of two 丸斗 *chü²*, to lay hold of, to seize. (W. 11 H). (See No. 139).

市 *shih⁴*, Phonetic, a market. (See No. 256). The market place is where each man is alert to his own interests and altercations which lead to disturbances are not uncommon. This symbol has no phonetic value but it does aid in explaining the meaning of the combination.

**689** 雜,儳,雑 *tsa²*, Mixed, confused.

隹 *chui¹*, Radical No. 172, a short-tailed bird. (See No. 21). In giving this character a radical the phonetic was destroyed; 集 *chi²*, in the old writing is 雧 a flock of birds on a tree, a collection or a coming together. 集 is the logical phonetic and the radical should be 衣 *i¹*, clothing; but the latter is written in an unusual form and consequently the above radical was adopted. A garment made of odds and ends of cloth, thus the idea of mixed or confused is set forth.

**690** 姐

*chieh³*, Elder sister.

女 *nü³*, Radical No. 38, a woman. (See No. 16).
且,且 *ch'ieh³*, Phonetic, a square bench. It resembles a chair without a back. This is a very

common article of furniture. Women were regarded more or less as chattels and the make up of this character was not regarded as humiliating.

**691 妹**

女 未

*mei⁴*, A younger sister.

女 *nü³*, Radical No. 38, a woman. (See No. 16).

未 *wei⁴*, Phonetic, not yet; a tree in full leaf and branch, but probably not of large size. (See No. 524). With the addition of the radical for girl or woman the character for younger sister is formed.

**692 賽**

寒, 窵

*sai⁴*, To contest, to rival.

貝 *pei⁴*, Radical No. 154, precious (See No. 38).

寒, 窵 *sai¹*, Phonetic, to wall in, to shut up, to cork. An empty space ᐧ ᐱ, is filled with bricks, 工 *kung¹*, by the 𐅂 hands of the workmen (W. 47 T). When 貝 *pei⁴*, a reward, is added, it gives the idea of competition to the labor; the one who works best is rewarded.

**693 遣**

辶, 辵

畳, 甞

*ch'ien³*, To depute, to send.

辶, 辵 *cho⁴* Radical No. 162, to run fast and stop, to go. (See No. 10).

畳, 甞 *ch'ien³* Phonetic, to carry earth in a 臾 *k'ui⁴*, basket, for erecting a wall, 𠂤 (W. 111 C). This being an important undertaking, an officer was deputed who had charge of the construction. The sending of a person to have charge is implied when the radical 辶 *cho⁴* is added to the phonetic.

**694 豫**

*yü⁴*, Prepared before hand, already.

豕 *shih³* Radical No. 152, a pig. (See No. 221).

予, 予 *yü²* Phonetic, to pass from one hand to another, to hand down, to give; I, me. (W. 95 A). The seal writing depicts one hand giving to another. This may be just a repetition of the act of passing from one hand to another, as a person, at times, will do unconsciously, when the mind is occupied. Add the radical plus the part which makes it an elephant 象 and we have a symbol which is suggestive of the archaic meaning, viz., excursions back and forth, indecision. A caged elephant goes from one side of the cage to the other for hours without stopping. He is all ready to escape at the first opportunity.

**695 備**

*pei⁴*, Complete, to prepare.

人, 亻 *jên²*, Radical No. 9, a man.

蒲, 葡 *pei⁴* Phonetic, to prepare, to make ready. This is composed of 敬 尚 *ching⁴*, deferential behaviour, (See No. 407) contracted, the 口 being replaced by 用 *yung⁴*. The *ching* 丬 indicates how the preparation is to be made, viz., with decorum, and 用 indicates that what is prepared is wanted for use. (W. 54 G). This phonetic was originally used for the preparation of the household necessities by the women. It has had many different writings. The addition of the radical is modern.

**696 曠**

*k'uang⁴*, Waste, wilds, desert.

日 *jih⁴*, Radical No. 72, the sun (See No. 12).

廣 *kuang³*, Phonetic, broad, enlarged, a large hall. From 广 *yên³*, a covering, a shelter; and 黃 *huang²*, yellow, the hue of loess. (See No. 207).

A yellow or imperial house is naturally made large, spacious. (W. 171 A). It is evident that 黃 *huang²* was originally used as a synonym of earth or soil, and thus 廣 *kuang³*, a hall, resembles 堂 *t'ang²*, a hall (See No. 408), as they both are used for holding large assemblies and both have the earth as the floor. *Kuang³* is not now used for a hall, as *t'ang²* fulfills all the requirements, and 廣 *kuang³* is used for broad. When the sun is added it is the symbol for a desert or barren waste. A hall, notwithstanding it has the earth for a floor, is non-productive; and 曠 *k'uang⁴* is a large, barren tract of earth with the sky for a covering and the sun the only occupant.

697 野 *yêh³*, A waste, a desert, savage, rude, wild, rustic.

里,里 *li³*, Radical No. 166, cultivated fields. (See No. 82).

予,予 *yü²* Phonetic, To pass something from one hand to the other, to hand over. (See No. 694). There is a reading of 野 which is *yü²*, but it is archaic. 段氏說文 Tuan Shih Shuo Wen has a good description of this character 邑外謂之郊 郊外謂之牧, 牧外謂之野. " Beyond the limits of the city it is called 郊 *chiao¹*; beyond the limits of the *chiao*[1] it is called pasture, 牧 *mu*[4] ; beyond the pasture it is called 野 *yêh*[3]." A pasture region was not maintained in all cases outside the limits of the *chiao*[1], and in such cases the *yeh*[3] was immediately beyond the limits of the *chiao*[1]. The 郊 *chiao*[1] was where intercourse 交 *chiao*[1], with the barbarians was held. They were not allowed inside the 邑 *i*[4] lest they should learn of its vulnerable points and thus attack the stronghold. This character was originally written 壄 indicating that it was covered with forests. After the forests were cleared off the composition was changed to the present form, which is 土 *t'u*[3] land for fields 田 *t'ien*[2]. During the feudal times the 野 *yêh*[3] was given into the charge of the military to manage, and timber, grain and straw were demanded as taxes. There were three grades of grain tax, one for farming land, one for buildings and another for living in the district in idleness. The 予 *yü*[2] indicates that the squatters or occupants handed over to the proper authorities the taxes or a rent.

698 施, 㪫  *shih*[1], To bestow.

方 *fang*[1], Radical, No. 70, square (See No. 503).

This radical has been given to the character because the original classifier is not among the modern radicals and it is now written 𣃘 *yên*[3], the old form is 㫃. It is a banyan tree with branches hanging down and striking root, 入. As this tree has many of these accessory trunks it is here used as a symbol for many. (W. 117 B).

也, 它 *yêh*³, Phonetic, also. (Archaic, a drinking vessel.) This combination indicates a pouring out 也 at frequent intervals 尥 as wine. at a feast; or something freely given, 施. (W. 107, B).

**699 悔**

*hui*³, To repent, to regret.

忄, 心 *hsin*¹, Radical No. 61, the heart (See No. 18).

每, 莽 *mei*³, Phonetic, each, every, many. (See No. 269). The combination of radical and phonetic implies that mistakes or crimes are committed through thoughtlessness and when one repents it is because his heart swarms 每 *mei*³ (archaic meaning) with the thoughts of his misconduct and causes him regret.

**700 改**

*kai*³, To change, to alter, to correct, another.

攴 *p'u*¹ Radical No. 66, to tap, to rap (See No. 17).

己 *i*³ Phonetic, exhalation of breath. As exhalation is immediately followed by inhalation, this symbol was adopted as appropriate for, "to change."
(W. 85 B and No. 191.)

**701 駱**

*lo*⁴, A camel.

馬 *ma*³, Radical No. 187, a horse (See No. 261).

各 *ko*⁴, Phonetic, to go on one's way without heeding others. (See No. 272).

The camel is a beast of burden for which 馬 *ma*³ is a generic symbol. The camel moves along the road apparently oblivious to his surroundings ; thus the combination is a happy one.

**702 駝**

*t'o*², A camel; to bear on the back, (of an animal).

馬 *ma*³, Radical No. 187, a horse (See No. 261).

它, 它 *t'o*² Phonetic, another. Archaic meaning, a cobra, or snake that raises its head from its coil, enlarges its neck and darts out its tongue, (W. 108 A). The head of this reptile being large attracted attention, as it seemed more than the body could support. Many of the characters which use this as a phonetic have the meaning of to bear or sustain. The camel is generally used as a pack animal.

**703 腰**

*yao*¹, The loins, the waist.

月, 肉 *jou*⁴, Radical No. 130, meat, (See No. 133).

要 *yao*⁴, Phonetic, to want, to need. Archaic, the loins, the waist. (See No. 16). Because the original meaning was usurped by its present meaning, in order to make a character for the waist the radical for flesh was added.

**704 蟲**

*ch'ung*², An insect, a reptile (See No. 232).

虫 ℘ *ch'ung*² Radical No. 142, a worm, a snake, probably the cobra.

蚰 *k'un*¹, Phonetic, insects that are numerous at certain seasons of the year, such as flies, lice, locusts, mosquitoes and silk worms. (W. 110 C). This phonetic is more of a classifier than a phonetic and when the radical is added the character takes the sound of the radical.

The multiplication of one symbol indicates that the character is used for something which occurs in swarms or great numbers.

705 蜜     $mi^4$, Honey.

虫 $ch'ung^2$ Radical No. 142. An insect, a worm. (See No. 232).

宓 $mi^4$, Phonetic, quiet, close, still, silent, secret. From 宀 $mien^2$, a sheltered place, and 必 $pi^4$ (See No. 504). When one is in a dilemma, or has to decide (戈 shoot) between two, (八 $pa^1$ to divide), modes of action, a quiet or secret place is desirable. Both these qualities are included in the phonetic. When 虫 $ch'ung^2$, here used for a bee, is added we have the character for honey. The bees make their honey in the darkness of a hollow tree or other secret place.

706 彎     $wan^1$, To draw a bow, bent, curved.

弓 $kung^1$, Radical No. 57, a bow (See No. 55).

龻 蠻 戀 $luan^4$ Phonetic, to adjust, to quarrel. The oldest writing represents a hand 爪 disentangling three threads 龻; their lower ends were contracted into 十 $shih^2$, ten. A later writing has 言 $yen^2$, word, taking the place of the middle thread, as the untangling of thread, it done in common, often leads to impatient words and reciprocal fault finding; thus the meaning of quarreling was developed. (W. 92 D).

In shooting an arrow the bending of the bow is very marked and so 弓 *kung*[1] is a fitting radical for the character meaning, bent, curved 彎.

**707** 解, 觧
角, 肏

*chieh*[3], To loosen, to explain, to open, to untie.

*chiao*[3], Radical No. 148, a horn. (See No. 250)

𧢲 The phonetic of this character is made up of two radicals which do not occur together in any other character and consequently it has no pronunciation. 長箋 說文 gives the following explanation, 從刀判牛角 "Dividing a cow's horn with a knife." Horn is put to a number of uses and this has been true for thousands of years. A horn being hard it was a difficult operation to divide it; thus a symbol which represents dividing a horn is used as the symbol for to open. A bodkin, 刀, made from the horn, 角 of an ox, 牛, and used to untie 解 knots.

**708** 配
酉, 酉
妃

*p'ei*[4], A mate, to pair, marriage.

*yu*[3], Radical No. 164, a jug for holding wine.

*fei*[1], Phonetic, imperial concubine. A woman 女 belonging to oneself 已. Contracted to 已 *chi*[3]. This combination of radical and phonetic was used for the wine 酉 *yu*[3] drunk at a wedding feast 妃 (contracted), and eventually it assumed the meaning of mate or pair. (W. 84 A).

**709** 利    *li*[4], Gain, interest profit, acute. Archaic, to cut grain.

刀, 刂   *tao*[1], Radical, No. 18, a knife, a reaping hook. (See No. 37).

禾, 禾   *ho*[2], Phonetic, standing grain. (See No. 556). In order to secure the benefits 利 *li*[4], from the ripened grain it was necessary to reap it, in other words to cut 刀 the stalks 禾.

**710** 勒    *le,*[1, 2, 4], *lei*[4], To bridle, to curb, to restrain, to force.

力   *li*[4], Radical, No. 19, strength, force. (See No. 212).

革, 革, 革   *ko*[2], Phonetic, hides, skins with the hair on. (See No. 163). Leather or rawhide is exceedingly strong, and with the addition of 力 *li*[4], strength, a good symbol for to curb or restrain is formed.

**711** 裂    *lieh*, To crack, to split, to rip open.

衣   *i*, Radical No. 145, clothing. (See No. 51).

列   *lieh*[4], Phonetic, to divide, seriatim. The original writing of this phonetic was 剡 剹, a river, 巛, *ch'uan*[1] (See No. 598) which on account of breaking its banks has caused great destruction 歹 *tai*[3], by cutting 刀, 刂, new channels through the fields. 歹 *tai*[3] is 𣥠 or 歺 in seal writing; these are the human bones as they are found after the flesh has decayed; a symbol of misfortune. Rivers have been the cause of much misfortune in China by their forming new channels.

The addition of the radical 衣 *i*[1], formed a character which originally meant the remnants of cloth left after a garment was cut out ; another old meaning was the sound of the tearing of cloth ; but it is now used only for the meaning given above.

**712 彷**

彳 *ch'ih*[4], Radical No. 60, to step with the left foot.

口.屶.兓.方 *fang*[1] Phonetic, square. (See No. 503).

This seems to be a simple phonetic, but the Shuo Wen says that the symbol is composed of two boats tied together forming a square, therefore the boats must have been similar in shape and size, thus they resembled each other. The radical 彳 may have been selected because a step with the left foot is naturally succeeded by one like it with the right foot.

**713 彿**

彳 *ch'ih*[4] Radical No. 60, a step with the left foot. (See No. 78).

弗.弗 *fu*[4] Phonetic, (See No. 554).

This phonetic may have been selected as the two rods or bows which are tied together are of equal strength and thus neutralize each other, consequently they are similar or alike. For the use of the radical see No. 712.

**714 鴿**

鳥 *niao*[3], Radical No. 196, a bird. (See No. 628).

合 *ho*[2], Phonetic, harmony, agreement. (See No.

103). The fact that doves are not quarrelsome caused the selection of this phonetic.

**715** 催

*ts'ui*[1], To urge, to hasten.

人 *jên*[2], Radical No. 9, a man.

崔 *ts'ui*[1], Phonetic, very high, a high mountain ; a surname. This phonetic is made up of 山 shan, a mountain, and 隹 *chui*[1], a short-tailed bird. Grouse do not live on the low hills but are found on the higher hills and mountains, as they there find more seclusion and shelter. The addition of the radical for man may have been suggested by the energy required if one wishes to follow a flock of rock grouse up a mountain ; if this is tried the appropriateness of the composition of 催 is never again questioned.

**716** 獸

*shou*[4], An animal, a brute.

犬, 犭 *ch'üan*[3] Radical No. 94, a dog, a pictorial representation of the animal. (See No. 424).

嘼, 獸 *shou*[4] Phonetic, the domestic animals distinguished from 禽 *ch'in*[1], wild animals. The domestic animals were 馬 *ma*[3], 牛 *niu*[2], 羊 *yang*[2], 鷄 *chi*[1], 犬 *ch'üan*[3] 豕 *shih*[3], the horse, cow, sheep, chicken, dog and pig. The archaic writing depicts two ears, then the head and below are the hind legs and a tail. (W. 23. I) This symbol was sufficient to convey the idea of domestic animal but when the radical for dog is added it means wild animals chased by dogs. The pictorial effect is unfortunately entirely lost in the modern writing.

**717** 伺

伊, 人　*jên²*, Radical No. 9, a man.

司, 司　*szŭ⁴*, To wait upon, to examine, to spy.

*szŭ¹*, Phonetic, to manage. This is 后 *hou⁴*, (a man 尸 who orders 口, a prince, and by extension, a princess) reversed to indicate the subordinate or servant who receives orders. It is the imprint of the prince. The prince has informed his minister of his desire, impressed or imprinted his ideas on him, and the latter puts them into execution. When the radical for man is added the character represents the superior 亻 with his attendant 司 who waits upon him.

**718** 烈

巛, 火　*huo³*, Radical No. 86, fire. (See No. 482).

列　*lieh⁴*, Burning, fiery, virtuous.

*lieh⁴*, Phonetic, to arrange in order (See No. 711). With the radical 火 we have the fierceness of fire added to floods.

**719** 網

糸　*mi⁴ ssŭ¹* Radical No. 120, silk. (See No. 8).

罔　*wang³*, A net.

*wang³*, Phonetic, a net, to capture with a net. The idea of capturing or taking is set forth by 亡 *wang²*, to destroy, (See No. 123). Owing to the 网 *wang³* being written in an abbreviated form, the radical for silk is placed at the side.

**720** 稍

*shao¹*, A little, to diminish.

禾 *ho²*, Radical No. 115, standing grain. (See No. 556).

肖 *hsiao⁴* Phonetic, like, similar. The archaic meaning was, to be like one's father, not a degenerate. The idea of small is attached to this phonetic as the child is smaller than the parent. A small piece of the father's flesh. " A chip off the old block." When 禾 *ho²*, a stalk of grain, a very small thing, is added the character stands for the above.

**721** 雅

*ya³*, Elegant, decorous, polished, cultured.

隹 *chui¹* Radical, No. 172, a short-tailed bird. (See No. 21).

牙 *ya²*, Phonetic, a tooth. (See No. 97).

There is evidence that this character was originally written 雅 but 互 *hu⁴*, reciprocal, being very similar to 牙 *ya²*, the latter has entirely supplanted the old form and 牙 *ya²*, has the advantage of being a perfect phonetic but, devoid of any suggestion of elegance, 互 *hu⁴*, conveys the ideas of satisfaction. A person who is reciprocal is courteous and is generally in high favor.

**722** 招

*chao¹*, To beckon, to call, to proclaim.

扌,手 *shou³*, Radical No. 64, the hand. (See No. 53).

召 *chao⁴*, Phonetic, to summon, to call. The archaic meaning was to criticise,—to use the mouth as a knife 刀. With the addition of the radical 手 it has the meaning of to beckon 招, as the hand is used in that act. This is a term used in summoning a person to appear at court.

**723** 呼

*hu*[1, 2], To call, to expel the breath.

口 *k'ou*[3], Radical No. 30, the mouth.

乎, 兮 *hu*[1, 2] Phonetic, an exclamation; an interrogative, a sigh; a sound which is uttered after the completion of a sentence. The 兮 *ch'iao*[3] is the breath meeting with an obstruction. The 八 is composed of ノ *p'ieh*[1], a sign of action and 八 *pa*[1], to disperse or scatter. The obstruction is overcome. The difference between impeded respiration and unimpeded, is taken as a symbol for wonderful. (See No. 258, 853). The radical for mouth is added to indicate a call.

**724** 息, 憩

*hsi*[4], To produce interest, to stop, a full breath, respiration.

心 *hsin*[1], Radical No. 61, the heart. (See No. 18).

自 *tzŭ*[4], Phonetic, self, the nose (See No. 104). The Chinese believe that during a full breath the 氣 *ch'i*[4] of the heart is expelled when the outside air is brought in through the nose 自 and goes to the heart 心. As breathing is necessary for the maintenance of life, the meaning was extended to interest on a loan, a requirement necessary for the continuance of the loan.

**725** 訓

*hsün*[4], To instruct, to teach, to exhort, to persuade.

言 *yên*[2], Radical No. 149, a word. (See No. 10).

川 *ch'uan*[1], Phonetic, a river. (See No. 598). Instruction should be continuous as the flow of a river, a continual flow of words. " For it is precept upon precept, precept upon precept ; line upon line, line upon line ; here a little, there a little."

**726 權**

ch'üan², Authority, power ; the pee of a steel-yard.

**木** mu⁴, Radical No. 75, wood. (See No. 22).

**雚, 霍** kuan⁴ Phonetic, the heron. (See No. 428, 511).

At first glance it is difficult to understand why 雚 is used as the phonetic of this character, but a study of the characters which use this phonetic, plus the habits of the bird as set forth in 桂氏, Kuei Shih Shuo Wen, aid in the understanding of its use. The heron is supposed to an-nounce by his call the approach of rain ; hence he is possessed of great intelligence. He stands by the hour in the water mo-tionless, watching for food ; when within reach, action is prompt and sure. His common name is 老等, " the old waiter," or " patient waiter." Probably the poised attitude suggested the use of this phonetic with wood 木, (the steelyard beam being made of wood), as a fitting symbol, for the pee on the steelyard. The string suspending the pee resembles the long neck and its shape is not unlike the body of the bird. The pee only indicates the weight when in precisely the correct posi-tion, thus it is just and unwavering. For these reasons, authority and ability to give a just decision, are given to this character by extension.

**727** 柄

*ping³*, Authority, a handle.

木 *mu¹*, Radical No. 75, wood (See No. 22).

丙 *ping³* Phonetic, the 3rd of the ten stems, referring to fire. (See No. 437).

Fire has authority over wood, hence the combination, to the Chinese mind, is suggestive of authority. Wood, in a sense, is the handle by which fire can secure a hold on the structure.

**728** 污浮汗

*wu¹*, Foul, unclean, stagnant water.

氵,水 *shui³*, Radical No. 85. (See No. 79).

夸 *k'ua¹*, Phonetic, to boast, to overpraise.

亐,亐,于 *yü²* Phonetic, the breath, 亐 having overcome an obstruction,—spreads in all directions. —It seems reasonable to think that this character was originally written 㳕 i.e. 杅 *yü²*, a basin, a tub, with the addition of water 氵; it is the symbol of water which has been used for washing.

**729** 附

*fu⁴*, To be near, to follow, to lean on, possessed by.

阝,阜 *fu⁴ fou⁴* Radical No. 170, a mound. (See No. 493).

付 *fu⁴*, Phonetic, to give. (See No. 672).

Tuan Shih 段氏 Shuo Wen explains this character more fully than the others. 阝阜 *fou⁴* is a mound or small hill. A foothill looks up to the mountain, a small state must do the same with reference to a large, powerful state, and is obliged to adopt the customs and usages of the latter and pay it tribute, 付.

**730**

*mieh*⁴, To put out (as a fire), to destroy, to exterminate.

氵,水 *shui*³, Radical No. 85, water (See No. 79).

威 *mieh*⁴ Phonetic, to extinguish or kill; 戌 *hsü*¹ to wound 一 *i*¹, with a halberd 戉 *yüeh*, and 火 fire. This phonetic was originally the full character, but later water was added to indicate the substance used to extinguish fire. (W. 71 P.)

**731** 責,責

*tse*², *chai*² To reprove, to punish, to lay a charge on; duty, to be responsible.

貝 *pei*⁴, Radical No. 154, valuable. (See No. 38).

主,束,朿 *tz'u*⁴ Phonetic, thorns. It represents a thorny tree. The modern writing entirely changes this phonetic so that no trace of thorns remains. There are two meanings of this character: 1. To reprove or to punish. The thorns 朿 *tz'u*⁴, indicate torture, and 貝 *pei*⁴ indicates a fine. 2. The care and worry, 朿 *tz'u*⁴, of property, 貝 *pei*⁴. The possession of property brings responsibility. (W. 120 H.)

**732** 抽

*ch'ou*¹, To draw out, to shrink, to levy.

扌,手 *shou*³, Radical No. 64, the hand. (See No. 53).

由,甶 *yu*², Phonetic, from, origin. The old writing represents a sprout which is drawing its strength and nourishment from the seed. There is another old writing of 抽 which has 畱 畱 *liu*², to keep, retain, for phonetic; when 扌 *shou*³ is added, 擂, the idea is that the hand is taking away a part, but something is still left, *liu*² 留, = 畱.

**733** 陣 邑

*chen*[4], To arrange, to form into ranks, a regiment of soldiers.

陳 陳 *ch'en*[2], To arrange, to state to a superior, old, stale.

陣 阝, 阜 *fu*[4] Radical, No. 170, an elevation. (See No. 493).

There are two phonetics in the old writings of this character. One is 申 邑 *shen*[1]. Chalfant regards this as a symbol for a thunderbolt, something terrible; the shock of their serried phalanx, the ancient warriors may have been pleased to liken to a thunderbolt. The other form is 東 東, not 東 *tung*[4], east, but two hands supporting or planting a tree. It seems to indicate the planting of trees on a hillside, perhaps a park. The present forms of the character seem to be a combination of these two old forms. (W 50 H.)

**734**  瘋

*feng*[1], Leprosy, scrofula, paralysis, insanity.

疒 *ni*[4] Radical No. 104, sickness. (See No. 593).

風 *feng*[1], Phonetic, wind.

The Chinese divided the wind into eight kinds, east, west, north, south, and northeast, etc. Some were regarded as having good and some as having bad influences. This is not an old character and is not described in the 說文, but leprosy or insanity was supposed to be caused by bad 疒 wind. Rabies in dogs is attributed to the evil influences of a certain kind of wind.

**735**  驚

*ching*[1], Terrified, alarmed.

馬 *ma³*, Radical, No. 187, a horse. (See No. 261).

敬 *ching⁴*, Phonetic, to reverence. (See No. 407).

The terror 敬 which a horse 馬 experiences in the presence of that which he regards as being more powerful than himself.

**736** 訝

*ya⁴*, To wonder at, admire, to take exceptions to.

言 *yen²*, Radical No. 149, a word. (See No. 10).

牙 *ya²*, Phonetic, a tooth. (See No. 97).

Tuan Shih 段氏 says that this character, originally written 迓, meant to meet, or receive a guest; when one meets a noted person there is a feeling of awe or fear. It now is used for surprised, or to wonder at.

**737** 徧

*pien⁴*; *p'ien⁴*, Everywhere.

彳 *ch'ih⁴* Radical No. 60, a footprint of the left foot, or a step with the left foot.

扁 *pien³*, Phonetic, flat; an inscription hung over the door. Kuei Shih's Shuo Wen 桂氏說文 explains this phonetic as the official register of the inhabitants of the Empire, 戶朋者. Therefore it must include all. With the addition of 彳 *ch'ih⁴*, to go, the idea of going to every house in the land is set forth.

**738** 躺

*t'ang³*, To lie down, to lie.

身 *shen¹*, Radical No. 158, the body. (See No. 291).

尚 *shang⁴*, Phonetic, a house. (See No. 52).

This is an unauthorized character and is not found in old dictionaries. The etymology of it is not difficult. When lying down 躺 persons desire a roof 尚 above them to protect their bodies 身 from heat, cold or storms.

**739 拉**

手 *la¹*, To draw, to pull, to lead.
手 *shou³*, Radical No. 64, the hand. (See No. 53).
立 *li⁴*, Phonetic, to set up, to rise, instantly. (See No. 216).

The old writing of this character was 拹 *la¹*, which indicated the putting forth of great strength, but as the three 力 *li⁴* characters were more difficult to write than 立 *li⁴*, to stand, the latter was substituted, and its use is explained thus: in exerting great strength in pulling one has to stop and take a firm stand.

**740 扶**

*fu²*, To uphold, to help.
手 *shou³*, Radical No. 64, the hand. (See No. 53).
夫 *fu¹*, Phonetic, a husband, a man. (See No. 234). Kuei Shih 桂氏說文 says 夫, 丈夫 議 a husband. The hand of the husband assists the wife and the meaning is now extended to any kind of assistance.

**741 退**

*t'ui⁴*, To retreat, to decline.
辶 *cho⁴* Radical, No. 162, action. (See No. 10).
艮,𣆅 *ts'ui⁴* Phonetic; to refuse, to retreat; to have walked with difficulty 夊 all day long ⊖, and refuse to go farther, or to go backward on account of the difficulties of advancing. This phonetic may have been suggested because the sun, each morning, slowly ascends until midday, when the indications are that it will continue to go

higher ; but at noon it starts to descend. With the addition of ⻌ it forms the character for to retreat. Compare No. 402, to advance.

**742** 聚, 𦐊

*chü*[4], To gather, to assemble.

耳 *er*[3], Radical, No. 128, the ear. (See No. 71).

取, 𦐆 *ch'ü*[3], Phonetic, to lay hands on, to take. (See No. 578). The oldest use of this phonetic was for the cutting off of the left ear of captives and presenting them to the officer in command ; this was evidence of the number of captives taken. The meaning gradually extended to the holding of persons and things in general. When three men 乑 *chung*[4] are added it is the symbol of an assembly brought together 又 by the desire of people to hear 耳 what is to be said ; thus the speaker, figuratively, holds his audience by the ear. This character is not composed of radical and phonetic as most characters are, as the radical is part of the phonetic and the three men are still unaccounted for, but their presence has a logical significance. (W. 27 K.)

**743** 集, 雧

*chi*[2], To assemble, to collect, a fair.

隹 *chui*[1] Radical No. 172, a short-tailed bird. (See No. 21).

木 *mu*[4], Phonetic, wood or tree. This character was originally written △ three lines coming together at the ends forming a triangle. It was afterwards supplanted by a tree with three birds on it, and later the number was reduced to one. (W. 14 A, 119 G).

**744** 伴

イ,人
牛

*pan⁴*, A comrade. to attend on.

*jên²*, Radical No. 9, a man.

*pan⁴*, Phonetic, half. (See No. 118).

When イ *jên²* is added to this phonetic the idea is set forth that two persons are usually seen together and are regarded as a pair and one is the half of the pair. A single man 人 is but half 牛 a |man. The usage is not limited to two persons, only ; it is applied to several persons whose vocation necessitates their being together.

**745** 追

辶 阜

*chui¹*, To pursue, to follow.

*cho⁴* Radical No. 162, to go, or to pursue. (See No. 10).

*tui¹*, Phonetic, a terrace, ramparts, a city. (See No. 310) With the addition of 辶 *cho⁴* the idea may have been to follow the person or enemy even down to his stronghold, to his ramparts. This phonetic is also used for troops which guard the city and thus this character is sometimes explained as the legion on the march pursuing an enemy. (W. 86 B).

**746** 鄰

邑, 阝
舜

*lin²*, Near, contiguous, neighbor.

*i⁴*, Radical No. 163, a city. (See No. 11).

*lin²* Phonetic, an ignis fatuus. (See No. 588). The reason for using this phonetic in the character for "near" is owing to the necessity of being within close proximity to an ignis fatuus before it is seen. A city which is not farther away than this light is visible must be close at hand.

**747**

*chieh²*, Pure, clean, neat, tidy.

水, 氵 *shui³*, Radical No. 85, water. (See No. 79).

絜 *chieh²* Phonetic, to adjust, to regulate.

Tuan Shih 叚氏 says that 㓞 *ch'i⁴* in this combination indicates the cutting of a bundle of hemp threads, thus making them of one length and the 糸 signifies that they are tied up into bundles after having been washed 氵 and cleansed.

**748** 嚴

*yên²*, Stern, majestic, strict, tight.

口 *k'ou³*, Radical No. 30, the mouth. (See No. 17).

厰, 嚴 *yên²* Phonetic, to lay hold of a person and force him to move forward. The modern writing is quite different from the original; that shows a hand striking 殳 *shu²* a bear 耳 厓 (as in 敢 *kan³* see No. 545) in a cave 厂 *yen³*, accompanied with great outcries 㗊 *hsüan¹*. The modern meaning emphasises the sternness of outcry, such as is heard in the court when the magistrate browbeats a witness. (W. 146 H).

**749** 囑

*chu³*, To order, to enjoin upon.

口 *k'ou³*, Radical No. 30, the mouth. (See No. 17).

屬, 屬 *shu²* Phonetic, a tail, an appendage. This is made up of 尾 *wei³*, tail, contracted, and 蜀 *shu³*, a silkworm in the process of spinning its thread ; as the worm is constantly moving during this operation, this part of the phonetic indicates motion. Thus the two parts indicate a tail which is constantly wagging. When 口 *k'ou*³ is added it seems to indicate a last injunction, an appendage or command added after the business has been talked through. For another meaning of 蜀 *shu*³ see No. 800.

**750 謹**

*chin*³, Watchful, respectful.

言 *yên*², Radical No. 149, words. (See No. 10).

堇,蓳 *chin*³ Phonetic, yellow, 黃 contracted and earth 土, potter's clay, loess. (W. 171 B.) When 言 *yen*² is added the idea may have been that one should be as careful and watchful as to what he says as a potter is in shaping the clay.

**751 慎**

*shên*⁴, Caution, attentive.

忄,心 *hsin*¹, Radical No. 61, the heart. (See No. 18).

眞 *chên*¹, Phonetic, true. (See No. 218). A true heart is cautious and attentive.

**752 摩**

*mo*¹ ², To feel, to rub with the hand, to caress.

手 *shou*³, Radical, No. 64, the hand. (See No. 53).

麻 *ma*², Phonetic, hemp. (See No. 24). Painters use wads of hemp for rubbing oil into wood and for painting.

It is probable that this character was formerly written 攠 as 磨 *mo*², to grind, and the character under consideration are sometimes interchanged. 摩 may have been first used as the symbol for rubbing the hands together, the hands acting as the upper and nether mill-stones 石 and gradually it was used for any kind of rubbing.

**753** 證

chêng⁴, Evidence, proof.

言 yên², Radical No. 149, word.  (See No. 10).

登 têng¹, Phonetic, to ascend.  (See No. 240 and 243).

This phonetic indicates climbing to a high platform and 證 is to proclaim, from a high platform, to publish abroad.

**754** 據

chü⁴, Evidence, according to.

手 shou³. Radical No. 64, the hand.  (See No. 53).

豦 chü⁴ Phonetic, wild boar, to fight, to struggle. A wild boar 豕, shih³, and a tiger 虎 hu³ fighting, and neither one letting go his grip on the other.  (W. 69 D.)  With the addition of hand the idea of holding firmly is set forth.  Evidence is that which a person affirms and holds without wavering in spite of any opposition.

**755** 揚

yang², To display, to publish ; to extend ; to winnow.

扌,手 shou³; Radical No. 64, the hand.  (See No. 53).

昜,昜 yang², Phonetic, to expand, glorious.  (See No. 541) The hand placed beside the phonetic indicates that something is exhibited in bright light in order that all may know and understand.

**756** 折

ch'ai¹, To break, to destroy.

扌,手 shou³, Radical No. 64, the hand.

斥,斥 ch'ih⁴, Phonetic, to attack.  (See No. 288) an abbreviation of 庐.  This means to attack, 並 i⁴ (it is 干 kan¹ doubled and means that it is repeated attacks) a man in his own house 广 yen³. When the hand is added it stands for to break or to destroy. (W. 102. D).

**757** 卧

臥 wo⁴, To lie down.

臣 ch'ên², Radical No. 131, a minister, a statesman. (See No. 120).

亻,人 jên², Phonetic, a man. The proper position for a man in the presence of an official was the prone posture, and the above symbol is used for, "to lie down." (W. 82 F).

**758** 褥

ju⁴, A mattress, a cushion.

衤,衣 i¹, Radical No. 145, clothing. (See No. 51).

辱,辱 ju⁴, Phonetic, to shame, to insult, to reveal with the hand 寸 彐 a disgraceful condition, 辰 ch'ên², to be pregnant (See No. 122). The 辱 ju⁴ seems to be a simple phonetic and the radical 衣 indicates that the mattress is made of cloth.

**759** 縋

chui⁴, A cord, to let down by a rope.

糸 ssü¹, mi⁴ Radical No. 120, silk. (See No. 8).

追 chui¹, Phonetic, to pursue, to follow. (See No. 745).

The radical here indicates a rope or cord and the article suspended follows the lowering or raising of the rope.

**760** 税

shui⁴, Tax, duty on merchandise.

禾 ho², Radical No. 115, growing grain. (See No. 556).

兌,兌 tui⁴, Phonetic, to exchange, to barter. (See

No. 72). The character indicates the giving of grain 禾 *ho²* to the government for the privileges derived.

**761** 吏, 吏

*li¹*, An officer, a magistrate. (See No. 231).

口 *k'ou³*, Radical No. 30, the mouth. (See No. 17).

丈 *chang⁴*, Phonetic, ten feet. (See No. 368).

In the seal writing the basis of the character 吏 is 芻 史 *shih³*, a scribe, a hand holding a stylus. This is also the character for history, as it was the work of the scribes to record history. 吏 *li⁴* has one stroke above the 史 ; this is a contraction of 上 *shang⁴*. Thus this character stands for those scribes who were directors or rulers of the literati.

**762** 席

*hsi²*, A mat, a table, a repast, a feast.

巾 *chin¹*, Radical No. 50, a napkin, a towel. (See No. 143).

庶 *shu⁴* Phonetic, all (contracted) ; all the individuals of the house gathered about the light of the hearth to eat. In ancient times meals were served on a flat surface made of stone, and the family partook while reclining. The 庶 is composed of 广 *yên³*, the house, and 苂 *kuang⁴*, light. The light of the fire was all the illumination they had. The 巾 *chin¹* was originally written 囷 and is described as being a flat stone on which the meal was served. This eventually gave place to a mat. 庶 *shu⁴* is a logical element rather than a phonetic.

**763** 康

广 *k'ang*[1], Joy, peace, repose ; healthy, delightful.

*yên*[3] Radical No. 53, a shelter. (See No. 132). The phonetic is not easily separated, as it is only in the modern writing that 广 *yên*[3] arbitrarily appears. 庚 甬 *kêng*[1] (a pestle in two hands) is the hulling of rice, and 康 蘭 is the same, save that in the latter rice 米 is represented. A grain of rice was firm and could stand the violence to which it was subjected in the process of hulling. The meaning of peace, repose, and satisfaction is supposed to refer to the rest which came after the labor of hulling the daily portion of rice. (W. 102 B).

**764** 健

亻,人 *chien*[4], Strong, vigorous.

*jên*[2], Radical No. 9, a man.

建,逮 *chien*[4], Phonetic, to write regulations 聿 *yü*[4] (See No. 7), for the march 辶 辵 *yin*[3] (archaic ; long strides, 彳 *ch'ih*[4] lengthened out). (W. 169 B). A man who was able to fulfil the regulations was strong and vigorous.

**765** 禁

示 *chin*[4], To prohibit.

*shih*[4], Radical No. 111, to reveal. (See No. 164).

林 *lin*[2], Phonetic, a forest ; indicated by doubling the radical for tree. 禁 bad omens 示 from trees 林. (W. 119 M). The 示 when seen was regarded as a revelation of divine or supernatural disapproval, and thus the character stands for prohibition

**766** 郎

*lang²*, A son, a bridegroom, gentleman, secretary.

邑, 阝 *i⁴*, Radical No. 163, a city. (See No. 11).

良 *liang²*, Phonetic, good. (See No. 445).

The character 郎 was formerly the name of a city—a city of excellence. The meaning given above was an expression of the hope of the family in the son or bridegroom, that he would bring benefits equal to that of a powerful city.

**767** 陪

*p'ei⁴*, To entertain, to visit with, to aid, to match; to add earth about the roots of plants.

阜, 阝 *fu⁴* Radical No. 170, a mound. (See No. 493).

音, 吞, 商 *t'ou⁴* Phonetic, to cut a speaker short by interrupting him. The dot ` on the top indicates the interruption, and the 否 *fou³* is an adverb of negation i.e. saying 口 no 不. This seems like a strange phonetic to be used in a character which means "to visit with," but persons when chatting are constantly interrupting one another as they speak, in order to get the real meaning, or to correct a wrong statement. If one is not on intimate terms with the speaker this is not possible.

**768** 服, 艒

*fu²*, To manage a boat (archaic), to yield to, to assent, to serve, clothes.

月 *yüeh¹*, Radical No. 74, moon. (See No. 43).

艮, 反 *fu²* Phonetic, to hold the seal, authority.

In the modern writing 月 *yüeh¹* has supplanted 舟 *chou¹*, a boat, and consequently the etymology is not apparent without a study of the old writing which represents the hand 又 which wields the authority 卩 on the boat 舟, the captain. The character also sets forth the opposite of to govern, viz., to be governed ; this is the action of the boat under the direction of the captain, to yield, to assent to ; to be attached to, as to a girdle, therefore, clothes.

**769** 袋, 帒

衣   *tai⁴*, A bag, a pocket, a purse, sash.

衣   *i¹*, Radical No. 145, clothing. (See No. 51).

巾   *chin¹*, Radical No. 50, cloth. (See No. 143).

代   *tai⁴*, Phonetic, a substitute. Order 弋 of succession or substitution of men ; a reign ; to supersede ; a dynasty.

It may have been the custom, when one 亻 *jên²* got a substitute to give him a tally 弋 *i⁴*, (See No. 576) which when presented allowed him to occupy the position of the one for whom he was substituting. The addition of 衣 or 巾 may have been suggested when trying to carry grain or fine material, a cloth 巾 or the clothing 衣 when used to carry it could take the place of many persons.

**770** 招

扌, 手   *ch'ia¹*, To pinch, to claw ; to twist.

扌, 手   *shou³*, Radical No. 64, the hand. (See No. 53).

臽   *hsien⁴* Phonetic, a pit, a pitfall, a snare. This comes from 臼 *chiu⁴*, a mortar, or hole in the ground or rock for pounding grain. 臽 *hsien⁴* is a pitfall or trap with a man in it. When 扌 *shou³* is added the idea is that with the hand something is held secure as if in a trap.

**771**  *sui*⁴, Head of grain, ear.

禾 *ho*⁴ Radical No. 115, standing grain. (See No. 556).

惠 *hui*⁴ Phonetic, grace, kindly. (See No. 385) This is not the original phonetic of this character, but it has become generally used. It may be that it was used as a recognition of the grace of heaven, 天 *t'ien*¹, in giving the increase of the field; or the gracious part of the standing grain is that where the seed is borne. The original writing was 釆 畧 *sui*⁴, a hand gathering the heads of grain.

**772** 衛

*wei*⁴, To escort, to defend, a military station, Tientsin.

行 *hsing*² , Radical No. 144, to walk. (See No. 161).

韋, 韋 *wei*⁴ Phonetic, refractory; thongs, rawhide. Two men pulling 夊 in opposite directions on an object 〇, or hide, in tanning it. 夊 = 夊 中 the reverse of 屮 牛. The indicates opposition, refractory. Compare 舛 屮 牛 *ch'üan*³, opposition, error. The refractory have to be bound with leather thongs, hence the meaning leather. As leather is strong and used to protect delicate articles it is here a suggestive phonetic. The addition of the radical 行 indicates the guarding of something while on the march.

**773** 缺

*ch'üeh*¹, Deficient, a vacancy; broken, defective.

缶, 击 *fou*³ Radical, No. 121, earthenware. (See No. 264).

夬, 叏 *chüeh*[2] Phonetic, to divide, to **break**. (See No. 109). A dish 缶 *fou*[3], which is broken 夬 is deficient.

**774** 乏

一 *fa*[2]. In want, poor, weary.

*p'ieh*[1] Radical, No. 4, a stroke to the left. (See No. 176).

之, 屮 *chih*[1], Phonetic, a 止 屮 *chih*[3] written backwards. The explanation is : a person who 止 stopped before reaching the line 一. The inference is that he was exhausted. 乏 has nothing to do with the sign of the possessive 之 屮 *chih*[1].

**775** 飢, 饑

*chi*[1], Dearth, hungry.

食 *shih*[2], Radical No. 184, food, to eat. (See No. 75).

几 *chi*[1], Phonetic, a small table ; a contraction for 幾.

幾 *chi*[1, 3], Phonetic, little. (See No. 34). When food 食 is scarce 幾 a small table 几, is large enough. When food is scarce 幾 it is a time of dearth 飢. The character's original meaning seems to have been dearth or famine and hungry is an extension, as hunger is the common condition during famine.

**776** 餓

*o*[4], *e*[4], Hungry.

食 *shih*[2], Radical No. 184, food, to eat. (See No. 75).

我 *wo*[3], Phonetic, I. (See No. 2). This character according to Kuei Shih Shuo Wen 桂氏 說 文 was originally written 饿 *o*[4], 劢 魟 *szŭ*[4], to feed, and 我 me. It was contracted to the present form.

**777 枯**

k'u¹, Dry, decayed, withered, (as a palsied limb).

木 mu⁴, Radical No. 75, wood. (See No. 22).

古 ku³, Old. Phonetic. (See No. 17). Old wood is probably decayed.

**778 窺**

k'uei¹, To peep, to spy.

穴 hsüeh⁴, Radical No. 116, a cave. (See No. 97).

規 觖 kuei¹, Phonetic, to shoot an arrow (archaic); rule, custom. (See No. 529). To shoot 觖 a glance through an opening 穴 hsüeh⁴. The present writing of 規 breaks up the etymology, as the 夫 fu should be 矢 shih³. In archery the eye aims along the arrow shaft; but here the eye shoots a glance through an opening.

**779 控**

k'ung⁴, To rein in, to draw a bow, to check, to accuse.

手, 扌 shou³, Radical No. 64, the hand. (See No. 53).

空 k'ung¹, Phonetic, vacant, empty. (See No. 302).

This phonetic plus the radical seems to have been first used for drawing the bow; in shooting an arrow one increases the vacant space 空 k'ung¹, between the string and the bow. In prosecuting a person it was not unlike shooting an arrow at him; if the accusation was substantiated, the defendant suffered perhaps more than if hit by an arrow.

**780** 周, 冑

chou[1], Completely, to extend everywhere.

口 k'ou[3] Radical No. 30, the mouth. (See No. 17). Here it is a modern replacement of 及 contracted to 𠃓. This character is a primitive compound which cannot be broken up into radical and phonetic. It is 用 用 yung[1] (See No. 476) and 及 chi[2], to reach to, contracted, (See No. 324). Every bull's eye has been hit. Efficiency is expressed in this character.

**781** 圍

wei[2], To surround, to inclose.

囗 wei[2] Radical No. 31, an enclosure. (See No. 28).

韋 wei[2] Phonetic, thongs, rawhide, refractory. (See No. 772). The meaning of the phonetic may be that 圍 is a leather case protecting that which is precious, but more probably it means refractory, 韋 and therefore when it is in 囗 it means "incarcerated."

**782** 愁

ch'ou[2], Grieved, sad.

心 hsin[1], Radical No. 61, the heart. (See No. 18).

秋 ch'iu[1], Phonetic, autumn, harvest. (See No. 169).

In the autumn the grain is often blighted with frost and appears as if scorched with fire 火. When one's desires are thus blighted, it causes sadness of heart.

**783** 硬

ying[4], Hard, obstinate.

石 shih[2], Radical No. 112, stone. (See No. 42).

更 keng[1,4], Phonetic, to change. (See No. 226). With the addition of stone 石 shih[2] the idea is to change and become hard like stone.  This refers either to a physical or mental change.

**784 伸**

人,亻 *jen²*, Phonetic No. 9, a man.

申 *shen¹*, To stretch out, to explain.

申 *shen¹*, Phonetic, to extend, to stretch.  (See No. 227) A man who is taking a rope and measuring off a fathom, six feet, with his outstretched arms.  A man who is able to explain or straighten out the tangled cord.

**785 希**

*hsi¹*, Rare, seldom.

巾 *chin¹*, Radical No. 50, cloth.   (See No. 143).
The phonetic here is not a character which is separated from the radical.  It represents the texture of cloth 乂 and the 巾 *chin¹* was placed below.  As the threads are clearly seen it conveys the idea of loose as opposed to close ; thus by extension scattered, rare, seldom.   (W. 39 G).

**786 律**

*lü⁴*, Statute, law.

彳 *ch'ih⁴* Radical No. 60, to step with the left foot.

聿 *yü⁴* Phonetic, to write.   (See No. 7).
With the addition of 彳 *ch'ih⁴* the character is used for written regulations for the march, and by extension, law.

**787 黨**

*tang⁸*, A clan, a faction, an associate, a cabal.

黑 *hei¹*, Radical, No. 203, black.   (See No. 178).

尚 *shang⁴*, Phonetic, a house.   (See No. 52).
The Shuo Wen says that the 黑 indicates that the members of this society are all smoked with one smoke, that is that they

meet together in the same room. They
meet in the dark 黑, secretly, form a cabal.
The 尚 shang⁴ here represents the leader
of the clan or association.

**788** 擁

yung¹,³, To crowd, to gather in a crowd, to
embrace.

手, 扌 shou³, Radical No. 64, the hand.

邕, 雍 yung¹ Phonetic, a city; harmony, union; the
wagtail. The first is the old form of the
character, a city 邑 with a moat 巛 em-
bracing it, but the second form is now in
general use. 巛 = 亠 and 邑 = 阝 as in 鄉.
With 隹 it means the bird that haunts the
borders of moats and ponds in harmonious
flocks, the wagtail. (W. 12 G). This
phonetic is used to express harmony of
action, and with the addition of the
radical 手 it means to jam or press as a
crowd, and embrace with the arms.

**789** 擠

chi³, To crowd, to press out.

手 扌 shou², Radical No. 64, the hand. (See No. 53).

齊 ch'i², Phonetic, even, together. (See No. 455).
The hands 手 working together 齊, to
crowd, to press 擠.

**790** 俯

fu³, To stoop, to bow, to condescend.

人, 亻 jen², Radical No. 9, a man.

府 fu³, Phonetic, a palace. (See No. 388).
This is not an old character, but it has
come into general use. The etymology is
apparent: When a man 人 comes to an
official department 府 to pay his taxes 付,
the customs of China require him to show

respect and reverence to the official in charge. Thus by extension to bow and condescend, 俯.

**791** 伏

*fu*⁴, To fall prostrate, to fall on the face, to lie in ambush ; a decade in dog days ; to subject.

人, 亻 *jen*², Radical No. 9, a man.

犬 *ch'üan*³ Phonetic, a dog, a pictorial representation. 伏 is a man 人 taking the cringing attitude of a dog 犬 or compelling another to take it, i.e. to humble or subject another. (See No. 647) (W. 25 E).

**792** 顯

*hsien*³ Conspicuous, to make plain, glorious.

頁 *yeh*⁴, Radical No. 181, the head, a page, a man. (See No. 105).

㬎 *hsien*³ Phonetic, motes in a sunbeam, volatile, minute, fibrous. When a sunbeam 日 shines into a dark room, small motes like silk fibres, 絲 *ssu*¹, become visible 顯 floating in it. When 頁 *yeh*⁴, the head, is added the original idea was that the decorations of the hat were very apparent. The character is now used for anything conspicuous.

**793** 露

*lou*⁴, *lu*⁴, Dew ; *lou*⁴, plain, to expose, to disclose.

雨 *yü*³, Radical No. 173, rain. (See No. 61).

路 *lu*⁴, Phonetic, road. (See No. 279). 桂 氏 Kuei Shih say's—露者陰之液也露從地出 "Dew is the secretion of the dark, female power of nature, dew comes from the earth." *Lu*⁴ 路 seems to be used for earth 地 as rain from the earth instead of the ordinary rain of heaven. Rain that wets the feet only, as when walking in grass wet with dew.

"The dew is the path 路 of the rain 雨, and when it falls on grass it turns it white disclosing each stem and leaf."

**794 狂**

犭, 犬   *k'uang*[2], Mad, wild, raging ; presumptuous.

犭, 犬   *ch'üan*[3] Radical No. 94, a dog, a pictorial character.

王, 坒   *wang*[3] Phonetic, rambling. (See No. 350).

This character indicates that dogs have suffered from rabies in China from the very beginning of their civilization. This character is described as a mad dog. The animal wanders around from place to place without any definite aim, and thus this is a very apt phonetic for this disease. The character is not confined to this one disease, it is at present. used for any kind of mania.

**795 喻**

  *yü*[4], To instruct, to illustrate.

口   *k'ou*[3], Radical No. 30, the mouth.

俞, 兪   *yü*[2] Phonetic, a small boat, a primitive barge, sampan, 三板, *san*[1] *pan*[3], 舟之始也. " The commencement of boat-building." Joining 亼 *chi*[2] of planks to form a boat 月 to sail the rivers 巜 *kuai*[4]. With the addition of 口 *k'ou*[3], the mouth, the idea is conveyed of giving instructions in the building of the boat ; by extension instructions of any kind.

**796 捆**

  *k'un*[3], To bind, to hamper.

手 shou³, Radical No. 64, the hand. (See No. 53).

困,圀 k'un⁴, Phonetic, confined. There are two writings of this phonetic I. 朱, to stop and rest by a tree, to take a nap under a tree ; II. 困 a tree which is hemmed in 口 wei², by rocks or large trees, and thus restricted in growth, or wilting from confinement. This last is the one which is in general use. The addition of hand implies that there is an act of repression. It seems probable that these were two different characters but they have become merged into one. The reason for this view is, the two meanings, viz., sleepy and cramped and hemmed in. The first seal writing is in accord with the idea of sleepy, to stop it under a tree 木 and take a nap. It is difficult to explain why this character should have the two meanings had it sprung from one symbol.

797 擔

tan¹·⁴, To carry a burden on a pole, a load or burden.

手,才 shou³, Radical No. 64, the hand. (See No. 53).

詹 chan¹ Phonetic, to talk impudently. (W. 59 H).

This is from 产 wei², a man 人 standing on a dangerous crag 厂 (See No. 634), and 八 pa¹, to scatter, and 言 yên², words ; to recklessly scatter indiscreet words. The radical 手 indicates that the character was first used as a verb. One who talks indiscreetly has a heavy, dangerous burden to bear and this eventually has been extended to mean a burden of any kind. (W. 59 H).

**798 苗**

miao², A sprout, the sprout of grain ; wild tribes.

卄 ts'ao³, Radical No. 140, grass. (See No. 22).

田 t'ien², Phonetic, a field. (See No. 212).

The sprouting vegetation 艸 of the cultivated field 田. That which is planted just .appearing above the ground, 苗. (W. 149 B).

**799 曬 晒**

shai⁴, Bright sunlight, to dry in the sun.

日 jih⁴, Radical No. 72, the sun. (See No. 12).

麗 li⁴,¹, Phonetic, elegant. This phonetic originally meant antelope, deer, 鹿 etc., animals which lived in droves, but it early took on the meaning of elegant, perhaps owing to the graceful appearance of the animals. The upper part 丽 li⁴, is a primitive representing decoration. These animals were decorated with horns. 鹿 lu⁴ deer is a picture 鹿 of horns, body, feet and tail.

西 hsi¹, Phonetic, west.. (See No. 26). The western sun is much warmer than the eastern, thus this is a suggestive addition to the character, but, like the other phonetic, is without phonetic significance.

**800 獨**

tu², Solitary, only, childless.

犬, 犭, 犮 ch'üan Radical No. 94, a dog. A pictorial representation.

蜀, 罒 shu⁸ Phonetic, a silkworm spinning its thread. (See No. 749) (W. 54 I). If a silkworm is spinning a cocoon it is working alone and for itself, and when this phonetic is used in this combination the idea of "solitary" is derived from the above fact. As dogs do not usually roam about in packs the dog radical is appropriate to form the character for solitary or alone.

**801** 奥, 奧

ao⁴, The southwest corner of a room, where the Lares were placed, mysterious.

大 ta⁴, Radical No. 37, large. (See No. 54).

This character cannot be broken up into radical and phonetic. The above radical is arbitrarily given to it in the modern writing. The Shuo Wen says the character stands for the south-west corner of the room ∩ mien², the dark corner, where one is obliged to grope with the hands 月 in order to differentiate 釆 pien⁴ the articles. 釆 pien⁴ is the track of a wild animal and these were easily distinguished, the one from the other, only by hunters or those who frequently saw them; thus this is a symbol for discrimination (See No. 837). As there was more or less obscurity about such a corner, by extension the character has acquired the meaning of mysterious. (W. 123 F).

**802** 祕 秘

mi⁴, pi⁴, Secret, private, divine.

示 shih⁴, Radical No. 113, spiritual influences. (See No. 164). Written 礻 with a pen 祕.

禾 ho², Radical No. 115, standing grain. (See No. 556).

必 pi⁴, Phonetic, must. (See No. 504).

祕 *pi⁴* originally was used as a term for a god or deity and the manifestations of his will must 必 be complied with. 秘 is another writing of the same character. The meaning of secret may have originated from the fact that the will of the gods could not be known unless set forth by revelation or omen.

**803 暫**

日 *jih⁴*, Radical No. 72, the sun. (See No. 12).

斬, 斬 *chan³*, Phonetic, to decapitate, to cut in two.

*chan⁴*, A part of a day, briefly, temporarily.

This phonetic is a war chariot with scythes according to the Shuo Wen. It may have been used to exterminate captives, and so, by extension this symbol 斬 came to mean beheading by an executioner. The character may mean to whirl or brandish 車 a battle axe 斤. (W. 128 A). See 漸 (No. 812). When a day 日 *jih⁴* is divided the time is necessarily short.

**804 逼 偪**

辶 *cho⁴* Radical No. 162. (See No. 10).

畐 *fu²* Phonetic, abundance. (See No. 267). The

*pi⁴*, To press upon, to ill use.

character 逼 should be written 偪 *pi⁴*. When there is an abundance of men, a crowd of people, they press one another, and if the throng is great the weaker ones suffer from the pressure; a very suggestive symbol for oppression.

**805 跌**

*tieh¹*, To stumble, to fall.

足 *tsu²*, Radical No. 157, the foot. (See No. 484).

失 *shih¹*, Phonetic, to lose, to err, a fault. (See No. 566). An error 失 of the foot 足, a mis-step, leads to a fall 跌.

**806** 私

私 *szŭ¹*, Personal, selfish, secret.

禾 *ho²*, Radical No. 115, standing grain. (See No. 556).

厶 *szŭ¹* Phonetic, private, selfish. (See No. 569). Grain 禾 was used for paying taxes and the residue was personal 厶 property 私. By extension, selfish.

**807** 慾

慾 *yü⁴*, Passion, lust.

心 *hsin¹*, Radical No. 61, the heart.

欲 *yü⁴*, Phonetic, to long for, to desire. This is made up of 谷 *ch'iao⁴*, (See No. 135) the upper lip, or the flesh 八 above the mouth, 口 *k'ou³*. In this phonetic the upper lip seems to be regarded as the center of self-restraint. The 欠 *ch'ien⁴* indicates a deficiency of restraint which allows desire to gain the mastery. When 心 *hsin¹* is added it stands for passion **or lust.**

**808** 掩

掩 *yên³*, To screen, to hide from view, to shade.

手 *shou³*, Radical No. 64, the hand. (See No. 53).

奄, 奄 *yên³* Phonetic, a man making a long stride, quickly; by extension, to cover, remain. The old writing, depicts a man making a stride 大 and covering ground the length of the outstretched arms, a fathom. 申 *shên²*, (See No. 784). When hand 扌 *shou³*, is added the hand covers or screens from view.

**809** 隱

阝, 阜    *yin*³, Retired, in private life.

*fu*⁴ Radical No. 170, a mound. (See No. 493).

㥯 *yin*³ Phonetic, careful, care, taking an interest in, freedom from care; to enjoy the results of the work 工 *kung*¹ of one's hands ⺤ ⺕. The 心 *hsin*¹ indicates peace of mind of one who has what he needs and desires nothing else (W. 49 G). The 阝 *fu*⁴ is a modern substitution, meaning place, where formerly was written ㄴ a hiding place.

**810** 瞞

目    *man*², To deceive, to conceal.

*mu*⁴, Radical No. 109, the eye. (See No. 102).

萳 *man*² Phonetic, equality. (See No. 306). When both eyelids are closed (equally tight), then one cannot see. An old meaning of this character 瞞 was to close the eyes. It now means to hoodwink or to cause one to have closed eyes to the real condition of affairs.

**811** 芽

⺿    *ya*², To sprout, to bud, a germ, a shoot.

*ts'ao*³ Radical No. 140, grass or vegetation. (See No. 22).

牙 *ya*², Phonetic, a tooth. (See No. 97).
Dentition is an interesting process and is watched by those interested in children. The sprouting of seeds seemed to the originators of this character to have a striking resemblance to that process; it occurs at the commencement of the new life and the germs appear like teeth just showing above the gums.

**812** 漸

水, 氵    *chien*[4], Gradually, by degrees.

   *shui*[3], Radical No. 85, water. (See No. 79).

斬    *chan*[3], Phonetic, decapitate, to cut in two. (See No. 803). Water cuts its way through great rocks but ages are required in the process. This impressed the scribes and they adopted this process as a symbol for gradually.

**813** 穀

穀

禾    *ku*[3], Grain, cereal.

   *ho*[2], Radical No. 115, standing grain. (See No. 556).

殼,殼    *ch'iao*[1] *k'o*[1], Phonetic, a cover 冂 and vegetation 士, 屮 *chih*[1]. By extension, the husk of grain, the shell of nuts or of an egg. The 殳 *shu*[1], to strike, (See No. 165) is added, as frequently the husk requires much harsh treatment, before it is removed from the grain.

**814** 粒

米    *li*[4], A kernel (of grain).

   *mi*[3], Radical No. 119, rice, small grains. (See No. 47).

立    *li*[4], Phonetic, to establish, to stand. (See No. 216). Grain in bulk cannot be piled up unless it is in a bin; it is only a single kernel 粒 that can stand 立 alone without support.

**815** 枝

木    *chih*[1], A branch of a tree.

   *mu*[4], Radical No. 75, a tree, cr wood. (See No. 22).

支, 夊, 枲    *chih*[1], Phonetic, a bow, a branch, to advance money; the 65th Radical.

This phonetic originally was used for the branch of a tree. The old writing shows a hand with a branch as if stripping it from a tree. The radical 木 is a modern superfluous addition.

**816 蔭**

艹, 艸 *yin⁴*, Shady, to shelter.
*ts'ao³* Radical No. 140, grass. (See No. 22).

陰 *yin¹*, Phonetic, shade, dark, Hades, female, secret, cloudy. This symbol often refers to the sky as being overcast; now 今 *chin¹*, it is cloudy 云 *yün²*. The 阝 *fu⁴*, high, is superfluous. When 艹 is added it indicates that the shade comes from trees or some thatched or artificial shelter.

**817 涼**

氵, 水 *liang²*, Cool, fresh, cloudy.
*shui³*, Radical No. 85, water. (See No. 79).

京 *ching¹*, Phonetic, the capital. (See No. 98). The capital is the most important place in the Empire, and by extension it is most desirable; cool water is most desirable and refreshing.

**818 渡**

氵, 水 *tu⁴*, A ferry, to ford, to cross a ferry.
*shui³*, Radical No. 85, water. (See No. 79).

度 *tu⁴*, Phonetic, to measure, a degree; capacity; to cross. This phonetic is made up of 庶 *shu⁴*, contracted, (See No. 762), and 又 *yu⁴*, the right hand which measures by spans. (W. 24 M). The important thing in fording a stream is to be sure that the water 水 is not deeper than you are able 度 to ford, 渡: or, to pass across 度 water 水.

**819** 暴, 暴

pao⁴, To expose to the direct sunlight ; violent, cruel.

日 jih⁴, Radical No. 72, the sun. (See No. 12). This character does not divide into radical and phonetic. The old writing shows definitely the idea which the character was intended to convey; which was to spread 臼 grain 米 out 出 in the sun 日 to dry. On account of the strength of sunlight it has come to mean violent or cruel.

**820** 波

po¹, A wave, a ripple.

氵, 水 shui³, Radical No. 85, water, (See No. 79).

皮 p'i², Phonetic, the skin. (See No. 224). The waves and ripples are like a superficial layer, 皮 p'i², of the water. (See No. 832).

**821** 浪

lang⁴, Waves, profligate.

氵, 水 shui³, Radical No. 85, water. (See No. 79).

良 liang², Phonetic, good ; the original nature of a thing. (See No. 445).

It is the nature 良 of water 水 to form waves, the waves 浪 seem impertinent, rude, lawless, profligate 浪.

**822** 枕

chên³, A pillow, to pillow ; to sleep.

木 mu⁴, Radical No. 75, wood, (of which pillows are made in China) (See No. 22).

尢, 冘 yin² Phonetic, to go away, to withdraw ; a man 儿 who walks out of a space 冖 冂 (See W. 34 E). When wood 木 mu⁴ is added it forms the character for pillow and is thus explained : when the head is pillowed (asleep) the man makes journeys 冘 yin² all over the world in his dreams.

823 靜 *ching*⁴, Quiet, still ; clean.

青 *ch'ing*¹, Radical No. 174, pure, fresh. (See No. 63).

爭 *chêng*¹, Phonetic, to wrangle, to contest. (See No. 315). This character 靜 was originally used for thoroughly 爭 blended colors 青 *ch'ing*¹, but it is now used for quiet or still. The proper character for this was 竫 *ching*⁴, a cessation 立 *li*⁴, of wrangling 爭 *chêng*¹ ; but in modern composition the proper character is never used.

824 膽 *tan*³, The gall, courage.

肉.月 *jou*⁴, Radical No. 130, meat. (See No. 133).

詹 *chan*¹ Phonetic, to talk indiscreetly, oversee. (See No. 797). The reason for this combination of radical and phonetic may have been :—if a man does indulge in indiscreet statements, he not only needs to be a man of muscle 月 *jou*⁴, in order to stand by these statements, but also a man of courage or gall. The gall bladder is considered to be the seat of courage.

825 怯 *ch'ieh*⁴, Timorous, cowardly.

心, 忄 *hsin*¹, Radical No. 61, the heart. (See No. 18).

去 *ch'ü*⁴, Phonetic, to go. (See No. 67). If the heart 心 is gone 去 there is no courage.

826 懼 *chü*⁴, Afraid, to fear, to stand in awe of.

心, 忄 *hsin*¹, Radical No. 61, the heart. (See No. 18).

瞿, 瞿 *ch'ü*² Phonetic, the timid look 朋 of the bird 隹, needed to preserve life, looking to right and to left. When a hawk has caught his prey, he is on the alert while devouring it, lest an enemy should attack him. With the addition of 忄 *hsin¹*, heart, the timidity of the bird is referred to the emotions.

**827 迎**

*ying²*, To go out and receive, as a guest.

辶 *cho⁴* Radical No. 162, to run and stop. (See No. 10).

卬,阝 *ang²* Phonetic, high, noble. A high dignitary an official who holds the seal 卪. Here the seal 卪 stands for the official. (See No. 42). The other part of the phonetic is 𠂉 匕, a man facing the opposite way from the usual position. This man is looking up to the official as if desiring to attain to the rank of the latter. When 辶 *cho⁴* is added the idea of respectfully going out to meet a guest or high dignitary is expressed. 仰 *yang³*, to look up, has the same phonetic. (See W. 26 G).

**828 鏈**

*lien²*, Lead or tin ore ; *lien⁴*, a chain.

金 *chin¹*, Radical No. 167, metal. (See No. 13).

連 *lien²*, Phonetic, to connect. (See No. 499). This phonetic is suggestive of a chain as it is used for things connected. The chain 鏈 is made of many rings of metal 金 connected 連 like a string of carts, 車, going 辶 one after the other.

**829 屢**

*lü³*, Many times, repeatedly.

尸 *shih¹*, Radical No. 44, a person in the recumbent posture. (See No. 449)

婁 *lou²* Phonetic, the part of the palace where

women are confined. (See No. 392). The idea of the phonetic here is not the same as that in 樓 *lou²*. This 屢 *lü³* is a very old character and it is easiest to explain it by commencing with the 尸 *shih¹*, which is a contraction of 屋 *wu¹*, a room ; (See No. 337). 毋 *wu²*, a negative ; 中, 女, *chung¹ nü³* are two characters used in the 八卦 *pa¹ kua⁴*, which indicate an empty space ; and it indicates that in this room 屋, where the women were confined, there was no 毋 furniture, it was empty. The character eventually came to mean a space as opposed to a solid substance and was used for the holes in the lattice windows. From this the idea of "frequent" is derived, as in a window there are many of these spaces.

**830** 羣

*ch'ün²*, A flock, a herd, a multitude, all.

羊 *yang²*, Radical No. 123, a sheep. (See No. 253).

君, 君 *chün¹*, Phonetic, a princely man. It is composed of 尹 *yin³*, and 口 *k'ou³* ; a magistrate 尹 who holds in his hand ⺕ authority 丿 and who utters 口 his decrees or orders. As sheep are orderly in their actions the above phonetic was adopted with 羊 *yang²*, sheep, for a flock of sheep. It now means a flock of any kind.

**831** 緣

*yüan²*, A hem of a garment, a collar, **a** cause, a connection, because.

糸 *szŭ¹*, Radical No. 120, silk. (See No. 8).

彖 *t'uan*[3] Phonetic, pigs with bristles. By extension, accessories, as bristles are accessory to the pig. (W. 68 I). When silk 糸 is added it is used for the trimmings of a garment. The bristles of the pig were regarded as decoration and harmonized with his general appearance.

**832 坡**

*p'o*[1], A declivity, a mound, a hill.

土 *t'u*[3], Radical No. 32, the earth. (See No. 13).

皮 *p'i*[2], Phonetic, skin. (See No. 224). The use of this phonetic plus 土 *t'u*[3], earth, for a hill, and plus 氵 *shui*[3], for a wave (See No. 820) leads to the supposition that the two characters were originated by the same scribe. The wave is an elevation on the surface of the water and a hill is an elevation on the surface of the earth. In skinning an animal the skin is prone to lie in wrinkles ; this may have suggested its use as a phonetic in the two instances.

**833 闖**

*ch'uang*[3,4], To push ahead, to bolt out or in ; rudely.

門 *mên*[2], Radical No. 169, a door. (See No. 5).

馬 *ma*[3], Phonetic, a horse. (See No. 261). Without phonetic force, but it is suggestive of dashing forward ; if once a horse 馬 strikes the side of a door 門 when going through, he will ever afterward go through with a rush 闖.

**834 投**

*t'ou*[2], To throw at, to give over, to join.

手　shou³, Radical No. 64, the hand. (See No. 53).
殳　shu¹,² Phonetic, the right hand making a quick
motion, to strike. (See No. 165). With
the addition of shou³ 扌 the hand, a good
character for to throw is formed and to
give over or to join must mean that one
throws himself on the mercy of another,
as the prodigal did in the far country.

835 痊　ch'üan², Cured, recovered.
疒　ni⁴, Radical No. 104, sickness. (See No. 593).
全　ch'üan², Phonetic, entire, finished. (See No.
552).
This character is not found in the Shuo
Wen, but it is not difficult to see the idea
of its composition: when the disease 疒
ni⁴ has run its course 全 ch'üan², the
patient recovers.

836 源　yüan², A fountain, the source.
水, 氵 · shui³, Radical No. 85, water.
原, 厵 · yüan², Phonetic, the origin, a spring. (See
No. 653). The modern character has 氵
shui³, water, added, owing to the present
writing of the phonetic having no suggestion of water left in it. The original
character depicted the streams issuing
from under a ledge of rock.

837 繙　fan¹, To interpret, to translate.
糸　szŭ¹, Radical No. 120, silk. (See No. 8).
番, 釆 fan¹, Phonetic, the tracks of a wild beast,
aborigines, discrimination. The ⊕ is the
ball of the foot and the rest of the

symbol is the imprints of the claws 釆 (cf. No. 801). Hunters became expert at recognizing the footprints of the various animals and could tell at a glance what beast made them.

The character for " to interpret or translate" should be written 譒 *fan¹*, but through the carelessness of some scribe 繙 *fan¹* was substituted. It was probably used first for translating the writing of some tribe or person who wrote different symbols from those in common use. Observe that 審 *shên³*, to judge or investigate, uses the same phonetic: the judge in his courtroom 宀 *mien²*, investigates 番 *fan¹* the testimony and pronounces sentence accordingly.

**838** 閨

*kuei¹*, Women's rooms, women, female, girl.

門 *mên¹*, Radical No. 169, door. (See No. 5).

圭 *kuei¹*, Phonetic, a small stone scepter or baton, anciently given to nobles as a sign of rank. (See No. 161). The character 閨 *kuei¹* seems to have been first used to indicate the door of a feudal lord in distinction from the large door used by the 王 *wang²*, the prince, and it was afterwards used to designate the door of the women's apartment, and finally was used for women in general.

**839** 嚷

*jang³*, To clamor, to cry out, to scold.

口 *k'ou³*, Radical No. 30, the mouth.

襄,𤕠,𤔔 *hsiang¹* Phonetic; to remove, to assist, to perfect. It is necessary to study the old writing. It is to take off one's outer garment 衣 *i*[1] and assist 𠬪 in a common piece of work 工 *kung*[1]. The 吅 *hsüan*[1] indicates that there is much discussion, perhaps many orders given. 𠬪, seen only in oldest writing, was changed into 已 *chi*[3] and indicated disorder or confusion. (W. 16 I. and 72 H.) With the addition of 口 *k'ou*[3], mouth, to this already boisterous phonetic we have a strong character for clamor. The modern writing gives but little clue to the original composition.

**840** 攆

才, 手 *shou*[3], Radical No. 64, the hand. (See No. 53).

輦 輦 *nien*[3], Phonetic, the Emperor's chariot. When the Emperor went on the street the ordinary traffic was suspended and the streets must be vacated. The addition of hand 扌 *shou*[3] to this phonetic may have formed the character adopted for the clearing of the thoroughfare for the passage of the Emperor's chariot. It was drawn by two men 夫. (W. 60 M).

*nien*[3], To expel, to drive out.

**841** 厭, 厭

厂 *han*[4] Radical No. 27, a projecting cliff.

猒, 猒 *yên*[4] Phonetic, to be satiated, 甘 *kan*[1], with dog 犬 *ch'üan*[3], meat 月 *jou*[4].

*yên*[4], To dislike, to loathe.

The 㠯 *i*[3] and 甘 *kan*[1] of the old forms have been changed to 日 in the modern character. Satiety seems to have been the aim in the ancient feast; it is indicated by 㠯 *i*[3], belching. By extension, the 厭

_yen_⁴ means disgust, aversion. 厂 _han_⁴ represents the retreat from the place of feasting. (W. 65 G).

**842**

棄, 棄, 㐫    _ch'i_⁴, To reject, to discard.

木   _mu_⁴, Radical No. 75, wood. (See No. 22).

This character does not exhibit radical and phonetic. The seal writing represents a newborn child in a scoop and two hands in the act of throwing it away. (W. 94 G.) This indicates that infanticide has long been practiced in this country.

**843**

拐    _kuai_³, A staff, a crutch.

手, 扌   _shou_³, Radical No. 64, the hand. (See No. 53).

另   _ling_⁴, Phonetic, separate, extra. (See No. 474). As a staff is something used by man in walking and is not a part of himself, this phonetic aids in explaining the character but is without phonetic force.

**844**

塵    _ch'ên_², Dust, the world.

土   _t'u_³, Radical No. 33, earth. (See No. 13).

鹿, 麤   _lu_⁴, Phonetic, a deer, an antelope, a gazelle. On the upper part are the horns, below are the feet and the body is in the middle. The original writing of 塵 _ch'ên_² was not always the same. 麤 indicated the dust which a herd of deer or elk caused to rise when they ran. There is now but one 鹿 deer.

**845**

躱    _to_⁴,³, To stamp, to knock off (from the feet).

足   _tsu_², Radical No. 157, the foot. (See No. 484).

朵   _to_³, Phonetic, bushes with branches hanging with flowers. (See No. 581). When foot is added to this phonetic, there is the idea of something hanging or adhering to it, which can be removed by a stamp of the foot.

**846** 油

yu², Oil.

氵,水 shui³, Radical No. 85, water. (See No. 79).

由 yu², Phonetic, from, origin. (See No. 732). This was originally the name of a river and it was adopted as the character for oil. There is no etymological ground for this use.

**847** 婦

fu⁴, A wife, a married woman.

女 nü³, Radical No. 38, a woman. (See No. 16).

帚 chou³ Phonetic, a dusting cloth attached to a handle. Invented in the 21st century B. C. When 女 nü³, a woman, is added it is used as the character for a married woman or wife, the one who handles the broom-stick. (W. 44 K).

**848** 畏, 畏

wei⁴, To dread, to respect, to be in awe of.

田 t'ien², Radical No. 102, field. (See No. 212). This character cannot be divided into radical and phonetic. Originally the 田 t'ien² field, was 甶 由 fu⁴, a demon's head, and 爪 chao³, claw, and finally 刀 人 jên², a man, a frightened man, was added as a demon's head and a tiger's claws are most fear-inspiring objects to man. This character has undergone so great a change in modern writing that the etymology is entirely lost.

**849** 護

hu⁴, To protect, to defend.

言 yên², Radical No. 149, a word. (See No. 10).

蒦 huo⁴ Phonetic, to hold a bird 萑 in the hand 又 to protect it. This is a bird of the falcon or hawk tribe, carried on the arm 又. According to 桂氏說文 Kuei⁴ Shih⁴ Shuo¹ Wên², the bird is eminently able to foresee good fortune or calamity, and there is an intimation that they were kept and protected in order to secure good fortune. With the addition of word, 言 yên², the character stands for protection or, to defend.

**850** 游

yu², To float, to rove, to travel.

氵,水 shui³, Radical No. 85, water. (See No. 79).

斿 yu² Phonetic, the motion of the arms of a swimmer; fluttering of a flag. The phonetic is a contraction of 㳺 yu², a swimmer. The 㫃 yên³ (See No. 698) a fluttering motion, here means the overhand swimming strokes. The 子 � tzŭ³, a child, indicates that the legs of the swimmer are hidden by the water and thus invisible as those of a child wrapped in long clothing. The water radical 氵 shui³, is a recent addition. By extension this character is used for the verb, to travel.

**851** 移

i², Stalks standing so close together that they require to be transplanted, to move.

禾 ho², Radical No. 115, standing grain. (See No. 556).

多 to¹, Phonetic, many. (See No. 184). This phonetic assists in explaining the meaning of the character, but has no value as a phonetic. When plants are crowded 多 and their growth is thus stunted, the farmer often transplants 移 and so allows room for development.

**852** 恰

心, 忄  *hsin¹*, Radical No. 61, the heart. (See No. 18).

合  *ho²*, Phonetic, joining, union, harmony. (See No. 103). That which occurs just at the right time or just when it·is wanted, 忄 *hsin¹*, is called timely.

*ch'ia⁴*, Timely.

**853** 巧

工  *kung¹*, Radical No. 48, work, workman, time of work. (See No. 89).

丂  *ch'iao³* Phonetic, difficulty in breathing, air which has met with an obstruction. (See No. 258). This is a phonetic which indicates curves and waves of air; these curves and twists plus 工 *kung¹*, a representation of the square, when brought together, are used for skilful. as a workman who can combine curves and angles in his work must be skilful.

*ch'iao³*, Skillful, lucky.

**854** 排

手, 扌  *shou³*, Radical No. 64, the hand. (See No. 53).

非  *fei¹*, Phonetic, a primitive with two sides opposite to each other. (See No. 276). The objects are placed in a certain position with reference to each other and with the addition of hand this forms the character to arrange.

*p'ai²*, To arrange.

855 誓

*shih⁴*, To swear, an oath.

言 *yên²*, Radical No. 149, word. (See No. 10).

折.斦.㪿 *shê²*, Phonetic, to break, to cut in two. In the oldest writing this phonetic represents an ax which has cut a branch in two. In ancient times when one desired to affirm a statement as true, he took an ax and cut a branch in two, the idea being that he expected such a retribution if his statement was not true. With the addition of 言 *yên²*, word, this character is used for an oath.

856 擘

*pai¹*, To break apart with the hand (as bread).

手 *shou³*, Radical No. 64, the hand. (See No. 53).

辟.辟 *pi⁴ p'i⁴*, Phonetic, a prince, a man who pronounces 口 the sentence 尸 on criminals 辛 *hsin¹* (See No. 274).

The 尸 *chieh²*, seal, has been changed to 尸 *shih¹*, in the modern writing. As the sentence was generally death, the character also means to kill by cutting asunder. When hand is added it means to break open with the hand; a case where the addition of a radical very materially reduces the original severity of the phonetic.

857 岸

*an⁴*, The bank, the shore.

山.山 *shan¹*, Radical No. 46, a mountain, a pictorial representation in the old writing.

干 *kan¹*, Phonetic, arms. (See No. 110). Here the idea is that arms 干 *kan¹*, are used for defense. The radical 山 *shan¹*, a mountain, should also include 厂 *han*⁴, a projecting cliff, as mountains and the cliffs are the guardians against the encroachment of the sea.

**858** 搖

*yao*², To shake, to sway to and fro.

扌 手 *shou*³, Radical, No. 64, the hand. (See No. 53).

备, 图 *yao*² Phonetic, an earthen vessel for cooking or keeping meat. (W. 130 C). There is no explanation of why this phonetic is used with the radical 扌 hand, *shou*³, for the verb to move, and consequently it must be regarded as a simple phonetic.

**859** 慌

*huang*¹, Agitated, apprehensive, to scare; very.

忄, 心 *hsin*¹, Radical No. 61, the heart. (See No. 18).

荒 *huang*¹, Phonetic, barren, wild, reckless. (See No. 639). This is a good phonetic and when heart 忄 *hsin*¹, is added the condition of the barren and worthless land is transferred to the heart. It suggests the idea of being " scared out of one's wits."

**860** 愚

*yü*², Silly, stupid.

心 *hsin*¹, Radical No. 61, the heart. (See No. 18).

禺, 禺 *yü*² Phonetic, a monkey. In the old writing the head resembles that of a demon. (See No. 447). It has a prehensile tail (W. 23 E). For some reason a monkey is regarded as stupid, thus when heart is added the character indicates a monkey's heart—stupid.

**861** 拘

*chü*¹, To grasp, to restrain.

扌, 手 *shou*³, Radical No. 64, the hand. (See No. 53).

句 *chü*⁴, Phonetic, a sentence; (See No. 80) to admonish or warn, and with the addition of 才 *shou*³, the hand, to lay hold on one, to prevent his going. 句 *chü*⁴ is not originally from 勹 *pao*¹, as stated under the 80th character, but from 丩 , 糾 *chiu*¹, a primitive representing a creeping plant twining over and circling round other things. That 丩 *chiu*¹ is here written precisely like 勹 *pao*¹, to wrap, is misleading. Because the tendril 丩 *chiu*¹ and the placenta 勹 *pao*¹ both have the idea of to wrap, or contain, the modern forms are often identical and they are used interchangeably.

862 守

shou³, To keep, to guard.

宀 *mien*² Radical No. 40, a house.

寸 *ts'un*⁴, Phonetic, an inch, a measure, a hand. (See No. 69). It is without phonetic value but it explains the use of the character. The 宀 *mien*² is an official's residence and here the law 寸 *ts'un*⁴, is kept and used in the administration of the office. Another explanation is that 宀 *mien*² is a house on the frontier where soldiers are stationed to protect the frontier from encroachment.

863 遺

*i*², To bequeath, to lose, to give.

辶, 辵 *cho*⁴ Radical No. 162, to run and stop. (See No. 10).

貴 *kuei*⁴, Phonetic, honorable. This is from 臾 *k'uei*⁴, a basket, (See No. 693) and 貝 *pei*⁴, precious, a basketful 虫 of precious things, 貝, valuable. This character has undergone many changes and the present writing does not indicate the original meaning. Kang Hsi gives three old writings which are obsolete. The best way to remember the character is to regard the valuables 貴 *kuei*[4] as moving 辶, changing hands, either as a present or bequeathed 遺.

**864** 脣

月,肉 *jou*[4], Radical No. 130, meat, flesh.

辰,辰 *ch'ên*[2], Phonetic, time, 7 to 9 a.m. (See No. 122) 長箋說文 Ch'ang[2] Chien[1] Shuo[4] Wên[2] gives the following explanation:—辰, 辰 *ch'ên*[2] is from 乙 *i*[1], germination (it represents the germ striving to get thru the ground); and 匕 *hua*[4], an inverted man, change; (See No. 488; the seed is being changed into a plant,) and 二 old writing of 上 *shang*[4], up; (the plant is growing up out of the ground); and 厂 *han*[4] indicating that at first the sprout is covered with the earth. As this is the season when vegetation commences to grow it is a most important time for farmers. Why this was selected as the phonetic for lips is not apparent, unless the cotyledons of plants such as beans reminded the scribes of the lips.

**865** 枉

*ch'ün*[2], The lips.

木 *mu*[4], Radical No. 75, wood. (See No. 22).

*wang*[3], Crooked; wrong, a grievance.

王, 坓 *wang*³ Phonetic, vegetation which grows here and there without any order. (See No. 350). With the addition of tree 木 *mu*⁴ this irregular growth is transferred to the tree and this is a symbol of a crooked, wrong or unnatural growth, a tree so contorted that it is useless for building purposes.

**866** 誡

*chieh*¹, To prohibit, to caution ; a precept.

言 *yên*², Radical No. 149, a word.   (See No. 10).

戒, 㦢 *chieh*⁴, Phonetic, to warn, to caution. This phonetic is made up of two hands 𠈌 and a halberd 戈   It implies an ocular warning.  When 言 *yên*² is added it implies a verbal warning.  (W. 47 E).

**867** 廢

*fei*⁴, Ruined, a house in ruins, useless ; to abandon.

广 *yên*³ Radical No. 53, a covering, a shelter, a house.

發 *fa*¹, Phonetic, to shoot an arrow, to send forth. (See No. 214).  Some explain this phonetic as 癶 *po*⁴, to separate the feet, to place the feet apart as one does when shooting an arrow 殳 from a bow 弓.  When shooting the arrow is sent away, is lost ; this is the idea stressed in this combination ; and when 广 *yên*³, a house, is added it indicates an abandoned house ; one which owing to its location or for other reasons cannot be used.

**868** 藉

*chieh*⁴, To borrow, to avail oneself of ; by means of.

艹 ts'ao³, Radical No. 140, grass or vegetation. (See No. 22).

耤, 藉 chi² Phonetic, a field plowed by the Emperor, appanage, to borrow. This is made up of 素, 耒 lei³, a harrow (See No. 601) and 昝, 昔 hsi¹, dried meat old, ancient. (See No. 222). The crops from the Imperial field were used in sacrifices. This phonetic is made up of the products of the field, grain, and the results of the chase, dried meat; in a word, the articles used as food. By planting and hunting one could supply himself with these articles and the original meaning was, "to avail oneself of," and this meaning was extended to "borrow." It is now written with the grass radical when used in this sense.

**869** 穢

hui⁴, Weeds growing among grain, dirty, unclean.

禾 ho², Radical No. 115, standing grain. (See No. 556).

歲 sui⁴, Phonetic, a harvest, a year. (See No. 197). As Jupiter's phases indicated whether or not war was to be waged, it thus decided whether the crops 禾 ho² were properly cared for; when war was being carried on the weeds were not removed and thus the fields were dirty, as the men were called away from their agricultural pursuits.

肚

tu⁴, The belly.

月 肉 jou⁴, Radical No. 130, meat, flesh. (See No. 133).

土 *t'u³*, Phonetic, earth. (See No. 13). This character is not found in the Shuo Wen and hence is probably a modern invention. The 土 *t'u³* is a simple phonetic.

**871** 苟

*kou³*, Illicit, careless, if.

艹 *ts'ao³*, Radical No. 140, grass. (See No. 22).

句 *kou¹*, Phonetic ; curved, crooked, a hook ; to entice ; to cross out from a list. This is composed of 丩 , 乭 *chiu¹*. a creeping vine, (See No. 861), and 口 *k'ou³*, mouth. This phonetic is often written 勾 *kou¹*. Because a creeping vine extends its growth in any direction, it is regarded as being selfish, careless, and by extension illicit.

**872** 偷

*t'ou¹*, To steal, to pilfer, secretly, stealthily.

亻, 人 *jên²*, Radical No. 9, a man.

俞, 龠 *yü²* Phonetic, a small boat. (See No. 795).

The original writing of this character 媮 was 媮 *t'ou¹*, and it has to be looked up still in the Shuo Wen under 女 *nü³*, woman, where it says the vulgar writing is 偷 *t'ou¹*. It is evidence that the incongruity of using 女 *nü³*, when in the courts and jails ninety-nine out of a hundred thieves are men, was recognized and consequently the 女 *nü³* was replaced by 亻 *jên²*, a person of either sex. Why 龠 was used as phonetic is not apparent ; perhaps boat-women were notorious for their thieving propensities.

**873** 妒

*tu⁴*, Jealous, envious.

女 *nü³*, Radical No. 38, a woman, a girl. (See No. 16).

戶 *hu⁴*, Phonetic, a single door. (See No. 480).
This is another instance where women are maligned by the scribes as if jealousy were confined to the female portion of the human race. The Shuo Wen says that 妒 *tu* is the jealousy of women and 懯 *chi⁴* the jealousy of men. If this is correct why is 女 *nü³* used in both characters? The present character represents a woman back of a 戶 door giving vent to her jealousy where she is not seen by others.

**874 渣**

*cha¹*, Sediment, dregs.

氵,水 *shui³*, Radical No. 85, water. (See No. 79).

查 *ch'a²*, Phonetic, a proper name. (See No. 397).
It was at one time used as the character for a railing and also for the foundation of a pillar, but none of these meanings aid in the explanation of the present combination, therefore it has to be put in the class of simple phonetics.

**875 境**

*ching⁴*, A region, a place; state or condition.

土 *t'u³*, Radical No. 32, earth. (See No. 13).

竟 *ching⁴*, Phonetic, the end, limits; boundaries where the pronunciations 音 *yin¹*, of men 儿 differ; only, nothing but. With the addition of 土 *t'u³*, earth, the stress is removed from the boundaries, to the region in which the language is the same.

**876 楚**

*ch'u³*, Painful, distressing; orderly, well-done.

木 *mu*⁴, Radical No. 75, wood, tree. (See No. 22).

楚, 楚 *ch'u*³, Phonetic, a place planted with trees. This phonetic contains the radical, the upper part is a grove or forest 林 *lin*². The lower part is 疋 *shu*², the foot in motion. (W. 112 C, 119 N). It is a difficult thing to walk through a thicket. The idea of orderly may have been suggested by the regular order of the trees which were planted in the grove.

877 悟 *wu*⁴, To awaken, to discern ; to recover.

忄, 心 *hsin*¹, Radical No. 61, the heart. (See No. 18).

吾 *wu*² Phonetic, I, my. It is composed of 五 *wu*³ five (See No. 30), and 口 *k'ou*³ the mouth, 吾 *wu*⁴ is a very lofty appellation for I, myself, as it represents the creation of all things 五, by the word of my mouth 口, but man has ever been prone to elevate himself and with the addition of 忄 *hsin*¹, heart, consciousness, we have the symbol for, to discern.

878 漂 *p'iao*¹, To float, to drift.

水, 氵 *shui*³, Radical No. 85, water. (See No. 79).

票 *p'iao*⁴, Phonetic, a signal, a ticket. (See No. 255). The old writing represents smoke floating in the air as a signal; when 氵 *shui*³, water, is added, the floating is transferred from the air to the water.

879 遮 *chê*¹, To cover, to hide, to screen, to intercept.

辶, 辵 *cho*⁴ Radical No. 162, to run and stop (See No. 10).

庶 *shu*⁴ Phonetic, all (See No. 762). If a person

left or went away from, 辶 *cho*⁴, the light
of the hearth 庶 he was not seen, as
this was all the light in the house at
night.

**880** 彩     *ts'ai*³, Variegated, gay, ornamented with
diverse colors.

彡 *shan*¹ Radical No. 59, to adorn with feathers
or colored hair. It is intended to represent feathers or long hair.

采, 采 *ts'ai*³, Phonetic, to pluck with the fingers 爪
fruit or flowers from a tree 木; to choose.
(W. 49 B). With the addition of 彡 *shan*¹,
to adorn with feathers or long hair, we
have flowers and long hair or feathers;
thus the character contains all the natural
articles for ornamentation.

**881** 擋     *tang*³, To obstruct, to withstand.

扌,手 *shou*³, Radical No. 64, the hand. (See No. 53).

當 *tang*¹, Phonetic, to be equal to. (See No. 478).
A hand 扌 *shou*³, must be equal to 當 the
requirements before it can obstruct or
withstand 擋.

**882** 獄     *yü*⁴, That which decides who is right in a
quarrel; a prison, a jail.

犬 *ch'üan*³ Radical No. 94, a dog, a pictorial
representation.
The Shuo Wen explains this character as
being two dogs 犬 犬 *ch'üan*³. The phonetic
is 言 *yên*² but though it has no phonetic
force, it assists in explaining the meaning.
The two dogs personate two criminals
who are mutually incriminating each

other 言 yên², in order to secure a lighter sentence. This is not a pleasant pastime and is an apt symbol for Hades or prison.

**883 嫁**

chia⁴, To marry a husband.

女 nü³, Radical No. 38, a woman. (See No. 16).

家 chia¹, Phonetic, a home, a family. (See No. 221). The bride leaves the parental roof and a new home 家 chia¹, is started. This combination of radical and phonetic forms a good character for the above meaning.

**884 撇**

p'ieh¹, To throw away, to give up.

扌,手 shou³, Radical No. 64, the hand. (See No. 53).

敝 pi⁴, Phonetic, mean, poor, ruined. (See No. 211). With the hand 扌 shou³, added, which indicates the action of discarding or throwing away worn out clothing 敝 we have a very good symbol for the above meaning 撇.

**885 殿,臀**

tien⁴, A grand hall, a palace.

殳 shu¹ Radical No. 79, the right hand making a jerky motion. (See No. 165).

屍 t'un² The phonetic is not now used as a character; the buttocks. The explanation given in Chu Shih 朱氏 Shuo Wên is as follows: 盜賊繫囚榜笞臀以臀爲之 "A thief is bound and spanked in the hall." The second 臀 is here used for 殿 tien⁴. A place for the administration of punishment seems to have originally been the chief use of the 殿 tien⁴, but as their civilization advanced it was used for large gatherings of any kind. (W. 22 D).

**886** 籬

*li²*, A fence, to inclose.

竹 *chu²*, Radical No. 118, bamboo. (See No. 7).

離 *li²*, Phonetic, to part, to separate. (See No. 351).

To separate off, 離 *li²*, a plot of land with a bamboo 竹 *chu²* fence is the explanation of this character.

**887** 笆

*pa¹*, A bamboo hedge; a species of bamboo with spines.

⺮, 竹 *chu²*, Radical No. 118, bamboo (See No. 7).

巴 *pa¹*, Phonetic, a kind of boa (See No. 53).

It may be that a serpent 巴 was selected for the phonetic because it, like a hedge, has length without much width; and 竹 *chu²*, bamboo, is a common material for a hedge, or a fence.

**888** 葡

*p'u²*, The vine.

卄, 艸 *ts'ao³*, Radical No. 140, grass or vegetation. (See No. 22).

匍, 匐 *p'u²*, Phonetic, to fall prostrate; to crawl, as a child. The 勹 *pao¹* here takes the place of 丩, 昌 *chiu¹* of the original writing. The reason for this change is that 勹 *pao¹* is one of the 214 radicals and 丩 *chiu¹* is not. Thus the meaning was a vine which spreads 甫, *fu³*. (See No. 416).

**889** 萄

*t'ao²*, The grape.

卄, 艸 *ts'ao³*, Radical No. 140, vegetation. (See No. 22).

**匋,匋** *t'ao²*, Phonetic, a furnace for pottery. This seems to be a simple phonetic. It is a pictorial representation of a kiln 勹 with porcelain ware 缶 inside. (W. 54 D). 匋 is a recent character, coined about 100 B.C. An emperor of the Han Dynasty in 138 B.C. sent 張騫 Chang¹ Ch'ien¹, to the region of the Caspian Sea on a mission and this man brought back grapes, alfalfa and large horses. He saw that grapes were good for men and alfalfa was good for animals. This man also established a trade route to that part of the world. (See Giles' Biographical Dictionary, under Chang⁴ Ch'ien 張騫, and K'ang Hsi's Dictionary under 匋 *t'ao²*.)

890 **壓**

*ya¹*, To press down, to repress.

**土.** *t'u³*, Radical No. 32, the earth.

**厭** *yên⁴*, Phonetic, to dislike, to loathe, to be satiated. (See No. 841). This phonetic represents a man whose stomach is distended and uncomfortable. The addition of 土 *t'u³* earth, may imply that a hole is to be filled with earth 土 and solidly packed 壓 as an over-distended stomach is packed with food.

891 **鞭**

*pien¹*, A whip.

**革** *kê²*, Radical No. 177, to skin. (See No. 163).

**便** *pien⁴*, Phonetic, convenient, ready. (See No· 492). The 鞭 was originally an instrument of torture, but it is now used as a whip for animals. A convenient 便 piece of leather 革 may stimulate, in some, recollections of a slipper sole.

**892 您** nin², You. (A polite term). This is an unauthorized character.

心 hsin¹, Radical No. 61, the heart.

你 ni³, Phonetic, you. (See No. 3). The addition of heart 心 hsin¹, is intended as a mark of respect. Some think that the origin of 您 nin², was from 你老 ni³ lao³ which in the spoken language was contracted to nin⁻, and this character was coined for the new sound.

**893 盪** t'ang⁴, A bath tub.

皿 min³, Radical No. 108, a dish or vessel.

湯 t'ang¹, Phonetic, hot water, broth, 皿 min³ and 湯 t'ang¹, form a good character for the above ; also read tang⁴.

**894 形** hsing², Form, figure, shape.

彡 shan¹ Radical No. 59, feathers, long hair. (See No. 415).

开, 幵 ch'ien¹ Phonetic, two shields of equal height. (See No. 235). Shields with decorations in various designs were common. An article if not decorated is spoken of as lacking in appearance or shape.

**895 俩** lia³, Two, a couple. (An unauthorized character).

人, 亻 jên², Radical No. 9, a man.

兩 liang³, Phonetic, two, a pair, an ounce. (See No. 35).

It is probable that this character was originally used for two men, but it is now used for two of anything.

**896** 景

> *ching³*, Bright sunlight ; a view ; appearance ; circumstances.

日 *jih⁴*, Radical No. 72, the sun.  (See No. 12).

京 *ching¹*, Phonetic, the capital.  (See No. 98).
> When the sun, 日 *jih⁴*, is high, 京 *ching¹* then one can get a view of the landscape or can learn the appearance of the surroundings.

**897** 務

> *wu⁴*, To use great effort and bend the mind to a subject, to strive after ; business, duty, must.

力 *li⁴*, Radical, No. 19, strength.  (See No. 212).

敄 *wu⁴* Phonetic, to display one's skill in wielding, 攴 *p'u¹*, arms, 矛 *mao²*, (a three pronged halberd).  The 力 *li⁴*, strength, is a modern addition.

**898** 介, 乔

> *chieh⁴*, Boundaries which separate men, one alone; an assistant, one who waits on, to assist ; petty.

人 *jên²*, Radical No. 9, a man.

八 *pa¹*, Phonetic, eight.  (See No. 32).  It has no phonetic power, but in the seal writing it helps to explain the meaning of the character.  Man, 人 *jên²*, is in the center and the 八 *pa¹*, separates him from others.  The meaning of to assist has been added without logical sanction.

**899** 紹

> *shao⁴*, To connect, to join, to tie together, to hand down as a trade.

糸 *szŭ¹*, Radical No. 120, silk.  (See No. 8).

召 *chao⁴*, Phonetic, to summon, to call.  (See No. 722).  The original meaning seems to have been a father summoning, 召 *chao*[4], his son and requesting him to continue, 糸 *szŭ*[1], the family trade or profession.

**900 極,櫃**

    *chī*[2], Utmost, very.

木 *mu*[4], Radical No. 75, wood. (See No. 22).

亟 *chī*[4] Phonetic, haste, urgent, a struggle for life. A man who watches for the favorable opportunity of heaven—and the advantages of earth.—A man is seen in the seal writing, between heaven and earth 二 *erh*[4] (the radical); he is striving with voice 口, and hand, 又, to gain his end. (W. 2 D). With the addition of 木 *mu*[4], a tree, the character stands for extreme, the very top. The tree, in its position between heaven and earth, attains to a much higher altitude than does man.

**901 盼**

    *p'an*[4], To look at, to hope for.

目 *mu*[4], Radical No. 109, the eye. (See No. 102).

分 *fên*[1], Phonetic, to divide. (See No. 181).

When one hopes 盼 for something the eye 目, *mu*[4], is prone to spend a portion 分 *fên*[1], of its time looking for it.

**902 股**

    *ku*[3], The thighs, the haunches, the rump; a division, share; a band, a gang; a strand of a rope.

肉,月 *jou*[4], Radical No. 130, meat. (See No. 133).

殳 *shu*[1] Phonetic, a long pole projecting before a war-chariot, a spear, to kill. (See No. 165). The meaning in 股 seems to be taken from the first definition given, the thighs are an extension of the body. The idea of a strand or a part or share seems to come from an ancient usage of the word ; the Shuo Wen says that the 殳 *shu*[1] is here used for 殊 *shu*[1], different, to distinguish between. The fibers of a rope are divided into strands, and a business concern is made up of a certain number of shares.

**903 礦**

*kung*[3], A mine.

石 *shih*[2], Radical No. 112, stone. (See No. 42).

廣 *kuang*[3], Phonetic, broad. (See No. 696). The Shuo Wen says that this should be written 礦. Here 黄, *huang*[2], (See No. 207), is used for 土, *t'u*[3], yellow earth, with 石, *shih*[2], metal-bearing stone. Another writing is 鑛.

**904 緒**

*hsü*[4], A thread, a clue, to succeed to.

糸 *szŭ*[1], Radical No. 120, silk. (See No. 8).

者, 崮 *chê*[3], Phonetic, this, that, it. This character was invented to represent a connection between what has already been said and what is to follow. The seal writing indicates that it reaches in two directions, two crossed branches, and beneath is 自 *tzŭ*[4], contracted, the starting point for what follows. Thus the composition of the character 緒 indicates the self 自 reaching in all directions in order to find a clue or trace 糸 of the thing desired.

**905 簡**

*chien*[3], A bamboo slip, to abridge, rude.

⺮, 竹 *chu*[2], Radical No. 118, bamboo. (See No. 7).

間 *chien*[1], Phonetic, between, among. (See No.

183). Strips were made of the part of the bamboo 竹 between 間 *chien¹*, the joints, and on these slips directions or descriptions were written; if the description was lengthy the slips were bound up in book form, but when the description was kept within the limits of one slip of bamboo it was regarded as abridged and eventually the above character took on that meaning.

**906 衙**

*ya²*, The house or office of an official; a tribunal.

行, 仝 *hsing²*, *hang²*, Radical No. 144, to walk, to act; read *hang²* a row, motion. (See No. 161).

吾 *wu²* Phonetic, I, my. (See No. 877). The original phonetic was 牙, *ya²*, a tooth, something to be dreaded; it represents the official. The radical 行 *hang²*, a row, in order, represents the underlings who are standing at their places in a row on either side of the official. It is difficult to explain how the writing was changed from 衙 to 衙.

**907 竟**

*ching⁴*, The end, finally, only.

立 *li⁴*, Radical No. 117, to stand. (See No. 216). By using 立 *li⁴*, as the radical the etymology has been destroyed. This character is very similar to 章 *chang¹*, a chapter. (See No. 87) 晉 *yin¹*, sound, should be the radical, and below this is man, 儿, 竟 *ching* (See No. 875). Another explanation is, 晉 indicates that this man

儿 was singing, he sent forth tones, 音 and we thought only of the melody 音; when the song is completed 竟 there is a sense of finality.

**908** 探

ts'ai³, To select, to pluck.

扌,手 shou³, Radical No. 64, the hand. (See No. 53).

采 ts'ai³, Phonetic, to gather, to pluck. (See No. 281). The addition of the 扌, t'i² shou³, contributes nothing.

**909** 項

hsiang⁴, The nape of the neck ; a sort : item, sum, income.

頁 yeh⁴, Radical No. 181, the head, a page of a book. (See No. 105).

工 kung¹, Phonetic, labor. (See No. 89). Owing to the head, neck and back forming a notch resembling one side of the radical kung¹, 工, this symbol was selected as the phonetic for the above character. Another reason given for the selection is that the nape of the neck is where burdens are carried, viz., where work, 工, kung¹, is done. (W. 82 A).

**910** 津

ching¹, A ford, a ferry, a narrows, a mart where boats stop.

氵,水 shui³, Radical No. 85, water. (See No. 79).

聿 yü¹,⁴ Phonetic, a stylus. (See No. 7). This phonetic was formerly 聿 chin¹, a stylus 聿 yü⁴ making marks 彡. It was contracted to 聿 yü⁴. There seems to be much evidence to the effect that originally this character was written 艜, a place where a boat was sure to be found for crossing a river. This being a clumsy character it was contracted until it assumed its present form.

**911** 託

言 *yên[2]*, Radical No. 149, a word. (See No. 10).

*t'o[1]*, To charge with, to entrust.

乇 *t'o[4]* Phonetic, to depend on, to engage a substitute. (See No. 624). By a word or command 言 the responsibility is changed 乇 *t'o[4]* from one person to another.

**912** 遊

*yu[2]*, To roam, to wander, to stroll, to travel.

辶, 辵 *cho[4]* Radical No. 162, to run and stop. (See No. 10).

斿 *yu[2]* Phonetic, the motion of the arms of a swimmer. (See No. 850). The character 遊 is often used for No. 850 游. The 辶 *cho[4]*, indicates movement, and for moving from place to place on land, is more logical than is 游 *yu[2]*.

**913** 機

*chi[1]*, A machine, a loom, to reveal, a spring.

木 *mu[4]*, Radical No. 75, wood. (See No. 22).

幾 *chi[1,3]*, Phonetic, few, nearly. (See No. 34). This phonetic plus wood is used for machine. The first machines probably were looms and these were constructed of wood. A few 幾 pieces of wood 木. which developed movement is a good symbol for a machine 機.

**914** 器

*ch'i[4]*, A utensil, an instrument.

犬 *ch'üan[3]* Radical No. 94, a dog, a pictoria representation.

㗊 *ch'i[1]* Phonetic, many mouths, clamor. Dishes

are spoken of as having mouths, thus each mouth represents a dish. The dog was added as he was kept to clean up the dishes after a meal. Another explanation is, the dog is watchful and careful of articles he is responsible for ; thus here the dog implies that utensils must be cared for. There is an old writing 甒 *ch'i*⁴, which has the radical 缶 *fou*³, porcelain, instead of 犬, *ch'üan*³, which is more logical, but owing to its being obsolete it does not help in remembering the construction of the character.

**915** 照

*chao*⁴, To illuminate, according to.

灬, 火 *huo*³, Radical No. 86, fire.   (See No. 482).

昭 *chao*¹, Phonetic, bright, to show forth. This phonetic is composed of the sun 日, *jih*⁴, and 召 *chao*⁴, to call or summon. (See No. 722). The sun 日 is that which calls 召 us in the morning owing to its brightness 昭. When 火 *huo*³, fire, is added, the character stands for, to illuminate 照.

**916** 精

*ching*¹, Unmixed, fine, essence, semen, vigor.

米 *mi*³, Radical No. 119, rice (See No. 47).

青 *ch'ing*¹, Phonetic, color of nature, green, blue, black.  (See No. 63). As rice grows in water the weeds or other grain which are found in wheat and oats cannot flourish in a paddy field ; therefore rice is seldom mixed with other grain, and consequently it is here used as a symbol of pure or unadulterated. 青 *ch'ing*¹ is also a symbol of purity and these two radicals when combined form the character for unmixed or fine.

**917** 聯

*lien*², To connect, to combine.

耳 *êr*³, Radical No. 128, the ear. (See No. 71).

絲 *kuan*¹ Phonetic, to run threads through the web. (See No. 95). With the addition of 耳 *êr*³, ear, one is inclined to believe, that this character was first used for the collecting of evidence, combining the statements of different individuals.

**918** 爽

*shuang*³, Cheerful, quick, crisp.

爻 *yao*² Radical No. 89, to mix, to lay crosswise.

大 *ta*⁴, Phonetic, large. (See No. 54),—without phonetic force. The two 爻 *yao*² represent the lattice work of a window and as this is large, 大, *ta*⁴. enough to admit light and air the occupants of the room are not gloomy and despondent. Or, a man 大 acting 爻 with both arms. (W. 39 O).

**919** 獲

*huo*⁴, To catch, to obtain.

犬, 犭 *ch'üan*³ Radical No. 94, a dog. Pictorial representation.

蒦, 萑 *huo*¹ Phonetic, to seize with the hand 又, as an owl 隹 *chui*¹ seizes its prey. With 犬 *ch'üan*³ added the character was probably first used for getting game in the chase with the help of a hound. It is now used for, getting or obtaining, in general. (W 103 C).

**920** 租

*tsu*¹, To rent ; or tax in kind from fields, to lease ; taxes.

禾 *ho²*, Radical No. 115, standing grain. (See No. 556).

且 *tsu³* Phonetic, a stand used in sacrifice (*tsu³*, archaic pronunciation, now read *ch'ieh³* and *chü¹*). In 長箋說文 is the following statement: 租 *tsu¹* was originally the land tax 田賦, *t'ien² fu⁴*. It was originally written 且 *tsu¹*. Land rent was spoken of as the portion of grain 禾, *ho²*, used as an offering in the ancestral temple. The character 租 is now used for any rent or tax.

921 顧

*ku⁴*, To look after, to regard, to consider.

頁 *yeh⁴*, Radical No. 181, the head, the page of a book. (See No. 105).

雇 *ku⁴*, Phonetic, to hire, to engage. (See No. 361). With 頁 *yeh⁴*, head, added the idea of, to look after or consider, is expressed. If a person heeded 顧 the migration of these birds 雇 as explained under No. 361, he took the warning to heart 頁 *yeh⁴*, and acted on it.

922 響

*hsiang*, Sound, noise, reverberation.

音 *yin¹*, Radical No. 180, a sound. (See No. 39).

鄉 *hsiang¹*, Phonetic, village, country, rustic. (See No. 466). The Chinese divide sound in to two kinds, 響 *hsiang³*, a nonmusical sound, and 音 *yin¹*, a musical sound. When a sound comes to the ear it is 聲 *shêng¹*. The etymology set forth in 長箋 說文 is that 鄉 *hsiang¹* is the abode of people and when 音 *yin¹* is added it stands for the home of sound or its origin. When one hears a sound he may go in that direction and may find it was a clock striking, and he will say 是 鐘 的 響.

**923** 決

*chüeh²*, To decide ; to pass sentence ; certainly.

冫 *ping¹*, Radical No. 15, ice. (See No. 516).

夬 *chüeh²*, Phonetic, to cut off, to decide, to settle, certainly. This phonetic is described under No. 109, an additional meaning seems reasonable according to 段 氏 說 文, to split with a wedge. The act of splitting a log is suddenly accomplished and once done there is no way of uniting it again. With ice as the radical it suggests a familiar winter sight, cracks or fissures in thick ice. With water which is also used as the radical, it indicates a break in a river bank, a condition once established, there was no question as to its existence.

**924** 掌

*chang³*, The palm of the hand, to control.

手 *shou³*, Radical No. 64, the hand. (See No. 53).

尚 *shang⁴*, Phonetic, a roof of a house. (See No. 52). When the hand is placed palm downwards and fingers act as pillars, the palm assumes the shape of a roof.

**925** 櫃

*kuei⁴*, A case with drawers, a chest, a treasury.

木 *mu⁴*, Radical No. 75, wood. (See No. 22).

匱 *kuei⁴, k'üei⁴*, Phonetic, a case with drawers. Read *k'uei⁴*, wearied. This phonetic is made up of 匚, *fang¹*, a wooden trough, a log hollowed out, by extension, a chest, a trunk, (W. 51 A), and 貴, *kuei⁴*, expensive, honorable. (See No. 863). This phonetic itself sets forth the meaning :—something valuable is placed in a chest or case, and the addition of 木, *mu*[4], is superfluous.

926 戚, 鏚

戈, 未 *ch'i*, [1,2,4,] A relative, grieved.

*ko*[1], Radical No. 62, a spear, a lance. (See No. 2). That which remains after taking out the radical is not a regular phonetic. The radical is not. the regular 戈, *ko*[1], as can be seen in the seal writing. The original meaning was a battle ax 戉, and it had 攴 *shu*[2], (contracted) to pick beans, (See No. 547) in the center. It may have been a weapon which was used both in military and agricultural pursuits, and so always at hand in time of war or peace ; hence its use as a symbol for relatives who are always at hand. The meaning of grieved is explained in the 說文 *Shuo Wen* thus :—Owing to its being a weapon of war, it caused a pang of regret to arise when seen.

927 幹, 斡

干 *kan*[4], To attend to, business.

*kan*[1], Radical No. 51, arms, a crime. (See No. 110).

倝, 覃 *kan*[4] Phonetic, the sun 日 penetrating into 入人, *ju*[1] the jungle 屮 and drawing up the vapor 丂. (See No. 137). The action of the sun is transferred to a man who has a 干 *kan*[1], a stick in hand. (See No. 110). The seal writing represents the overhanging branch about to take root, the form with 入 *ju*⁴, to enter, represents the tree as rooted and separated from the parent tree.

**928 濫**

水, 氵 *shui*³, Radical No. 85, water. (See No. 79).

監 *chien*¹, Phonetic, to watch, a prison. (See No. 294).

*lan*⁴, To overflow, profuse.

When the water of a river is confined within its banks it is where it should be, but when it breaks over 濫, it is like a criminal who has broken jail.

**929 虧**

虍 *hu*³ Radical No. 141, a tiger, a tiger skin. (See No. 258).

*k'uei*¹, Wanting, defective ; a grievance.

This cannot be broken up into radical and phonetic. Perhaps the character was coined to accord with the expression 行爲如虎 *hsing*² *wei*² *ju*² *hu*³, "He acts like a tiger," a man who is not governed by rules of propriety. The 隹 *chui*¹, a short-tailed bird, is used to impersonate a man.

丂, 丂 *yü*², is the breath overcoming an obstacle. Thus the character represents one who overcomes any compunctions of conscience and, like a tiger, forgets all kindnesses and does violence to friend or foe.

**930 狀**

犬 *ch'üan*³ Radical No. 94, a dog. Pictorial character.

爿 *ch'iang*² Phonetic, the left half of a tree. (See No. 84). The 說文, *Shuo Wen* explains

*chuang*⁴, Appearance, complaint, a law suit.

this character thus :—There is no animal the offspring of which more strikingly resemble in appearance the father or mother than the offspring of dogs ; therefore the selection of this radical. The one half of a log 片, also has a striking resemblance to the other half.

**931** 亂,𤔔

*luan⁴*, Confusion, disarranged, anarchy.

乙 *i¹* Radical No. 5, germination, movement. (See No. 137).

𤔔 *luan⁴* Phonetic, a thread 玄 being disentangled by two hands 𠬪. The rack H on which the thread is suspended is probably the loom. The ㄴ is 乙, *i¹*, which represents the thread being drawn out. (W. 90 B). (Archaic meaning, to put in order).

**932** 怨

*yüan⁴*, To dislike, ill will.

心 *hsin¹*, Radical No. 61, heart. (See No. 18).

夗 *yüan¹* Phonetic, to turn in bed, decency. (See No. 42). This character is explained by starting with 心 *hsin¹*, the heart; the feelings are hurt and consequently the person turns away 夕 *hsi¹*, acts as if it were night, and has nothing more to do 卩, 㔾 *chieh²*, with the one who has done the injury.

**933** 匯

*hui⁴*, Converge, deposit, a draft; to send money by draft.

匚 *fang¹* Radical No. 22, a chest, a log hollowed out. (W. 51 A).

淮 *huai²* Phonetic, the name of a large river in Honan and Anhwei. It may have received this name owing to the great number of water fowl in this region. The 匚 *fang*[1], a chest or receptacle, (See No. 925) indicates that a large amount of water must be confined with banks. The 滙 is an incorrect writing.

**934** 按

于 手 *an*[4,] *ên*[4], To lay hand on, according to.

*shou*[3], Radical No. 64, the hand. (See No. 53).

安 *an*[1], Phonetic, peace, quiet. This phonetic shows how women were regarded. If she, 女 was in the house 宀 all was peaceful, but if not, the opposite condition obtained as she would stir up trouble. The *Shuo Wen* says in explanation of 按 *an*[4]:—if one uses the hand and holds on to his goods, keeping them in their proper place, he also will receive advantage from this course of action.

**935** 減

水, 氵 *chien*[3], To lessen, to diminish.

*shui*[3], Radical No. 85, water. (See No. 79).

咸 *hsien*[2] Phonetic, to bite, to wound with the mouth ; modern meaning, all. (See No. 305). The *Shuo*[1] *Wên*[2] simply affirms that this character is arbitrarily used for the above meaning ; consequently no logical reason for the combination is set forth. Water is the radical and 咸 is a simple phonetic.

**936** 釐

里 *li*[2], A grain, a hundredth, tenth of a cash.

*li*[3], Radical No. 166, a village, a Chinese mile. (See No. 82).

氂,氂 *li*[2] Phonetic, to cut down, to diminish. This

is composed of 乇, to cut down a big tree 末 *wei*[1], 厂 represents its falling. (W. 120 C). This character was originally used for another meaning, but it has long been used for the above. A 里 is a plot of ground divided into small fields. The tree is fallen and split into small fragments and one of these can be regarded as a grain

937 單

*tan*[1], Single, odd, thin, only, but; a list, a bill.

口 *k'ou*[3], Radical No. 30. the mouth. (See No. 17). This is a character which originally represented a quarrel "", *hsüan*[1], two mouths, and an assault with a shovel 苹 *pan*[1] or pitchfork. (W. 72 E). It has long since lost this meaning and is used for single, odd, and so forth. The original meaning of the phonetic is seen in the following characters, 彈 *tan*[1] a crossbow, a bullet, a shell, and 戰 *chan*[4], to fight.

938 保

*pao*[3], To protect.

亻, 人 *jên*[2], Radical No. 9, a man.

呆 *tai*[1], Phonetic, an idiot. This was arbitrarily given to this character. The real phonetic is 禾 朵 *pao*[3]. A bird spreading its wings to cover its nest. Another older writing is 𤔔, a hen covering her young to protect them. This originally did not have a 亻 *jên*[2], at the side. The idea was to protect as a hen protects her young. (W. 94 C)

939 累, 纍

*lei*,[2,3,4] To connect, to implicate, often, weary.

糸 *szŭ*[1], Radical No. 120, silk. (See No. 141).

田 *t'ien²*, Phonetic, a field. (See No. 212). This was originally 畾 *lei²*, three articles connected or tied together. Because of the difficulty of writing, these have been reduced to 田 and the etymology lost. The 糸 was that which held the articles together.

**940 贅**

*chui⁴*, A pledge, to pawn, hanging on, repetition.

貝 *pei⁴*, Radical No. 154, precious. (See No. 38).

敖, 敖 *ao²* Phonetic, to go out for a stroll, it should be written 敖, to go out 出 for relaxation 放 *fang¹*, as animals are let out to pasture, and will return again. (See No. 147). With the addition of 貝 *pei⁴*, valuable, (See No. 38), it was used for a security left in the hands of a person from whom something has been borrowed.

The meaning of repetition may have originated owing to the repeated entreaty of the borrower to recover the article pledged before the loan was refunded.

**941 藏**

*ts'ang²*, To conceal, to store up.

艹 *ts'ao³*, Radical No. 140, grass. (See No. 22).

臧 *tsang¹* Phonetic, good, generous, compliance, the virtue of ministers. 爿 *ch'iang²*, which often means strength, and 戈 *ko¹*, weapon, when united form 戕 *ch'iang²*, to do violence to. When 臣 *ch'ên²*, a minister, is added this force and violence is only used in accordance with the benign purposes of the official who watches and defends the state. When 艹

ts'ao³, is added it means covered with grass, to store up, to conceal. Perhaps this phonetic was chosen owing to the mystery attending government action.

942 耗

hao⁴, To squander, to consume; bad.

耒 lei³, Radical No. 127, a plow. (See No. 601).

毛 mao², Phonetic, a hair. (See No. 254).

The *Shuo Wen* claims that the radical of this character should not be 耒 lei³ but 禾 ho², Thus the original idea was the beard or husk 毛 of grain 禾, the chaff; grain threshed and removed, nothing but the chaff 毛 remained.

943 漲

chang⁴, To overflow, an inundation.

水, 氵 shui³, Radical No. 85, water. (See No. 79).

張 chang¹, Phonetic, to draw a bow; to extend, increase; a classifier of tables; paper, a surname. (See No. 55).

Water 水 increases and extends 張 over the surface of the land.

944 扣

k'ou⁴, To knock, to deduct, to hook on, to buckle, to button, a discount.

手, 扌 shou³, Radical No. 64, the hand. (See No. 53).

口 k'ou³, Phonetic, the mouth. (See No. 17).

This combination 扣 was originally used for the governing of a horse with bit and bridle. The hand 手 exerted influence on the mouth 口 of the horse. The idea of to buckle or to button may have originated from the necessity of putting the bridle over the head of the beast.

The bridle once on the animal had to do what the driver desired. Discounts are exacted by those who have power over another.

**945 祥**

示 羊

hsiang², Felicity, good luck.

示 shih⁴, Radical No. 113, to show, a revelation. (See No. 164).

羊 yang², Phonetic, a sheep. (See No. 253). Most of the characters which have 羊, yang², for a phonetic have a good meaning. Thus, this combination stands for a fortunate or auspicious 羊 revelation 示.

**946 緞**

tuan⁴, Satin.

糸 szŭ¹, Radical No. 120, silk. (See No. 8).

段 tuan⁴, Phonetic, a fragment, a section. The left part of this phonetic is said to be a contraction of 耑 耑 tuan⁴, origin, a plant which develops both above and under the ground. The right side is 殳, shu². (See No. 165). This combination indicates that the plant has been violently torn to pieces. It may have been selected because in the manufacture of silk the cocoon is thrown into hot water; the chrysalis is killed, the thread unwound, thus destroying the cocoon.

**947 佩**

p'ei⁴, A pendant, to hang on the girdle, to esteem.

人, 亻 jên², Radical No. 9, man.

凧 The phonetic is not found in K'ang Hsi's dictionary. It is composed of 几 fan², all, and 巾 chin¹, cloth, and is supposed to represent the small ornaments hanging from the girdle 巾 *chin*[1], 從 八, 從 巾 (W. 21 D). When a gentleman went out he always wore ornaments on the girdle. These ornaments he selected because he admired them ; by extension this character is now used to express satisfaction with a person or things.

**948** 賺

*chuan*[4], To sell at a profit, to make money, gain.

貝 *pei*[4], Radical No. 154, precious. (See No. 38),

兼, 縑 *chien*[1], Phonetic, to join together ; together with, both. This is a hand holding two stalks of grain, a hand binding sheaves. (W. 44 I). The idea of this combination 賺 is to increase the investment 貝, to double 兼 it.

**949** 豁

*huo*[1], To open out, liberal ; to remit.

谷 *ku*[3], Radical No. 150, a valley. (See No. 579).

害 *hai*[4] *ho*[4], Phonetic, to injure. (See No. 436).

This character 豁 seems to have two explanations :

1. A person has met with misfortune 害 *hai*[4] or *ho*[4], and others have opened 谷 *ku*[3], their hand liberally for his assistance.
2. One has a calamity 害 *ho*[4], such as a harelip, 谷 *ch'iao*[4], the upper lip. A person who has a harelip is spoken of as a 豁子 *huo*[1] *tzŭ*[3]. (See No. 509). 谷 *ch'iao*[4] not being a radical 谷 *ku*[3], was substituted.

**950** 支, 枲, 寺

*chih*[1]. A bough, to prop up, a branch, to advance money, to draw money.

This is the 65th radical. The old writing represents a hand pulling a bough from a tree. (W. 43 C). The reason why this character is used to express giving out money is because the tree puts forth branches from the trunk. Note the phrase 多齡長支 *to¹ huo¹ ch'ang³ chih¹*, to generously overlook the debts of clerks, who have borrowed from the employer more money than their wages amount to. At the end of a prosperous year these sums are not collected.

**951 提**

才, 手 *shou³*, Radical No. 64, the hand. (See No. 53).

是 *shih⁴*, Phonetic, right. (See No. 12). Without phonetic significance. To take up 提 that which is proper 是 in order to teach or instruct.

*t'i²*, To take up, to suggest ; to bring forward.

**952 飾**

*shih⁴*, To paint, to ornament, to adorn, to pretend.

食 *shih² ⁴*, Radical No. 184, food, to eat ; eclipse. (See No. 75).

This character is an exception to the rule, as the radical is also the phonetic. In sacrificing an animal it was put before the gods and afterwards eaten. This accounts for the use of 食 *shih⁴*, as radical. The rest of the character is 㐁. The upper part is a man and the lower is a cloth ; before sacrificing the beast a man with a cloth cleansed it and thus improved its appearance. By extension, to adorn.

953 藝 $i^4$, Skill, an art.

艹 *ts'ao*³, Radical No. 140, grass. (See No. 22).

埶 $i^4$ Phonetic, to plant, to cultivate the ground. This is from 坴 *lu*⁴, mushroom. (See No. 485), and 土 *t'u*³ earth which form 坴 *lu*⁴, arable land, 陸 *lu*⁴, dry land, (mushrooms grow on high land), and 丮 *chi*⁴, to hold an instrument or utensil in the hand. Working the soil was the first art practiced by the Chinese. (See No. 139). The 艹 *ts'ao*³, and 云 *yün*² have been recently added, 云 *yün*², cloud, is composed of 二 *shang*⁴ (See No. 93), and 厶 vapor, rising and forming clouds. Thus the character for farming is composed of 艹 vegetation, 埶 tilling the soil and 云 clouds which give rain, without which all effort is vain.

954 鏨 *tsan*⁴, A fine chisel; to engrave.

金 *chin*¹, Radical No. 167, metal. (See No. 13).

斬 *chan*³ ⁴, Phonetic, to decapitate, to cut in two. (See No. 803). A metal instrument used for cutting. This utensil 鏨 is smaller than the ordinary carpenter's chisel; it is used in the manufacture of jewelry in the 首飾 *shou*³ *shih*⁴ shops.

955 拔 *pa*², To root up, to draw up or out; to elevate, promote.

扌, 手 *shou*³, Radical No. 64, the hand. (See No. 53).

犮 *pa*² Phonetic, a dog led by a leash. (See No. 626). This leash enabled one to pull or haul the dog around at will and thus the above meaning has been given to this combination.

**956 絲, 絲**

szŭ[1], Silk as it comes from the cocoons, fine, wire.

糸 szu[1] mi[4] Radical No. 120, silk. (See No. 8).

糸 mi[4] Phonetic. (See No. 141).

The second writing 絲 is not allowed by K'ang Hsi. This character was one of the original 540 radicals. The repetition of 糸 mi[4] indicates that it is not a single thread from a cocoon, but several, ten, are supposed to be required to form a 絲 szŭ[1]. In characters which use the 系 hsi[4] phonetic there is a figurative or real connection. 孫 sun[1], a grandson ; 縣 hsien[4], a district, (See No. 390) ; here the criminal's head is hung up for exhibition.

**957 銲**

han[4], To solder.

金 chin[1], Radical No. 167, metal. (See No. 13).

旱 han[4], Phonetic, the torrid effect of the sun, drought. (See No. 343). Great heat is required to melt the solder.

**958 邀**

yao[1], To engage, to seek, to invite.

辶 cho[4] Radical No. 162, to run and stop. (See No. 10).

敫 yao[4] Phonetic, to shine. This is made up from 放 fang[4], to liberate, (See No. 147 and No. 712) and 白 pai[2], white or light; the meaning is, to shine. When 辶 cho[4], is added the idea is to go to the one who can give you light or help. A person is engaged because he can give assistance, shed light, make conditions better.

**959** 搭

扌,手 shou³, Radical No. 64, the hand. (See No. 53).

荅 ta¹ Phonetic, vetch, peas, vegetation the branches of which get entangled, (W. 14 B). The pea vines and vetch extend, far from the stalk adding joint after joint and thus with the addition of 扌 shou³, a character is formed which means, to add to. This character is unauthorized.

*ta¹*, To add to, to pile up.

**960** 挪

扌,手 shou³, Radical No. 64, the hand. (See No. 53).

那,郍 na⁴, Phonetic, that ; a place 阝邑 where people wore skins with the hair out 冄 for cloth-ing. It may be that this people were nomadic and thus with the addition of hand the character is used for the above meanings. It is an unauthorized character.

*no²*, To move, to remove.

**961** 棧

木 mu⁴, Radical No. 75, wood. (See No. 22).

戔 chien¹ Phonetic, to destroy, narrow, small. (See No. 13). This character 棧 was origi-nally used for a small frame platform built in the camp to protect an officer while sleeping from attack, and from the moisture of the ground. It was also used for a lookout during military operations. By extension it is now used for a store-house, as goods in a 棧 chan⁴, are suppos-ed to be secure.

*chan⁴*, A storehouse.

**962** 散,糤

*san³,⁴*, Miscellaneous, to fall apart ; separate ; a powder.

支 *p'u*[1] Radical No. 66, (contracted) to tap, to rap. (See No. 17). The original phonetic is destroyed by using *p'u*[1] as the radical for classification in modern dictionaries. 肉, 月, *jou*[4], meat, should be the radical and 㪔 *san*[4], to beat 支 hemp stalks 㭊 *p'ai*[4] to cause the threads to separate, is the real phonetic. (See No. 24). When 月 *jou*[4], meat, is added the character was used for beating meat to cause it to separate into shreds for cooking. By extension it is now used for the separation of anything. (W. 79 H).

**963 卸**

*hsieh*[4], To lay aside, unload.

卩 *chieh*[2] Radical No. 26, a seal, a tally. (See No. 42). The phonetic part of this character is not used alone and therefore has no pronunciation. The upper part is 午 *wu*[3], (See No. 190), one of the twelve stems; each stem stands for an animal and the one which is associated with 午 *wu*[3], is the horse 馬 *ma*[3]. This stem is easier to write than horse and is therefore substituted for the latter. The 止 *chih*[3], to stop, with this stem implies stopping the horse and taking off his burden. The 卩 *chieh*[2], indicates that this is done at fixed intervals on the journey.

**964 物**

*wu*[4], A thing, an article.

牛, 牛 *niu*[2], Radical No. 93, a cow, an ox. (See No. 50).

勿, 冇 *wu*[4] Phonetic, a negative, do not; a flag with three pennons, usually used to indicate a prohibition. An ox, 牛, *niu²*, was the most valuable asset in ancient times. The addition of the flag to the ox may have indicated its importance—it was not to be disposed of. This character is now used for any article, regardless of value.

**965 糖**

米

唐,喬

*t'ang²*, Sugar, malt candy ; glazed with sugar.

*mi³* Radical No. 119 rice. (See No. 47).

*t'ang²* Phonetic, boasting talk, a dynasty ; the song 口 of men working 閂 in unison, as in pounding (rice) 庚 喬 *keng¹* with a heavy stone pestle 午 *kan¹*. This phonetic may have been selected as the preparing of grain for malt candy requires that it be crushed ; in this process large stone mortars may have been employed and several men manipulated the heavy pestles, who exerted strength according to the rhythm of a song. (W. 102 B). *Hsü Shih Shuo Wen* makes the following comment : 米糵煎也 *mi³ nieh⁴ chien¹ yeh³*, "After the rice has sprouted it is heated." 蔗蜜穀麥皆可造. "(Candy) can be made from cane, from honey, from millet and from wheat." The sugar (candy) made from millet and wheat was called 飴 *i²*. This indicates that as early as the Han Dynasty 200 B. C., the Chinese were making malt candy, but it was then a recent discovery, as the writer *Hsü Shih* says that 糖 *t'ang²*, is a character recently added.

**966 批**

*p'i¹*, To criticise, to arrange for the purchase of.

才, 手 *shou*[8], Radical No. 64, the hand. (See No. 53).

比, 仚 *pi*[8], Phonetic, to compare. Two 人 characters reversed and standing together as if comparing their height or strength. When 才 *shou*[8], is added the idea of criticising is given to this combination. In criticising one generally states what has been done and afterwards sets forth what should have been done; thus bringing out a comparison.

**967** 脾

*p'i*[2], The spleen, temper.

肉, 月 *jou*[4], Radical No. 130, meat. (See No. 133),

卑 *pei*[1], *p'i*[2] *pi*[1] Phonetic, *p'i*[2], lassitude, *pei*[1], base, low, vulgar, (See No. 526). This phonetic may have been given because the spleen is lax or soft in texture. The spleen was supposed to aid the stomach in the work of digestion. It is located on the left of the stomach and as 卑 *pei*[1], was a drinking vessel with a handle on the left, this may have been another reason for the use of this phonetic.

**968** 偶

*ou*[3], An image, a pair, paired; sudden, accidental.

人, 亻 *jên*[2], Radical No. 9, a man.

禺 *yü*[2] Phonetic, an image. (archaic) (See No. 860).

The origin of this phonetic is not the same as of the phonetic in the 860th character. The two are identical in modern writing and even in the old writing they are frequently interchanged. 寓 *yü*[4], to dwell in, is the correct writing for this charaeter according to the oldest authorities. When an image of a man was carved out of wood they believed that the spirit of the individual dwelt in this image. The 禺 *yü²*, impersonates the spirit. With the addition of 亻 *jên²*, there would be a pair. To use 偶 for "sudden" is arbitrary.

**969** 駕

*chia⁴*, To ride in a carriage, to harness ; Your Honour.

馬 *ma³*, Radical No. 187, a horse. (See No. 261).

加 *chia¹*, Phonetic, to add to. (See No. 318).

This combination was first used for harnessing animals to a vehicle:—to add 加 the horses 馬 to the carriage.

**970** 築

*chu²*, To harden by pounding, as a threshing floor, to make mud wails, to build.

竹 *chu²*, Radical No. 118, bamboo. (See No. 7).

巩 *k'ung³* Phonetie, to undertake. (See No. 518). This is not a complete phonetic as we have to add 木 *mu⁴*, wood, to it before it is finished. It was used for the ramparts or fortifications used in warfare, and the ⺮ *chu²*, was originally ⋀, wooden racks placed on top of the wall to prevent the enemy from climbing over. The 木 *mu⁴*, is said to be the short logs which were used to ram the earth into a solid mass.

**971** 委

*wei³*, To submit, a grievance ; to depute.

女 *nü³*, Radical No. 39, a woman. (See No. 16).

禾 朵 *ho²*, Phonetic, grain, (archaic phonetic 采 *sui⁴*), (See No. 771). This is a proper phonetic and indicates the heads of millet etc. being gathered. This character has two distinct meanings and may have originated in different places.

1. To submit. The heads of grain hung drooping : when 女 *nü*³, was added to this it was taken as the symbol of the proper attitude of woman, she should acquiesce even to unreasonable demands from her husband.

2. The grain 禾 *ho*², was stored at home and given into the care of the women when the male members of the household had to leave on business :—thus the meaning of depute.

**972** 遞

*ti*⁴, To hand to or transmit.

辶 *cho*⁴ Radical No, 162, to go. (See No. 10).

虒 *ti*¹ Phonetic, a beast like a tiger, with horns. An examination of the characters which use this phonetic show that there is no common idea attached to them. It is therefore necessary to regard it as a simple phonetic. It seems to have been used in connection with the sending of messages. The 辶 *cho*⁴, indicates that originally it might have necessitated a journey. At present it is used for, to hand to.

**973** 偏

*p'ien*¹, Inclined to one side ; partial prejudiced.

亻,人 *jên*², Radical No. 9, a man.

扁 *pien*⁴ Phonetic, a tablet hung over a door. From 戶 *hu*⁴ a door and 冊 *ts'e*⁴, inscribed bamboo slips. (W. 156 D). As these tablets are always hung with the lower edge against the wall and the upper edge some inches away from it, they are taken as the symbol for not straight, inclined. And when man, 亻, *jên²*, is added he takes on this quality of deflection.

**974 例**

亻人 *li⁴* Laws, regulations ; custom.
*jên²* Radical No. 9, a man.

列 *lieh⁴* Phonetic, to divide, seriatim, arrange in order. (See No. 711). This is not an old character. It is explained thus : the crimes 歹, *tai³*, of a man 亻 *jên²*, are separated 刂 *tao¹*, and placed in order 列 *lieh⁴*, and the law is administered accordingly.

**975 吞**

*t'un¹* To swallow, to gulp down ; to absorb, grasp.

口 *k'ou³*, Radical No. 30, the mouth. (See No. 17).

天 *t'ien¹*, Phonetic, the heaven. (See No. 113). This character 吞 is explained in two different ways : 天 *t'ien¹*, heaven, the sky, envelopes all. It appears like a huge mouth about to swallow everything. The second explanation commences with 一 *i¹*, one, and 大 *ta⁴*, great or large, and 口 *k'ou³*, swallowing in one big mouthful.

**976 弊**

*pi⁴*, Used up, deteriorated, vicious ; my ; mine.

廾 *kung³* Radical No. 55, hands joined and held up. (See No. 247).

敝 *pi⁴*, Phonetic, mean, poor, ruined, my, mine. (See No. 211). The character 弊 was originally written 獘 with 犬 *ch'üan³*, a dog, instead of 廾 *kung³*. It indicated that the dog was dead and useless. The old writing is now never seen. The present writing is two hands 廾 exhibiting a garment which has been worn to shreds 㡀, by beating 攵.

**977** 賧

*p'ei²*, Lose money; indemnify.

貝 *pei⁴*, Radical No. 154, precious. (See No. 38).

音 *t'ou⁴* Phonetic, to cut a speaker short. (See No. 332). Here the phonetic is used to indicate that something has been injured or a business has not been successful; with the addition of 貝 *pei⁴*, it indicates that money has been lost—by extension, the giving of money as indemnity.

**978** 償

*ch'ang²*, To restore, to forfeit, to atone.

亻, 人 *jên²*, Radical No. 9, a man.

賞 *shang³*, Phonetic, to bestow. (See No. 596). The addition of 亻 *jên²*, forms the character which is used for restoring or making amends.

**979** 眉, 睂

*mei²*, Eye brows.

目 *mu⁴*, Radical No. 109, the eye. (See No. 102). This is an old character and cannot be divided into radical and phonetic. The top of the old writing 𡿺 indicates the wrinkles above the eyebrows on the forehead: the ⼃ is the eyebrow and 目. ⊖ *mu⁴*, is the eye. The present form is an arbitrary modification, and the above features are largely lost.

**980** 佔

*chan⁴*, To usurp, to seize.

人, 亻 *jên²*, Radical No. 9, a man.

占 *chan¹·⁴*, Phonetic, to inquire about some enterprise by heating a tortoise shell, divination ; to usurp. (See No. 132). The 佔 is an unauthorized character and is not described in the Shuo Wen. It seems to have been invented to make a distinction between the two meanings of the character 占 *chan¹·⁴* the meaning of the 1st tone is to divine, of the 4th tone is to usurp.

**981** 賃

*lin⁴*, To lease, to rent.

貝 *pei⁴*, Radical No. 154, precious. (See No. 38).

任 *jên⁴*, Phonetic, a man — carrying a load suspended from the two ends of a pole Ⅰ, a load, a burden 壬. When 亻 *jên²*, is added the burden is transferred to another 人, hence the meaning, a trust, office. (W. 82 C). With the addition of 貝 *pei⁴*, there is an obligation of money which has been contracted for value received.

**982** 逛

*kuang⁴*, To ramble, to stroll.

辶 *cho⁴* Radical, No. 162, to go. (See No. 10).

狂 *k'uang²*, Phonetic, mad, wild, raging. (See No. 794). The 逛 is an unauthorized character. The combination indicates traveling in any direction the fancy may determine.

**983** 瓷

*t'zŭ²*, Porcelain, china ware.

瓦 *wa³*, Radical No. 98, tile. (See No. 558).

次 *t'zŭ⁴*, Phonetic, inferior. From 欠 *ch'ien⁴*, deficient. (See No. 273). With the addition of 二 *er⁴*, two, second, inferior. The first is regarded as the best, the second is inferior. Formerly vessels were made of gold, silver and wood ; when crockery ware was substituted it was regarded as inferior. 磁 is an unauthorized writing.

**984** 玩

*wan*[4], A toy, to play.

王.玉 *yü*[4], Radical, No. 96, jade. (See No. 124).

元 *yüan*[2], Phonetic, the first. (See No. 93).

Here this phonetic stands for the highest quality. When 玉 *yü*[4], jade, is added it implies the best jade. Cheap or inferior jade is not prized. Trinkets such as beads and rings have been used to designate rank from prehistoric times and the word 玩 *wan*[4], was first employed as the term for such articles, but is now used for toy or plaything.

**985** 篇

*p'ien*[1], The leaf of a book.

竹 *chu*[2], Radical No. 118, bamboo (See No. 7).

扁 *pien*[3], Phonetic, a tablet. (See No. 513). These tablets are made of board and are thin in comparison with their length and width. With the addition of bamboo 竹 this is the character for a leaf of a bamboo book. These books were made of slips of bamboo and tied together. After paper came into use for making books the same character was retained for leaf.

**986** 耍

*shua*[3], To sport, to fence, to play.

而 *êr*[2], Radical No. 126, the whiskers (archaic), (See No. 635).

女 *nü*[3], Phonetic, a woman. This is a modern

character. To play, to act. Chinese actors use false beards and others dress up in female costumes and personate women. Thus the two characters 而 *êr²*, whiskers, and 女 *nü³*, women, form the character for, to act. The character, by extension, is now used for practicing any handicraft as an occupation. (W. 164 A).

987 轉

*chuan³*, To turn over, to revolve ; to forward.

車 *chê¹*, Radical No. 159, a cart. (See No. 136).

專 *chuan¹*, Phonetic, singly, specially, bent on one object. (See No. 414). This phonetic plus cart 車 forms the character to revolve as the wheels of a cart have but a single function, i.e. to revolve.

988 遲

*ch'ih²*, Slow, late, steady ; to procrastinate.

辶 *cho⁴* Radical No. 162, to go. (See No. 10).

犀 *hsī¹* Phonetic, a rhinoceros. The 尸 *shih¹*, is the body and 牛 is a contraction of 毛 *mao²*, hair. These, when used together 屖 simply indicate that the animal has a tail. 牛 *niu²* added places the animal in the bovine class. (The Chinese are not very careful in their classification of animals.) This beast when not enraged moves about slowly. Thus 辶 *cho⁴*, to move, with the above phonetic makes a good character for slow.

989 慮

*lü⁴*, To care for, anxious ; to cogitate.

心 *hsin¹*, Radical No. 61, the heart. (See No. 18). This character cannot be divided into radical and phonetic. It is composed of

思 急 *szu*[1], to think, head and heart (See No. 45). When 虍 *hu*[2], tiger, (See No. 258), is added the idea is conveyed that the thoughts are turned to things which trouble—tigers are greatly dreaded.

**990** 販

具 反

*fan*[4], To traffic, to deal in.

具 *pei*[4], Radical No, 154, precious. (See No. 38).

反 *fan*[3], Phonetic, to turn. (See No. 75).

To turn goods into money 具 *pei*[4], is the purpose of a merchant.

**991** 脈

肉, 月 𠂤, 沠

*mo*[4] *mai*[4], The pulse.

肉, 月 *jou*[4], Radical No. 130, meat. (See No. 133).

𠂤, 沠 *p'ai*[4], Phonetic, water separating into smaller streams. This is 永 *yung*[4], a constantly flowing spring, reversed, the flow is still constant, but as it leaves the spring it divides up into several streams. (This character is also written with 血 as the radical.) The idea is that the pulse (arteries) break up into innumerable small arteries and are distributed through the flesh.

**992** 眷, 䀾

目 关

*chüan*[4], To love, to care for, family.

目 *mu*[4], Radical No. 109, the eye. (See No. 102).

关 *chüan*[4] Phonetic, to pick and cull. (W. 47 K). This is made up of 釆 *pien*[4], the tracks of a wild animal, (See No 801), to discriminate, and hands 廾, i. e. to select with the hands. Adding 目 *mu*[4], the eye, we have 眷 to look out for those whom one loves and is responsible for. In modern writing 关 *chüan* is identical with the phonetic of No. 609 膳

*shêng*$^4$ but the seal writing shows one to be from 火 *huo*$^3$ and the other from 釆 *pien*$^4$.

993 **碎**

*sui*$^4$, Bits, fragments, petty.

石 *shih*$^2$, Radical No. 112, a stone. (See No. 42).

卒, 卒 *tsu*$^{2, 4}$ Phonetic, to die. This is made up of 衣 *i*$^1$, clothing, and a /, a stroke across the back to indicate the wearer was a soldier. When a man swore allegiance to a prince or feudal lord he was regarded as having died; he was free from all previous obligation and he henceforth had no will of his own, he did what his lord bade him; he was but a fragment of a man, a stone 石 *shih*$^2$, is used for breaking or crushing.

994 **特**

*t'ê*$^4$, Specially, purposely, only.

牜, 牛 *niu*$^2$, Radical No. 93, ox. (See No. 50).

寺 *szŭ*$^4$, Phonetic, a court, a temple. (See No. 346). This character seems to indicate that in ancient times the Chinese were particular about the quality of animals used in sacrifice. The color was also decided on by the court 寺 *szŭ*$^4$. Thus 牜 *niu*$^2$, when added indicated an animal which, owing to its fulfilling all requirements, was set aside for a sacrifice; now by extension used for specially.

995 **任**

*jên*$^4$, A trust, responsibility, an office.

亻, 人 *jên*$^2$, Radical No. 9, a man.

壬 *jên*$^2$, Phonetic, a trust, office, (See No. 981)· Originally this character was used without the 亻 *jên*$^2$.

996 **舉**, 舉

*chü*$^3$, To raise, to lift up, to introduce to.

白 *chiu*[4] Radical No. 134, a mortar. (See No. 479). This is another character which has arbitrarily received a radical foreign to the original construction. The character is made up of 與 *yü*[3], to give, and 𡗜 𦥑 *shou*[3], hand the meaning is, to raise, to lift up, etc.

**997** 試

shih[4], To try, to test, to verify.
言 *yên*[2], Radical No. 149, a word. (See No. 10).
式 *shih*[4], Phonetic, a form, a pattern. (See No. 576). The 言 *yên*[2], word, seems to imply that the one who is to undertake to make an article according to the pattern is asking questions before he undertakes the task, thus securing the experience of others in addition to the ocular demonstration, thereby verifying his ideas as to the mode of procedure.

**998** 步

*pu*[4], A step, a pace, infantry. (See 484).
止 *chih*[3] Radical No. 77, to stop. (See No. 10). The phonetic part of this character is not used alone. It is 止 *chih*[3], to stop, inverted, which indicates the reverse of 止 *chih*[3], or to move. In walking first this foot is advancing while that is stationary ; then that foot is advancing while this is stationary.

**999** 丟

*tiu*[1], To cast away, to lose, to leave behind.
一 *i*[1], Radical No. 1, one. (See No. 19).
去 *ch'ü*[4], Phonetic, to go. (See No. 67). To go 去 *ch'ü*[4], once 一 *i*[1], to go one long journey and not return is to lose.

**1000** 久, 久

ﾉ

*chiu³*, A long time, long since.

*p'ieh¹* Radical No. 4, a stroke to the left. (See No. 176).

This cannot be broken up into radical and phonetic. The seal writing represents a man who is impeded in his walking by a train. Thus we have the idea of a long time, as it requires him to move slowly and much time is needed to walk a short distance.

**1001** 違

辶 *wei²*, To oppose, to disobey.

辶 *cho⁴* Radical No. 162, to go. (See No. 10).

韋 *wei²* Phonetic, thongs, refractory, a surname. (See No. 772). This phonetic is suggestive, when 辶 *cho*, is added it implies active disobedience, disorderliness.

**1002** 落

卄, 艸 *lo⁴*, To fall, to drop.

洛 *ts'ao³*, Radical No. 140, grass. (See No. 22).

*lo⁴* Phonetic (Archaic), a trench for irrigation, water 水 used by each man 各. Each man's field was separated from his neighbor's by these trenches; thus the idea of separation is conveyed. With the addition of ⺾ *ts'ao³*, it was used for the falling of leaves in the autumn; they fall when separated from the stem. (W. 31 B). Now this is used for the falling of anything.

# ALPHABETICAL INDEX.

| | | | | | | |
|---|---|---|---|---|---|---|
| **CH'IAO** | 妾 怯 {667, 177} | 夂 {168, 170} | 妻 910 | 殷 71 | 州 389 | 轉 987 |
| 丂 {258, 853} | 怯 825 | 支 {950, 815} | 禁 765 | 磬 71 | 周 {476, 780} | 尚 946 |
| 巧 853 | 遲 988 | 枝 815 | 董 750 | 卯 42 | 壺 {412, 684} | 賺 948 |
| 谷 135 | **CHIEN** | 止 {484, 128} | 謹 750 | **CHIU** | 帝 {405, 847} | **CH'UAN** |
| 雀 627 | 見 85 | 直 10 | **CH'IN** | 九 23 | | 巛 598 |
| 磬 813 | 戔 {13, 425} | 直 349 | 禽 {716, 83} | 丩 366 | **CH'OU** | 舛 {321, 588} |
| 喬 322 | 賤 679 | 直 {349, 99} | 親 309 | 久 {291, 1000} | ⇒ 438 | 串 57 |
| 橋 458 | 盬 120 | 知 100 | **CHING** | 白 {76, 479} | 抽 732 | 船 353 |
| **CHIEH** | 盬 294 | 紙 8 | 井 82 | 舊 395 | 愁 782 | 穿 97 |
| 丰 436 | 柬 619 | 隻 154 | 耕 601 | 酉 {477, 623} | 綢 476 | 叀 {204, 414} |
| 巴 42 | 揀 919 | 執 139 | 京 98 | 酒 589 | **CHU** | 傳 414 |
| 卩 {114, 42} | 建 764 | 稚 171 | 景 896 | 就 98 | 主 210 | **CHUANG** |
| 節 114 | 健 764 | 戠 39 | 競 537 | 救 150 | 佳 336 | 壯 355 |
| 介 {432, 898} | 間 183 | 職 39 | 淨 537 | **CH'IU** | 竹 7 | 裝 355 |
| 界 432 | 簡 905 | 治 450 | 靜 315 | 求 150 | 築 970 | 莊 605 |
| 頡 615 | 漸 812 | 至 88 | 竞 823 | 秋 169 | 猪 295 | 狀 930 |
| 纈 615 | 件 50 | **CH'IH** | 竟 {875, 907} | **CHIUNG** | 煮 401 | **CH'UANG** |
| 結 615 | 肩 652 | 彳 78 | 境 875 | 門 468 | 助 677 | 牀 84 |
| 絜 747 | 減 934 | 尺 375 | 至 136 | **CH'IUNG** | 囑 749 | 床 84 |
| 潔 747 | 兼 948 | 后 288 | 經 362 | 复 251 | 封 412 | 囪 230 |
| 戒 866 | **CH'IEN** | 庝 288 | 頸 362 | 窮 301 | **CH'U** | 囪 {287, 584} |
| 誡 866 | 千 59 | 吃 74 | 晴 159 | **CHO** | 出 46 | 窗 584 |
| 借 248 | 欠 {273, 571} | 赤 542 | 精 916 | 卓 {56, 631} | 初 115 | 闖 833 |
| 街 161 | 开 235 | 遲 988 | 敬 407 | 棹 56 | 處 409 | **CHUI** |
| 接 667 | 淺 425 | **CHIN** | 驚 735 | 之 10 | 處 409 | 隹 {21, 154} |
| 姐 690 | 錢 13 | 巾 143 | 津 910 | 乇 10 | 除 603 | 縋 759 |
| 解 707 | 前 108 | 今 18 | **CH'ING** | 着 333 | 楚 876 | 追 745 |
| 隔 536 | 乾 137 | 斤 419 | 青 {63, 159} | **CHOU** | **CHUA** | 贅 940 |
| 藉 868 | 遣 693 | 近 358 | 清 642 | 舟 {238, 108} | 爫 281 | **CH'UI** |
| **CH'IEH** | 僉 133 | 金 13 | 情 420 | | 爪 83 | 垂 {387, 352} |
| 且 {200, 690} | 竅 889 | 緊 120 | 請 63 | | **CHUAN** | |
| 切 557 | **CHIH** | 進 402 | 輕 136 | | 專 414 | |
| | 之 {27, 614} | 烝 648 | | | | |
| | | 盡 648 | | | | |

曉 77
鼻 390

**HSIEH**
些 20
邪 650
卸 963
鞋 163
鞵 163
寫 41
謝 342
歇 662

**HSIEN**
先 27
咸 {502, 305}
咠 770
現 124
鼎 {141, 792}
顯 792
閒 599
縣 390
綫 303

**HSIN**
忄 18
心 18
凶 45
辛 274
信 195
新 394

**HSING**
行 {30, 161}
省 391

幸 139
性 644
星 422
醒 422
刑 656
形 894
姓 206

**HSIU**
修 415

**HSIUNG**
兄 72

**HSÜ**
戌 {305, 730}
許 527
緒 904

**HSÜAN**
咺 {424, 428}

**HSÜEH**
穴 97
雪 438
血 462
學 462

**HSÜN**
訓 725

**HU**
戶 {480, 5}
乎 723
呼 723
互 721

虍 258
虎 258
壺 134
忽 669
胡 590
湖 590
護 849

**HUA**
匕 {20, 158}
化 488
花 488
話 73
畫 678

**HUAI**
襄 396
壞 396
淮 933

**HUAN**
奐 251
換 251
還 204
歡 511
覓 144

**HUANG**
皇 444
尨 639
荒 639
謊 639
慌 859
黃 {207, 696}

**HUI**
卉 525
回 62
灰 674
悔 699
惠 385
會 230
滙 933
穢 869

**HUN**
魂 447

**HUNG**
紅 89
哄 483

**HUO**
火 {169, 482}
伙 646
活 530
或 70
惑 659
禍 423
貨 519
豁 616
夒 949
雙 849
獲 919

**I**
一 {P x, 19}
乂 165
弋 576
乙 137
已 191

以 121
岇 288
圝 439
台 450
醫 439
衣 51
永 51
邑 11
異 311
椅 54
意 44
益 404
尾 510
義 471
議 471
易 597
移 851
遺 863
執 953
藝 953

**JAN**
肰 506
然 506

**JANG**
嚷 839

**JAO**
饒 514

**JÊ**
若 430
惹 430
熱 139

**JÊN**
人 3

亻 126
儿 27
尸 122
刃 37
忍 37
認 37
壬 995
任 {981, 995}
羊 139

**JIH**
日 12

**JOU**
肉 133

**JU**
入 35
如 {325, 521}
辱 758
褥 758

**JUNG**
容 579

**KA**
**KAI**
勾 271
改 700
該 487
概 528
蓋 335

**K'AI**
開 175

**KAN**
干 110
甘 23
斡 137
乾 137
幹 927
趕 343
感 502
敢 545

**K'AN**
凵 46
看 102
砍 571

**KANG**
**K'ANG**
康 763

**KAO**
告 203
羔 284
高 {142, 98}

**K'AO**
靠 276

**KÊ**
个 28
戈 2
個 28
箇 28
各 272
閣 498
革 163
哥 152

| LING | | | | | |
|---|---|---|---|---|---|
| 另 | 474 | | | | |
| 令 | {138, 61} | | | | |
| 領 | 472 | | | | |
| 零 | 61 | | | | |
| 霛 | 446 | | | | |
| 靈 | 446 | | | | |

**LIU**
六 31
流 629
霤 732
留 732

**LO**
勒 710
輅 701
羅 632
鑼 632

**LOU**
蔞 {198, 392}
樓 392
露 793

**LU**
先 485
坴 953
陸 953
鹿 844
甪 294
路 279
露 793
盧 320

**LUAN**
臠 931

亂 931
孌 706

**LUN**
侖 359
論 370
輪 359

**LUNG**
龍 286
攏 286
聾 592

**LÜ**
呂 301
慮 989
驢 320
律 786
屢 829

**LÜEH**
略 531

**LÜN**
侖 359

**MA**
馬 261
碼 261
罵 429
麻 24
麼 24

**MAI**
理 515
麥 575
脈 991
買 38
賣 220

**MAN**
萠 306
滿 306
瞞 810
曼 130
慢 130
饅 285

**MANG**
忙 676

**MAO**
毛 254
門 130
矛 897
白 244
冒 244
帽 244
帽 244

**MEI**
每 269
沒 79
美 345
妹 691
眉 979

**MÊN**
門 5
們 5

**MÊNG**
家 460
蒙 460
夢 572

**MI**
糸 {8, 213}
米 {47, 658}
迷 658
謎 705
祕 802
秘 802
蜜 705

**MIAO**
苗 798
廟 464

**MIEH**
滅 730
滅 730

**MIEN**
宀 1
丏 {575, 122}
麪 575
麵 575
免 {543, 107}
面 {486, 575}

**MIN**
皿 {233, 648}

**MING**
名 451
明 127
命 {551, 61}

**MO**
沒 79
末 665
抹 665
脈 991
麼 24
摩 752
磨 752
墨 382

**MU**
木 {22, 581}
母 269
目 {102, 547}
攵 79
牧 147
㤅 485
莫 523
墓 523

**NA**
那 11
拿 103

**NAI**
乃 581

**NAN**
男 212
南 347
難 398

**NAO**
鬧 688

**NEI**
內 468

**NÊNG**
能 357

**NI**
尼 278
呢 278
你 3
疒 {593, 437}

**NIANG**
娘 565

**NIAO**
鳥 {41, 628}

**NIEH**
幸 139

**NIEN**
年 110
念 18
輦 840
撵 840

**NIN**
你 892

**NIU**
牛 {50, 118}

**NO**
挪 960

**NUNG**
弄 467

**NÜ**
女 16

**OU**
偶 968

**PA**
八 {569, 3, 32}
巴 53
把 53
琶 53
笆 887
罷 {459, 328}
友 {626, 955}
扒 955

**P'A**
怕 372

**PAI**
白 {208, 6}
百 58
拜 188
敗 620
擺 328
擘 856

**P'AI**
舡 24
辰 991
排 854

**PAN**
半 118

伴 744
板 239
般 238
辦 274
草 937

**P'AN**
冸 24
盼 901
盤 238

**PANG**
邦 675
邦 675
幫 675

**P'ANG**
产 503
旁 503

**PAO**
勹 80
包 {495 327}
飽 681
報 376
保 938
寶 264
薄 416
暴 819

**P'AO**
泡 327
袍 51
跑 495

**PEI**
北 348

---

貝 38
倍 332
被 457
卑 526
碑 526
悲 540
備 695

**P'EI**
配 708
佩 947
陪 767
賠 977

**PÊN**
本 36

**P'ÊN**
盆 233

**P'ÊNG**
朋 48
鵬 48
硼 461

**PI**
匕 {491 348}
比 {323 966}
必 504
秘 802
俾 211
敝 211
弊 976
彼 489
辟 856
筆 7

---

偪 804
逼 804

**P'I**
匹 23
皮 224
批 966
脾 967
脖 856

**PIAO**
表 182
彪 {626 131}

**P'IAO**
票 255
漂 878

**P'IEH**
撇 176
撇 884

**PIEN**
采 801
更 492
鞭 891
扁 513
偏 737
遍 513
辦 {274 512}
辯 512
邊 104

**P'IEN**
偏 973
徧 737

---

篇 985
遍 513

**PING**
冫 {138 516}
兵 560
并 {235 461}
餅 235
丙 226
病 437
柄 727

**P'ING**
平 268
瓶 558

**PO**
癶 214
百 58
帛 675
波 820

**P'O**
坡 832
破 633

**PU**
卜 14
不 19
布 340
步 {197 998}
補 252

**P'U**
戈 {17 620}

---

父 17
匍 888
葡 888
舖 151
溥 416

**SA**
撒 638

**SAI**
寒 692
賽 692

**SAN**
三 P. xi
散 {638 962}
傘 685

**SAO**
掃 405

**SÊ**
嗇 454

**SHA**
杀 165
殺 165

**SHAI**
晒 799
曬 799

**SHAN**
三 415
山 857
善 537
扇 583

---

**SHANG**
上 91
尚 {410 408 52}
裳 52
賞 596
商 {262 475}
晌 189
傷 541
傷 541
錫 541

**SHAO**
勺 6
少 176
稍 720
紹 899
燒 482

**SHÊ**
舌 73
舍 40
捨 550
折 855
赦 542
射 342
嗇 454

**SHÊN**
申 {227 369}
伸 784
神 227
罙 140
深 140
身 291

---

甚 23
慎 751
桃 344
審 837

**SHÊNG**
生 15
升 607
省 391
聖 202
聲 71
勝 610
膡 609

**SHIH**
十 {p.xi 59}
士 {69 134}
尸 449
氏 8
示 164
礻 {227 164}
市 256
石 42
矢 100
失 566
世 426
家 {221 460}
式 576
試 997
時 125
詩 346
事 95
史 {96 231}

使 231, 食 75, 飾 952, 師 453, 獅 453, 是 12, 溼 141, 識 39, 拾 367, 濕 141, 實 421, 施 698, 誓 855

**SHOU**
手 53, 收 366, 受 463, 守 862, 首 101, 百 101, 獸 716, 熟 563, 壽 452

**SHU**
戌 34, 叉 {71, 165}, 疋 876, 乃 581, 朮 165, 叔 547, 束 619, 恕 521, 庶 762, 蜀 749, 屬 749

朓 563, 尌 412, 樹 412, 書 9, 數 198, 贖 485, 梳 549

**SHUA**
耍 986

**SHUANG**
雙 162, 爽 918

**SHUI**
水 79, 誰 21, 稅 760, 睡 434

**SHUN**
順 363, 隼 516

**SHUO**
說 72

**SO**
所 480, 負 680, 鎖 680

**SU**
俗 622, 訴 288, 穌 556

**SUAN**
算 247, 酸 664

**SUI**
碎 993, 采 771, 夊 170, 穗 771, 陸 493, 遺 493, 隨 493, 雖 505, 歲 869, 歲 {197, 869}

**SUN**
孫 956

**SUNG**
松 42, 送 94

**SZŬ**
山 {89, 569}, 私 806, 四 29, 死 {304, 299}, 寺 {125, 346}, 似 338, 司 717, 伺 717, 糸 8, 絲 {956, 141}

思 {45, 989}

**TA**
大 54, 打 155, 答 637, 苔 959, 搭 959

**T'A**
他 4

**TAI**
歹 711, 罪 396, 待 655, 代 769, 佾 769, 袋 769, 呆 938, 獃 711, 戴 544, 殆 311, 帶 143

**T'AI**
抬 174, 臺 580, 擡 174

**TAN**
丹 63, 旦 241, 但 241, 單 937, 彈 937

擔 797, 膽 824

**T'AN**
貪 574, 探 140, 談 517

**TANG**
當 478, 擋 881, 盪 893, 黨 787

**T'ANG**
堂 408, 躺 738, 趟 403, 唐 965, 糖 965, 盪 893

**TAO**
刁 37, 刀 37, 到 88, 倒 501, 道 101, 禱 452

**T'AO**
匐 889, 萄 889

**TE**
导 78, 得 78

慝 99, 德 {99, 442}

**T'Ê**
特 994

**TÊNG**
等 199, 登 240, 凳 240, 橙 240, 燈 243

**T'ÊNG**
疼 593

**TI**
氐 257, 底 257, 地 187, 弟 {86, 153}, 第 86, 的 6, 帝 217, 嚏 972, 遞 972

**T'I**
替 371, 提 {53, 951}, 剃 641, 體 292

**TIAO**
弔 266

吊 266, 掉 631

**T'IAO**
條 160, 挑 112

**TIEH**
跌 805, 迭 308

**T'IEH**
鐵 308, 貼 381

**TIEN**
店 132, 點 178, 典 386, 殿 885, 電 369

**T'IEN**
天 113, 田 {82, 201}, 甜 663

**TING**
丁 155, 頂 219, 釘 289, 定 259, 錠 259

**T'ING**
壬 22, 聽 99

亭 651
停 651
**TIU**
丢 999
**TO**
多 184
朵 581
躱 845
**T'O**
乇 624
托 624
託 911
它 702
駝 702
脫 534
**TOU**
斗 {117, 568}
豆 {105, 240}
都 270
鬥 688
**T'OU**
骰 613
否 767
音 {767, 332}
投 834
頭 105
儌 872
**TSA**
雜 689

**TSAI**
在 81
再 196
災 598
**T'SAI**
才 562
材 562
財 573
采 281
採 {908, 281}
彩 880
綵 281
裁 311
纔 277
**TSAN**
晉 185
咎 185
俗 185
贊 344
讚 344
鑒 954
**TSANG**
葬 299
髒 299
臟 941
**TS'ANG**
倉 666
藏 941
**TSAO**
早 {399, 111}

造 203
竈 69
遭 470
**TS'AO**
屮 22
艸 22
草 399
曹 470
**TSÊ**
責 731
**T'SÊ**
**TSÊN**
怎 293
**TSENG**
曾 {449, 230}
**TS'ENG**
層 449
曾 449
**TSO**
坐 66
座 192
作 149
昨 123
做 {17, 149}
**T'SO**
錯 222

**TSOU**
走 {42, 146}
**TSU**
足 {279, 484}
且 677
租 920
卒 993
**TS'U**
粗 200
**TSUI**
罪 331
觜 326
嘴 326
**TS'UI**
崔 715
催 715
艮 741
**TSUN**
尊 477
夋 664
**TS'UN**
寸 69
村 473
邨 473
**TSUNG**
總 287

**TS'UNG**
从 128
從 128
恩 {287, 586}
聰 586
**TU**
度 818
渡 818
肚 870
妒 873
都 270
督 547
獨 800
**T'U**
土 13
吐 570
辻 290
兔 277
充 {629, 549}
徒 290
**TUAN**
耑 946
短 393
段 946
緞 946
**T'UAN**
彖 831
**TUI**
自 310
兔 72
對 69

**T'UI**
艮 741
退 {595, 741}
腿 595
推 561
**T'UN**
吞 975
展 885
**TUNG**
冬 170
東 {22, 25}
動 179
董 22
懂 22
**T'UNG**
童 177
通 497
同 249
銅 249
**TZŬ**
字 1
自 104
茲 585
**T ZŬ**
次 983
姿 983
此 {20, 491}
束 731
慈 585

磁 983
賜 597
**WA**
瓦 558
**WAI**
外 14
**WAN**
丸 139
卍 60
完 93
玩 984
宛 42
碗 42
晚 107
萬 60
彎 706
**WANG**
尢 98
尪 {794, 350}
枉 865
往 350
王 444
望 660
亾 123
亡 123
忘 157
朢 660
罔 719
網 719
网 38
罒 38
囚 38
罓 38

**WEI**

| | |
|---|---|
| 口 | 28 |
| 广 | 634 |
| 危 | 634 |
| 未 | 524 |
| 位 | 216 |
| 為 | 83 |
| 爲 | 83 |
| 尾 | 510 |
| 畏 | 848 |
| 委 | 971 |
| 韋 | 772 |
| 圍 | 781 |
| 術 | 772 |
| 違 | 1001 |

**WÊN**

| | |
|---|---|
| 文 | 427 |
| 聞 | 65 |

**WO**

| | |
|---|---|
| 我 | 2 |
| 臥 | 757 |

**WU**

| | |
|---|---|
| 兀 | 77 |
| 午 | {527 / 190} |
| 无 | 507 |
| 五 | 30 |
| 巫 | 446 |

| | |
|---|---|
| 吾 | 877 |
| 悟 | 877 |
| 勿 | 964 |
| 物 | 964 |
| 戊 | 193 |
| 屋 | 337 |
| 武 | 640 |
| 惡 | 538 |
| 無 | 431 |
| 汗 | 728 |
| 污 | 728 |
| 洿 | 728 |
| 務 | 897 |
| 秋 | 897 |

**YA**

| | |
|---|---|
| 丫 | {670 / 163} |
| 牙 | 97 |
| 呀 | 533 |
| 雅 | 721 |
| 訝 | 736 |
| 芽 | 811 |
| 亞 | 538 |
| 衛 | 906 |
| 壓 | 890 |

**YANG**

| | |
|---|---|
| 央 | 441 |
| 羊 | 253 |
| 洋 | 253 |

| | |
|---|---|
| 業 | 283 |
| 樣 | 283 |
| 養 | 440 |
| 易 | 577 |
| 陽 | 577 |
| 揚 | 755 |
| 仰 | 827 |

**YAO**

| | |
|---|---|
| 幺 | 24 |
| 藥 | 456 |
| 樂 | 456 |
| 天 | {417 / 322} |
| 夭 | {77 / 514} |
| 堯 | 77 |
| 要 | 16 |
| 腰 | 703 |
| 备 | 858 |
| 搖 | 858 |
| 敫 | 958 |
| 邀 | 958 |

**YEH**

| | |
|---|---|
| 也 | 4 |
| 夜 | 173 |
| 耶 | 555 |
| 頁 | 105 |
| 野 | 697 |
| 舄 | 41 |

**YEN**

| | |
|---|---|
| 广 | {24 / 132} |
| 台 | 353 |
| 沿 | 353 |
| 扤 | 698 |
| 炎 | 178 |
| 言 | 10 |
| 眼 | 158 |
| 奄 | 808 |
| 掩 | 808 |
| 猒 | 841 |
| 厭 | 841 |
| 鼻 | 104 |
| 厰 | 748 |
| 嚴 | 748 |
| 鹽 | 294 |

**YIN**

| | |
|---|---|
| 尤 | 822 |
| 引 | 57 |
| 印 | 673 |
| 因 | 384 |
| 音 | 39 |
| 爯 | 809 |
| 隱 | 809 |
| 陰 | {30 / 816} |
| 蔭 | 816 |
| 銀 | 265 |

**YING**

| | |
|---|---|
| 迎 | 827 |
| 燚 | 683 |
| 英 | 441 |
| 雁 | 553 |
| 應 | 553 |
| 硬 | 783 |

**YU**

| | |
|---|---|
| 叉 | 43 |
| 友 | 49 |
| 絲 | 34 |
| 有 | 43 |
| 尤 | 98 |
| 由 | 732 |
| 油 | 846 |
| 酉 | {422 / 589} |
| 猶 | 623 |
| 攸 | 160 |
| 賣 | 485 |
| 郵 | 387 |
| 游 | 850 |
| 遊 | 912 |

**YUNG**

| | |
|---|---|
| 用 | {57 / 225} |
| 甬 | 497 |
| 永 | 283 |

| | |
|---|---|
| 雍 | 788 |
| 擁 | 788 |
| 邕 | 788 |

**YÜ**

| | |
|---|---|
| 卩 | 479 |
| 與 | 479 |
| 玉 | 124 |
| 余 | 40 |
| 余 | 603 |
| 聿 | 7 |
| 或 | 70 |
| 雨 | 61 |
| 予 | 284 |
| 豫 | 694 |
| 亏 | 694 |
| 于 | 728 |
| 禺 | 728 |
| 禺 | 860 |
| 愚 | 860 |
| 寓 | 968 |
| 欲 | 807 |
| 慾 | 807 |
| 俞 | 795 |
| 喻 | 795 |
| 獄 | 882 |
| 羽 | 583 |

**YÜAN**

| | |
|---|---|
| 元 | {93 / 263} |

| | |
|---|---|
| 夗 | 42 |
| 怨 | 932 |
| 袁 | {636 / 356} |
| 遠 | 356 |
| 園 | 636 |
| 原 | 653 |
| 源 | 836 |
| 願 | 653 |
| 員 | 418 |
| 圓 | 418 |
| 院 | 443 |
| 緣 | 831 |

**YÜEH**

| | |
|---|---|
| 曰 | 9 |
| 月 | 43 |
| 戉 | 329 |
| 越 | 329 |
| 兌 | {72 / 534} |
| 約 | 535 |
| 樂 | 456 |

**YÜN**

| | |
|---|---|
| 允 | 664 |
| 云 | {953 / 447} |

# INDEX BY NUMBER OF STROKES.

A letter c indicates that the character is colloquial.

# RADICAL INDEX

A CATALOG OF SELECTED
**DOVER BOOKS**
IN ALL FIELDS OF INTEREST

# A CATALOG OF SELECTED DOVER
# BOOKS IN ALL FIELDS OF INTEREST

DRAWINGS OF REMBRANDT, edited by Seymour Slive. Updated Lippmann, Hofstede de Groot edition, with definitive scholarly apparatus. All portraits, biblical sketches, landscapes, nudes. Oriental figures, classical studies, together with selection of work by followers. 550 illustrations. Total of 630pp. 9⅛ × 12¼.
21485-0, 21486-9 Pa., Two-vol. set $25.00

GHOST AND HORROR STORIES OF AMBROSE BIERCE, Ambrose Bierce. 24 tales vividly imagined, strangely prophetic, and decades ahead of their time in technical skill: "The Damned Thing," "An Inhabitant of Carcosa," "The Eyes of the Panther," "Moxon's Master," and 20 more. 199pp. 5⅜ × 8½. 20767-6 Pa. $3.95

ETHICAL WRITINGS OF MAIMONIDES, Maimonides. Most significant ethical works of great medieval sage, newly translated for utmost precision, readability. Laws Concerning Character Traits, Eight Chapters, more. 192pp. 5⅜ × 8½.
24522-5 Pa. $4.50

THE EXPLORATION OF THE COLORADO RIVER AND ITS CANYONS, J. W. Powell. Full text of Powell's 1,000-mile expedition down the fabled Colorado in 1869. Superb account of terrain, geology, vegetation, Indians, famine, mutiny, treacherous rapids, mighty canyons, during exploration of last unknown part of continental U.S. 400pp. 5⅜ × 8½. 20094-9 Pa. $6.95

HISTORY OF PHILOSOPHY, Julián Marías. Clearest one-volume history on the market. Every major philosopher and dozens of others, to Existentialism and later. 505pp. 5⅜ × 8½. 21739-6 Pa. $8.50

ALL ABOUT LIGHTNING, Martin A. Uman. Highly readable non-technical survey of nature and causes of lightning, thunderstorms, ball lightning, St. Elmo's Fire, much more. Illustrated. 192pp. 5⅜ × 8½. 25237-X Pa. $5.95

SAILING ALONE AROUND THE WORLD, Captain Joshua Slocum. First man to sail around the world, alone, in small boat. One of great feats of seamanship told in delightful manner. 67 illustrations. 294pp. 5⅜ × 8½. 20326-3 Pa. $4.95

LETTERS AND NOTES ON THE MANNERS, CUSTOMS AND CONDITIONS OF THE NORTH AMERICAN INDIANS, George Catlin. Classic account of life among Plains Indians: ceremonies, hunt, warfare, etc. 312 plates. 572pp. of text. 6⅛ × 9¼. 22118-0, 22119-9 Pa. Two-vol. set $15.90

ALASKA: The Harriman Expedition, 1899, John Burroughs, John Muir, et al. Informative, engrossing accounts of two-month, 9,000-mile expedition. Native peoples, wildlife, forests, geography, salmon industry, glaciers, more. Profusely illustrated. 240 black-and-white line drawings. 124 black-and-white photographs. 3 maps. Index. 576pp. 5⅜ × 8½. 25109-8 Pa. $11.95

AMERICAN CLIPPER SHIPS: 1833–1858, Octavius T. Howe & Frederick C. Matthews. Fully-illustrated, encyclopedic review of 352 clipper ships from the period of America's greatest maritime supremacy. Introduction. 109 halftones. 5 black-and-white line illustrations. Index. Total of 928pp. 5⅜ × 8½.
25115-2, 25116-0 Pa., Two-vol. set $17.90

TOWARDS A NEW ARCHITECTURE, Le Corbusier. Pioneering manifesto by great architect, near legendary founder of "International School." Technical and aesthetic theories, views on industry, economics, relation of form to function, "mass-production spirit," much more. Profusely illustrated. Unabridged translation of 13th French edition. Introduction by Frederick Etchells. 320pp. 6⅛ × 9¼. (Available in U.S. only)
25023-7 Pa. $8.95

THE BOOK OF KELLS, edited by Blanche Cirker. Inexpensive collection of 32 full-color, full-page plates from the greatest illuminated manuscript of the Middle Ages, painstakingly reproduced from rare facsimile edition. Publisher's Note. Captions. 32pp. 9⅜ × 12¼.
24345-1 Pa. $4.95

BEST SCIENCE FICTION STORIES OF H. G. WELLS, H. G. Wells. Full novel *The Invisible Man*, plus 17 short stories: "The Crystal Egg," "Aepyornis Island," "The Strange Orchid," etc. 303pp. 5⅜ × 8½. (Available in U.S. only)
21531-8 Pa. $4.95

AMERICAN SAILING SHIPS: Their Plans and History, Charles G. Davis. Photos, construction details of schooners, frigates, clippers, other sailcraft of 18th to early 20th centuries—plus entertaining discourse on design, rigging, nautical lore, much more. 137 black-and-white illustrations. 240pp. 6⅛ × 9¼.
24658-2 Pa. $5.95

ENTERTAINING MATHEMATICAL PUZZLES, Martin Gardner. Selection of author's favorite conundrums involving arithmetic, money, speed, etc., with lively commentary. Complete solutions. 112pp. 5⅜ × 8½. 25211-6 Pa. $2.95

THE WILL TO BELIEVE, HUMAN IMMORTALITY, William James. Two books bound together. Effect of irrational on logical, and arguments for human immortality. 402pp. 5⅜ × 8½. 20291-7 Pa. $7.50

THE HAUNTED MONASTERY and THE CHINESE MAZE MURDERS, Robert Van Gulik. 2 full novels by Van Gulik continue adventures of Judge Dee and his companions. An evil Taoist monastery, seemingly supernatural events; overgrown topiary maze that hides strange crimes. Set in 7th-century China. 27 illustrations. 328pp. 5⅜ × 8½. 23502-5 Pa. $5.95

CELEBRATED CASES OF JUDGE DEE (DEE GOONG AN), translated by Robert Van Gulik. Authentic 18th-century Chinese detective novel; Dee and associates solve three interlocked cases. Led to Van Gulik's own stories with same characters. Extensive introduction. 9 illustrations. 237pp. 5⅜ × 8½.
23337-5 Pa. $4.95

*Prices subject to change without notice.*
Available at your book dealer or write for free catalog to Dept. GI, Dover Publications, Inc., 31 East 2nd St., Mineola, N.Y. 11501. Dover publishes more than 175 books each year on science, elementary and advanced mathematics, biology, music, art, literary history, social sciences and other areas.